When Broadway Went to Hollywood

When Broadway Went to Hollywood

Ethan Mordden

OXFORD
UNIVERSITY PRESS

OXFORD
UNIVERSITY PRESS

Oxford University Press is a department of the University of Oxford.
It furthers the University's objective of excellence in research, scholarship,
and education by publishing worldwide. Oxford is a registered trade mark of
Oxford University Press in the UK and certain other countries.

Published in the United States of America by Oxford University Press
198 Madison Avenue, New York, NY 10016, United States of America.

Library of Congress Cataloging-in-Publication Data

Names: Mordden, Ethan
Title: When Broadway went to Hollywood / Ethan Mordden.
Description: New York, NY : Oxford University Press, [2016] | Includes
bibliographical references and index.
Identifiers: LCCN 2016012583| ISBN 9780199395408 (alk. paper) |
ISBN 9780199395422 (epub)
Subjects: LCSH: Motion picture music—United States—History and criticism. |
Musical films—United States—History and criticism.
Classification: LCC ML2075 .M652 2016 | DDC 791.43/6—dc23 LC record
available at http://lccn.loc.gov/2016012583

1 3 5 7 9 8 6 4 2
Printed by Sheridan Books, Inc., United States of America

To John Cronwell

CONTENTS

ACKNOWLEDGMENTS

To my friendly neighborhood agents Joe Spieler and Kent Wolf; to Ron Mandelbaum at Photofest; to Clint Bocock; to Ken Mandelbaum; to Matthew Kennedy; and to my fine editor at Oxford, Norman Hirschy.

When Broadway Went to Hollywood

✦

Introduction

This is not a book about the Hollywood musical.

This is also not a book about the music in the Hollywood musical.

This is a book about the work of primarily Broadway-identified songwriters in Hollywood. It treats both newly conceived films and adaptations of their stage shows. For example, in the case of Cole Porter, we will explore *Born To Dance* and *The Pirate* (because they were written for the screen) and *Can-Can* (as an adaptation of a Porter stage show). But we won't be concerned with *Jubilee* or *Out Of This World* (because these Porter stage shows were never filmed).

I need to emphasize this because, when I first told people about this project, some of them couldn't grasp its theme. They somehow heard only "Hollywood musicals" and thought the book was a history of the form. It isn't.

Or they somehow heard only "songwriters" and thought the book was about the music of Hollywood. It isn't.

Rather, we're going to follow the adventures of such figures as Jerome Kern, George and Ira Gershwin, Frank Loesser, and Jerry Herman when they trade in Broadway for Hollywood. We are not going to follow the adventures of such figures as Harry Warren or the team of Harry Revel and Mack Gordon (even though all three did some work for the stage), because Warren concentrated on writing for Warner Bros. and then MGM, and Gordon and Revel (as they were known) were Paramount and then Fox stalwarts.

However. In the book's first chapter, I do take some time to examine the formats of the earliest movie musicals, no matter who wrote them, because those first tries at making cinema out of story-and-song tell us how movie people regarded the music in musicals.

But then: what happens when writers used to the business of Broadway run into the very different business of Hollywood, with its often unmusical producer despots, its stacking of writing teams on a single project, its use of five or six songs per story where Broadway fits in a dozen or so, and its terror of characters bursting into song on the street, in your living room, near a cottage small by a waterfall? Did the movies give theatre writers a chance to expand their art? Did Broadway influence Hollywood, or vice versa? More and more, historians are combining stage and screen in their chronicles, so is there really one great epic that unites, say, *Show Boat* and *The Jazz Singer*, *Meet Me in St. Louis* and *St. Louis Woman*, *Funny Lady* and *Pacific Overtures*? Or are the Broadway and Hollywood musicals irreconcilable as artistic forms? And, finally, did any New York writer or writing team make a film musical as fulfilling as their stage shows were?

Decades ago, it was possible to write a succinct volume on either the stage or film musical. But by now the history is too big for a single book to be both comprehensive and detailed, and authors must select their examples. Therefore, I have made no attempt to cover every title that suits my survey. Further, I give more space to some films and less to others, for various reasons—and please note that this is not a reference work in the first place. Production data can be found at the Internet Movie Database and the Internet Broadway Database, both generally (though not invariably) reliable.

Meanwhile, this is probably the right time to lay out a very brief history of the Hollywood musical, thus:

1927: A silent with a few added sound sequences, *The Jazz Singer*, starts it all. The first movie vocalist: Al Jolson. The first big movie vocal: "Blue Skies," by Irving Berlin. And Hollywood sends to New York for composers and lyricists.

1929–1930: The first two years of regular sound production, stuffed with musicals: "All Talking, All Singing, All Dancing."

1931–1932: Too many musicals—and too many bad ones—inspire an audience boycott. "All Talking, No Singing" becomes an inviting sign on cinema marquees. Musicals in production are denuded of music, and big plans (RKO's more or less all-star *Babes in Toyland*, MGM's *The Merry Widow* for Lawrence Tibbett) are scrapped. The influx of New Yorkers becomes an exodus. "The party was over," says Oscar Hammerstein, "and we all came home."

1933–1939: Warner Bros.' *42nd Street* wins the public back, and the 1930s prove a golden age, led by RKO's set for Fred Astaire and Ginger Rogers and MGM's Eleanor Powell *Broadway Melody*s and Jeanette MacDonald-Nelson Eddy operettas. Among them, these three series use Kern, Berlin, Porter, the Gershwins,

Youmans, Friml, Romberg, and Victor Herbert—almost the executive board of the Broadway musical. Arlen and Harburg's *The Wizard of Oz* marks a culmination.

1940–1949: Musicals grow smoother and less daffy. Another golden age begins with MGM's Freed Unit story musicals like *Meet Me in St. Louis* and *The Pirate*, preferring character and situation numbers to Hollywood's favorite genre of song, the backstager's performance piece. Typical character or situation number (it's actually both): "The French Lesson," in *Good News*, because June Allyson is helping Peter Lawford pass his French exam to win the Big Game. Typical performance number: "Arthur Murray Taught Me Dancing in a Hurry," because *The Fleet's In* needs a specialty number for Betty Hutton. Hello, writers? She'll be on stage in a club, so any topic will work. Something on the current dance lesson craze? Do it!

1950–1959: Broadway adaptations become more popular than ever, often in reasonably faithful duplications. The break-up of the studio system, with its thriving music departments, means musicals become more difficult to organize and more expensive to produce, killing off the B-budget musical forever. Everything now aims at the formidable: *Oklahoma!* on its vast Todd-AO exhibition screen defines the era.

1960–1975: Formidable becomes the reigning genre in *West Side Story*, *My Fair Lady*, and, above all, *The Sound of Music*. Attempts to duplicate their success lead to a meltdown of reckless budgets, non-singing stars, and a failure to entertain. The traditional musical all but vanishes. There are exceptions, such as Bob Fosse's very altered view of Broadway's *Cabaret*, but the era is best summed up in Bette Midler's ironic comment on the spectacularly rotten *Lost Horizon*: "I never miss a Liv Ullmann musical."

1976–the present: After ceasing most musical production, Hollywood tentatively reconsiders. A show from the psychologically and artistically dense Stephen Sondheim atelier, *Into the Woods*, is filmed with great success. *Chicago* wins the Best Picture Oscar. These are special events, not a business-as-usual as in the days of Astaire and Rogers or MacDonald and Eddy. Nevertheless, musicals are back.

CHAPTER 1

cVo

The First Hollywood Musicals

To share in political and social power in America, a minority group must first assert a presence in the popular arts. In the nineteenth century, German and Scandinavian immigrants moved to farming communities in the midwest, isolated from show business (except in Chicago, Milwaukee, and a few nearby cities). The Irish, Italian, and Jewish newcomers, however, settled in the cities of the northeast and got into the entertainment business. By about 1920, as black talent began to slip out of the segregated "black time" into the "white time" of main-stage entertainment, minorities were hitting the big time, and New York was their headquarters.

It was as well the command-and-control center of American show biz, in not only vaudeville and theatre but popular music, records, and radio. New York was *the* twentieth-century American city, with its pride of skyscrapers, its professional "characters" from gangsters to opera stars, and its unique wisecrack humor, a flavorsome blend of Irish sarcasm and Jewish fatalism.

Samson Raphaelson's sentimental little play *The Jazz Singer* (1925) was very much a "New York" piece, as a kind of fable spanning the worlds of Broadway and the ghetto. The title means *The Pop Singer*, and the title role is virtually two different people: Jakie Rabinowitz when at home with his Jewish cantor father and Jack Robin on the stage. The work's conflict resides in Jack's belief that his wonderfully expressive way with a melody is akin to his father's wailing prayers. Raphaelson even has Jack demonstrate this, first singing a Hebrew canticle and then a pop song "to exactly the same tune"—as the stage directions demand—"and exactly the same plaintiveness but with a new rhythm and shaking his shoulders."

Cantor Rabinowitz furiously rejects the parallel, but the public must have been intrigued, for *The Jazz Singer* ran 303 performances—quite big for the day—and, after the usual tour, returned to town in the cavernous Century Theatre, suggesting a hot-ticket booking. Given that singing was the story's very substance, Raphaelson constructed a play with music, allowing Jack a solo called "Home Pals," an offstage prayer with choral backup, and "Dixie Mammy," also sung offstage. As Jack sings it (again, in the stage directions), it "has an evangelical terror, a fanatical frenzy...and has moments of staggering dramatic intensity." Now Raphaelson concludes his argument: "We are listening to a Cantor in blackface."

It's an arresting idea, because who ever considered the ontology of the Mammy Song—or the Moon Song, the Girl's Name Song, the New Dance Sensation, or any of the strait-format numbers that decorated American entertainment? Unfortunately, *The Jazz Singer* as a whole is maudlin and ordinary, with a "Here he comes now" before the star entrance and the same old musical-comedy jokes:

> JACK: I've been down to my father's farm where we have a black hen
>   that lays a white egg.
> STRAIGHT MAN: What's so wonderful about that?
> JACK: You go home and try it!

Still, *The Jazz Singer* was, if nothing else, a tale with an arresting conflict about music at its heart, which made it an ideal source when Warner Bros. shot the first movie musical. Then, too, *The Jazz Singer* was a backstager, with performing spots for Jack—and, in a way, a performing spot for Jakie, when he responds to the call of his forefathers, drops out of a show called *April Follies*, and substitutes in the synagogue for his ailing father.

Thus, the movie wouldn't have to explain where any of the accompaniments were coming from, whether orchestra, piano, or organ; it was an anxiety all over Hollywood in the first days of the musical. This is what made the backstager prominent, because if you're rehearsing, somewhere there's bound to be a piano, even if the public can't see it. And once the curtain goes up, there's an orchestra in the pit. But what if the film in question isn't a backstager? What if, God forbid, two sweethearts take a stroll in a forest and some crazy songwriter gives them a love song? Where was the orchestra supposed to be, sitting in the trees?

Yet more: Raphaelson's play was New Yorkist in tone, and New York was the nation's obsession and resentment, filled with folks who were "different"—like the Rabinowitzes, foreigners who came here yet stayed foreign. New York and its nonconformist carnival may have irritated a lot of red-state Americans, but it was a great movie city, because no matter what you put on the screen, the public believed it if it took place there: New York was stories. And it was show business, too. If Jakie Rabinowitz was a nobody, Jack Robin was a Broadway star, big stuff.

On Broadway, *The Jazz Singer*'s Jack/Jakie was George Jessel, an actor who could sing, but a "soft" talent, valid yet limited. Even so, Jessel was tapped to preserve his role on film. I have called *The Jazz Singer* the first musical, but it really was a part-talkie, a silent with a music-and-sound-effects track that, every so often, would give Jessel a song spot.

Then something happened. Historians tell us that Jessel made demands and Warner Bros. replaced him with Al Jolson—yet surely there was more to it than that. *The Jazz Singer* was planned to change the course of the movie business, and you don't make history with a soft talent. The vocals had to leap off the screen, take the audience into the future. Jolson had been an electric presence in entertainment for over a decade—didn't this mother of all musicals need electricity to establish the talkie in an industry that was all but unanimously against it because of the tremendous economic and technical problems? And didn't the Warners realize that Jessel was inadequate and Jolson was ideal?

So, what of *The Jazz Singer*'s numbers themselves? A hodgepodge by various writers, the score gathered up pre-existing songs, including the religious scenes and two pieces that Jolson had sung on Broadway in *Bombo* (1921), "Dirty Hands, Dirty Face" and "Toot Toot Tootsie (Goo'bye)." And then we come to "Blue Skies," by Irving Berlin. This is the song that invented the Hollywood musical, as the centerpiece of *The Jazz Singer*'s most effective sound sequence.

For now Jack ends a self-imposed exile to return to his place of origin. Critics think of *The Jazz Singer* as little more than a historical artifact, yet it is in fact quite artfully directed (by Alan Crosland). When Jack says farewell to his show-biz colleagues in a railroad yard, Jolson dances about waving his cap as their train departs. Behind him, another train passes in the opposite direction. It's no more than a moment, but it places Jolson at a kind of crossroads, like the one where Oedipus killed his father—and we can't fail to notice a heavily Oedipal undertone in *The Jazz Singer* in the first place.

Or we could view the train bit as simply that wonderful juxtaposition of moving objects that silent film reveled in. It intensifies the rhythm of the storytelling, as do title cards in ever larger lettering:

New York!
Broadway!
HOME!
MOTHER!

This leads into the "Blue Skies" episode, *The Jazz Singer*'s most discussed reel. Jack smothers his mom with love and then performs for her at the keyboard. Along the way, he breaks into a monologue about moving her to the Bronx and a perhaps tonier crowd than on the Lower East Side—"the Ginsburgs, the Guttenbergs, and the Goldbergs. Oh, a whole lot of Bergs. I dunno 'em all."

Jolson's manic confidence in this idiotic blather, the apparent surprise of the woman playing his mother (Eugenie Besserer, who nonetheless acts right along with him, albeit murmuring), and even the way Jolson flirts with her, noting, "You're getting kittenish," all suggest sheer improvisation. So does Jolson's ensuing rip into "Blue Skies," his left hand pounding away in "stride" style and his voice decorating the melody with scat tidbits. Now for another great touch from director Crosland: he frames a shot with Besserer at left and Jolson at right; at center, Jolson's father (Warner Oland) totters in in his usual bearded daze, realizes what's happening, and shouts, *"Stop!"*

The audio instantly switches back to pantomime-and-orchestra, but the history has been made. Lately, historians have doubted that the episode really was improvised. They say Besserer wasn't surprised, and she was murmuring because Jolson had the shot's only mike. And it wasn't Jolson playing the piano.

But it *was* Jolson singing, bringing the raved-up naturalism of his stage deportment onto the screen. In fact, Jolson's delivery of cheery or comic lines always sounded improvisational; one hears this in all his films. Like him or not, he has an energy that set the Hollywood musical on the way to the rest of its life. And it's worth noting that "Blue Skies"—the most significant of *The Jazz Singer*'s eleven vocal cuts—is the film's sole number written by a first-division Broadway songwriter.

One cannot imagine this scene with any other song, for Berlin gave its exuberant lyrics an irresistibly swinging setting that shows us why Jakie had to turn into Jack. The religious music that both unites and divides Jack and his father isn't meant to be heard outside of churchly precincts, but "jazz" reaches everyone everywhere.

And "Blue Skies" is sovereign jazz—which, again, simply means "popular music" in the context of the 1920s. It sounds like a made-to-order hit, and that's what it was: as an interpolation into a Ziegfeld flop with a Richard Rodgers and Lorenz Hart score called *Betsy* (1926). Its star, Belle Baker, begged Berlin for a dynamite number and he obliged. A grateful Ziegfeld arranged for a spotlight to beam upon Berlin as he took a bow during the number on the first night, while the show's nominal songwriters, who hadn't known their songs were going to be upstaged, were flabbergasted.

Well, Rodgers was. Hart simply shrugged: that's show biz. *Betsy* needed a quickmeup, and "Blue Skies" was the goods.

Yet it's an oxymoron of a song, for its A strains are in the minor, as if punning on "blue skies" (meaning "optimistic") and "blue" (meaning "sad"). Strange to tell, a contemporary news article by Edwin Schallert, unearthed and reprinted by Robert L. Carrington in *The Jazz Singer*'s published screenplay, reveals that the sequence was originally shot with an entirely different number, "It All Depends On You," by B. G. De Sylva, Lew Brown, and Ray Henderson. It's a fine song that had served Jolson well in another of his stage shows, *Big Boy* (1925), but it was too amiable a piece for this extraordinary scene.

Of course, Jolson had a packet of big-sing specialties he might have drawn on, but the most opportune—"Rockabye Your Baby With a Dixie Melody," from *Sinbad* (1918), "April Showers" (from *Bombo*), and "When the Red, Red, [*sic*] Robin Comes Bob, Bob, Bobbin' Along"—had already been used in Jolson's appearance in a program of Tin Pan Alley numbers released with a silent comedy with synchronized music, *The Better 'Ole* (1926). So the choice of "Blue Skies" was a kind of kismet, something inevitable that happens by accident.

The Jazz Singer was a roadshow, with tickets sold as if for Broadway, at higher prices and reserved seats. It more or less had to be, as theatres that showed it as a part-talkie needed to be wired for sound reproduction. (Most cinemas presented it as a silent, a few playing Jolson discs during his vocal sequences.) In all, *The Jazz Singer* was a revelation and a hit, and silent film had only two years left to live.

Its author hated it. "Dreadful" was Samson Raphaelson's verdict, in an interview quoted in the aforementioned Carringer edition of the screenplay.[1] "Silly," he said. "Maudlin." One could say as much of Raphaelson's play. Perhaps he was offended that his theme that blood destiny is an all but overwhelming force was changed in the film into an affirmation of the destiny of talent. Raphaelson didn't even approve of the movie's choice of songs, though he had to admit that "Blue Skies" hit the spot. And there is this odd bit: "From this particular [motion] picture," Raphaelson observes, "you wouldn't have much hope for the possibilities of [the sound] era."

---

1. The interview, from 1959, was part of the Columbia University Oral History series. A huge undertaking designed to explore the New Deal and the American civil rights, women's, and antiwar movements, the project also conversed with people in the arts, from Rudolf Friml to Stephen Sondheim, opera soprano Jarmila Novotna to Betty Comden and Adolph Green. Raphaelson's interview was conducted by Joan and Robert Franklin.

Is he kidding? Jolson's follow-up to *The Jazz Singer*, *The Singing Fool* (1928), turned out to be the biggest commercial hit between *The Birth of a Nation* (1915) and *Gone With the Wind* (1939), and suddenly all Hollywood was planning talkies. Though partly silent, *The Singing Fool* offered more dialogue than *The Jazz Singer*, and it, too, owned an outstanding number of Broadway authorship, the same "It All Depends On You" that was originally in the mother scene in *The Jazz Singer*, replaced by "Blue Skies."

On its own, "It All Depends On You" went so big that De Sylva, Brown, and Henderson published it with alternate covers, each one bearing a photograph of the number's many interpreters, including, besides Jolson himself, Hazel Hurd, Frank Munn, Jay C. Flippen, Rube Wolf, Tom Waring, even the Ipana Troubadours. The song's soft-grained tone is strengthened by its key position in *The Singing Fool*'s plot, for Al, as Jolson is called here, has written it to impress a blond gold digger (Josephine Dunn), sings it in a club, wows the usual Big Broadway Producer, and ends up spurning the nice dark-haired girl (Betty Bronson) when the blonde indicates an interest. Now it's time for the club manager (Arthur Housman) to sidle up to Bronson and utter the movie's theme line: "No matter how smart a guy is or how long he lives, he'll never know anything about women."

As with "Blue Skies," Jolson makes "It All Depends On You" entirely his own, demoting all the other cameos on the sheet-music covers to Etch-a-sketch status. In a word, he Jolsonizes the number, building up from a deceptively modest start to a second chorus more declaimed than sung and riddled with inserted words that tear the written lyrics into confetti. Not till the very last line does Jolson simply pronounce the words and sing the pitches (with an added high note).

Even so, *The Singing Fool*'s unqualified top hit was the sappy "Sonny Boy" (also by De Sylva, Brown, and Henderson), which Jolson sings to his toddler (David—generally known as Davey—Lee). What Jack Robin's mother was to *The Jazz Singer*, Sonny Boy is to *The Singing Fool*: a receptacle for the vast amount of love the insecure yet ebullient Jolson needs to express in manic worship. The mother thing was at least picturesque, if only to watch Eugenie Besserer squirming and mooing during the "Blue Skies" scene. But Jolson's relationship with Sonny Boy is revolting. Has there ever been a father so gluey and dippy, grabbing the kid, holding him, kissing him, calling him "sweetheart" and "darling" over and over?

Mind you, there's nothing untoward in Jolson's affection. There's just too much of it. And then of course Al's marriage has fallen apart (because he married the gold digger instead of the nice girl), he hits the skids, and Sonny Boy dies. Why? Because it's time to be sad in the cinema. Al returns to the stage to sing "Sonny Boy," now inspired to remake his life for the better.

Note that *The Singing Fool* is another backstager. Hollywood nourished a very greed for the form, remaking plots right into the 1950s. In fact, there were essentially only three:

PLOT A: Two women love the same man as they all put on the show.

PLOT B: A male star on the rise gets ego fever and deserts his true love, to reconcile with her after various hardships as they all put on the show.

PLOT C: The woman star becomes indisposed and her understudy wows the public as they all put on the show.

The Singing Fool is Plot B, but the first all-talkie musical, MGM's *The Broadway Melody* (1929) uses Plot A: freshly arrived in New York from the midwest, the two Mahoney Sisters join Francis Zanfield's latest super-production. Feisty sister Hank (Bessie Love) and Eddie (Charles King), Zanfield's star juvenile, have been a couple, but now Eddie falls for the other Mahoney, sister Queenie (Anita Page). It's a classic triangle, because Hank is the interesting one but Queenie the lovely one—in other words, the one the dull male will always go for. And while the girls are devoted to each other, Hank insists on sacrificing her happiness and renouncing Eddie: she departs on a long four shows a day vaudeville tour to let Eddie and Queenie start their life together.

But note that the movie doesn't fade out on an Eddie-Queenie kiss panel (as they put it in romance comic books). It ends as Hank, her new gal performing partner, and her ridiculously stuttering uncle of an agent (who keeps on trying to get a word out then settles for a synonym, in a comedy cliché of the time) are heading for the train station. It's a wildly offbeat ending for a film that won the Best Picture Oscar, especially as we keep noticing the sadly distracted look on Hank's face. Uncle gets off a last stutter joke, the partner lets out a giggle, and Hank manages a half-smile. Unlucky in love, lucky in vaudeville, and the camera takes a last look at bustling Times Square, the hub of the entertainment world. That's the Broadway melody.

This ironic fadeout is not simply a decoration: it is the very stuff of the film, which is at once silly, brutal, touching, and naturalistic to a fault. One scene in Hank's dressing room, in which she utterly loses control while contemplating what she must give up—love of Eddie because of her love of Queenie—got Bessie Love a Best Actress nomination. (She lost to Mary

Pickford, trying out an uncharacteristically serious role in *Coquette*.) In a way, Love was the woman equivalent of Al Jolson—not as a singer, but in the raw, explosive personality that put the talkie over as something beyond—and, yes, better than—silent film.

Many strains of realism run through *The Broadway Melody* along with strains of imaginative whimsey. A rich fancy pants tries to seduce Queenie with an oleaginous power personality that repels us. It's not simply irritating. It's disturbing, because this brilliantined creep keeps trying to take her over, to own her like a dog with a bone. It makes one want to shout at the screen in frustration. Yet, at the same time, the film shows us a flamboyant gay costume designer, and Zanfield has an amusing troop of yes-men backers, invariably in black tie and including one guy who's never seen sober. ("Come on, Unconscious," his buddy constantly tells him.) Or there's the dancer who taps in toe shoes. Or Zanfield himself (Eddie Kane), obviously a tintype of Florenz Ziegfeld but played with obtuse line readings and no involvement whatsoever in what is happening around him. It might be the worst performance ever in an MGM musical.

In other words, *The Broadway Melody* is a grabbag of art, now direly honest and now capricious or even prone to accident. Above all, it treats its tale to a realism all but unknown to the stage musical of the time. Yes, *Deep River* (1926) and *Show Boat* (1927) dealt with adult themes, and a number of twenties operettas saw the world from a liberals-versus-fascists viewpoint, as in *The New Moon* (1928). Even so, Broadway, whether in carefree musical comedy or the more evolved operetta, could not challenge the realism we see in parts—only parts, I repeat—of *The Broadway Melody*.

And that is because the Broadway musical and the Hollywood musical derive from antagonistically different sources. The former's origins lie in ancient burlesque and musical farce, forms that are essentially comic in every aspect. Fun stuff. But the movie musical's origins lie in the movies themselves, taking in genres from comedy and romance to drama and suspense; not all of these are "fun." So the movies grew up on their own, influenced by the theatre in various ways at various times but generally independent of it.

And yet: those New Yorkers did know how to talk. *The Broadway Melody* is obsessed with Manhattan, especially in the way it expresses itself. Plays of the 1920s had been featuring New York wisecrack humor, and *The Broadway Melody* is filled with it. With the wisecrack comes bad grammar; "ain't" and "he don't" saturate the early talkie. But the slang was wisecrack's glory: "jack" (for "money"), "crepehanger" (a pessimist), a "facial" (for "a sock in the nose"). Better yet, New York was the place where the music starts, and *The Broadway Melody* opens in a music publisher's office in full cry, with room after room of professionals trying things out—a singer here, instrumentalists there. A new song. An innovative arrangement. Above all, the central question:

What does the public want from the music it hears? Eddie knows, as he goes into a brand-new piece sure to put Zanfield's show over—"The Broadway Melody" itself. All the others gather around to hear, overseen by the publisher himself, a Mr. Gleason. He is in fact James Gleason, a playwright and actor strongly associated with New York wisecrack comedy and a co-author of this very screenplay, hired to juice it up with New York quips and taunts: Is zat so? Yes, *zat's so*! And note the self-effacing accompanist at the keyboard: it's the film's real-life composer, Nacio Herb Brown. As Eddie unveils his prodigy of a song, his little audience is transfixed, especially a young woman who picks up the rhythm, listens to the words, and utterly succumbs to its spell. New music is new life, and she, like everyone else, realizes how essential is the songwriter's art in the pursuit of success.

This place is Tin Pan Alley: Twenty-Eighth Street between Fifth and Sixth Avenues, where many music publishers were located. By synecdoche, the term encompassed the American popular-music business itself.[2] However, a revolution had occurred sometime before this, when Tin Pan Alley was taken over by Jerome Kern, the Gershwins, Vincent Youmans, Rodgers and Hart, Cole Porter, and others who wrote not one-off song hits but scores for Broadway shows. Around 1900, hit tunes had no connection with musicals or were interpolated into productions after shows were written, because Broadway's composer-lyricist teams generally lacked the skill—or whatever it was—to concoct a hit. There were exceptions, yes. But, in the main, the smash successes—such as "After the Ball," "Under the Bamboo Tree," "Meet Me in St. Louis, Louis," and "Yip-I-Addy-I-Ay!"—were heard on their own in vaudeville or were dropped into a Broadway show as a foreign element.

Then came the revolution, in about 1914, just as the one composer known for creating hit tunes for Broadway, Victor Herbert, began to lose influence. He was Old Music, sometimes European in flavor. The New Music was adventurous and the accompanying lyrics sophisticated and sly.

---

2. The Twenty-Eighth Street block's offices, through whose open windows passersby could hear a multitude of pianos and voices reviewing the latest would-be song hits, created an amusing cacophony—thus the "tin pan" description, as if an entire kitchen were being tossed. The address was current very early in the twentieth century only, because the music business followed the theatres, which moved up Broadway every generation or so. By the time of the talkie revolution, New York's theatre district stretched from Thirty-Ninth Street up to Central Park, and the music publishers were headquartered from about Thirty-Seventh Street to Fiftieth.

From Rodgers and Hart's "Manhattan" to Cole Porter's "Night and Day"—
not to mention George Gershwin's pop-classical *Rhapsody in Blue*—this
new collection of songwriters combined commercial success with distinction of style. The New Music left Tin Pan Alley behind, and we might call its
adherents "the Harms group," after their publishing house, T. B. Harms. Its
chief was Max Dreyfus, the least known name of all masterminds in the
making of Broadway musicals. Dreyfus put writers together, advised producers whom to hire, packaged orchestrators and dance arrangers, and
brewed nearly all music theatre in his cauldron.

So, when MGM needed a songwriting team for *The Broadway Melody*, the
studio came calling on the Harms group, right? After all, who would know
what a Broadway melody is better than one of Max Dreyfus' protégés? And
this was a historical commission, too, for the part-talkie musicals had assembled their scores from a variety of donors. *The Broadway Melody*, the
first all-talkie musical, would likewise boast the first score entirely written
for the specific occasion by a single team.

But MGM did not apply to Harms. Instead, the studio hired the aforementioned composer Nacio Herb Brown and lyricist Arthur Freed, both of
whom had been working separately for some eight or ten years in Los
Angeles. Freed had actually started as a musician. He was a song plugger
like the ones we see in *The Broadway Melody*'s opening sequence, auditioning the latest numbers for show-biz folk hunting hits for their act. A singer
and even composer as well, Freed ultimately found his niche writing words
to Brown's tunes, so Brown and Freed became a byline typical of the 1930s
screen musical: under contract to a single studio with little or no Broadway
work. Warner Bros. had Harry Warren and Al Dubin. Twentieth Century-
Fox had Harry Revel and Mack Gordon. Paramount had Ralph Rainger and
Leo Robin. And all these teams were, in essence, Tin Pan Alleymen. True,
their style was smartly evolved, for the New Music, extremely influential as
it was, inspired all songwriters. But the music that Hollywood wanted for
its musicals was not show music. It was hit music.

And what precisely did Tin Pan Alley want from a song? Here's one
recipe: a simple texture overall in both words and music, but with a kick.
Take for instance *The Broadway Melody*'s love ballad, "You Were Meant For
Me." It couldn't be simpler—its second line is "I was meant for you." Yet the
melody starts in not the tonic (as almost invariably in pop music), but the
supertonic sixth, not resolving to the tonic till the third measure. This gives
the song an airy quality, and the release is so chromatic that its first three
measures run down from (in F Major, the published key) D to F, skipping
only a single half-step. In all, the music is lithe and slithery, a glass of water
disguised as a love potion.

Of course, as a backstager, *The Broadway Melody* could program all the songs as performer spots—but on two occasions we get a number in a hotel room with no legitimate source of accompaniment. So Hollywood is already breaking away from its fear of The Orchestra From Nowhere. At some point, a musical is a musical, and this will be one of my throughlines in these pages: Hollywood's approach-avoidance relationship with the practices of the stage musical. Or, really, its love of New York's prestige and originality coupled with a fear of alienating the New York–hating public out in what we now call the red-state countryside.

These folks, curiously enough, knew of the Mahoney Sisters, and may even have seen them in vaudeville, for they were real people: Rosetta and Vivian Duncan, on whom MGM based the fictitious Mahoneys. The Duncans were not great talents, but they were great stars, because they had such terrific chemistry together, Rosetta's Hank-style command and Vivian's Queenie-esque sweetness dovetailing onstage exactly as Bessie Love and Anita Page do in the movie. The Duncans preferred vaudeville to Broadway, because the undemanding public of the smalltown variety theatres formed their core audience. Still, the Duncans did try a musical now and again, most famously *Topsy and Eva* (1925), based of course on *Uncle Tom's Cabin*, with Vivian as dear Little Eva and mischievous Rosetta as Topsy, in the usual blackface with a pride of braids sticking straight up from her head. The Duncans even wrote the show's songs, and they toured triumphantly in it for years while critics everywhere moaned in their seats and prayed for death.

With a worldwide gross of some twelve times its production cost and a Best Picture Oscar, *The Broadway Melody* was a genre success on the spectacular level: it infixed the New York backstager as an ideal platform for the Hollywood musical. As every studio readied imitations, MGM went to the film's source material and made a kind of second *Broadway Melody* starring the Duncans themselves: *It's a Great Life* (1929). For variation, the Plot A setup created a triangle balanced not on a guy (here Lawrence Gray) both girls love but on the Queenie figure. Thus, Gray and Rosetta fight over Vivian, Gray as her husband and Rosetta as her protective sister, who has taken an implacable dislike to Gray.

Modest in every respect, *It's a Great Life* is no *Broadway Melody*. Its backstage is distinctly smalltime, that of department-store-employee talent shows and third-rate vaudeville. Its score, too, mostly fumbles. Composer Dave Dreyer and lyricist Ballad MacDonald lacked initiative, and while MacDonald had done a lot of work on Broadway, Dreyer was strictly Tin Pan Alley; they're hard to characterize as a team. Nor does the script revel in the inflected wisenheimer chatter we enjoy from *The Broadway*

Melody's show folk. But then, MGM might have been holding down the soft pedal to soothe the feelings of those unsophisticated villagers out in the regions.

Indeed, MGM based *It's a Great Life* entirely on the Duncans' charm. Rosetta was a natural-born cutup, perfectly suited to the extemporaneous atmosphere that prevailed in old show business. Audiences liked seeing the stars working at the edge of a danger zone, impulsively riffing on some line or piece of business that wasn't in the script, and that extremely "live" ambiance is preserved in the very earliest talkies. After all, wasn't that why Al Jolson's dialogue in his "Blue Skies" sequence so excited the public? And the Duncans were of the same school.

For instance, at that department-store variety show, Lawrence Gray is at the keyboard accompanying Vivian, who is kitted out in recital-afternoon white, trimmed with huge roses and topped by a floppy hat. Her number is "Won't You Be My Lady Love?," dippy and sentimental. (You'll recall the genre if you're ninety years old; the verse begins "They were sitting by the river in a little birch canoe...") Director Sam Wood moves into the stage-left wings to show Rosetta, waiting to go on in a checked "mad little tyke" outfit, pridefully nodding to the other performers. That's my sister!

But nervous Vivian is troubled by the high soprano key—and, suddenly, Rosetta prances onstage, pretending to try to stop her singing in a babyish voice. Vivian murmurs, "Get me out of here," and Rosetta whispers, "Just do it, honey, they'll think it's part of the act." Rosetta starts to exit, but at a *pow!* high note from Vivian, Rosetta grabs her behind and goes flying off-stage as if shot. No, wait...she's back, still trying to "sabotage" the number. Vivian plays along, giggling—surely they can't have rehearsed this bit of "real-life" flummery—and now Rosetta makes another entrance, swaggering around in a mantilla and waving a vast feathered fan. Then another crazy entrance: Rosetta comes gliding in backward on tippy-toe, grabs Vivian's arm, and pulls her offstage right. Gray and the two girls take their bows, Gray signals for a speech, and, just as he opens his mouth, Rosetta snatches the stage away from him to announce an encore. There's just time for a sotto voce hate fight:

GRAY: Hey, Dizzy, you're gonna clown yourself into a flop.
ROSETTA: Say, I just clowned you outta one!

And she looks tougher than he does.

Here we reach the film's key number, "I'm Following You," which the Duncans deliver in close harmony. This is where the sisters go deep Duncan on us, not just musically but lovingly, making the song—which is about the steadfast nature of their bond—a valentine to each other. Now the use of Tin Pan Alleymen instead of the more resourceful talents of the Harms group makes sense: the squonky "Won't You Be My Lady Love?" and the endearing "I'm Following You" function, in the most basic, uninflected way, as a set: first, the sentimental clichés; second, the honesty. It's an irresistible sequence, combining the amateurish and expert at once; it almost suggests that all of us have a show-biz chromosome, needing only luck and timing—and personal support—to develop it.

On the other hand, Hollywood's early-talkie emphasis on scores by the second or third rank becomes monotonous, especially in films that use them as mere backstage punctuation of the dialogue scenes. Thus, Paramount's *The Dance of Life* (1929) counts some six new songs (along with older ones) that are no more than decoration. Drawn from George Manker Watters and Arthur Hopkins' stage hit *Burlesque* (1927),[3] *The Dance of Life* used the original playscript with occasional departures to give it air, and even hired Broadway's male lead, Hal Skelly, now opposite Nancy Carroll. Like many early talkies, *The Dance of Life* needed two directors, a movie veteran (A. Edward Sutherland) to frame the action optically and a stage veteran (John Cromwell, who became one of Hollywood's top directors of non-musical drama) to get actors who were routined in the silent arts to stop pantomiming all over the place and start picking up their dialogue cues. You're in the talkies now: don't show me how you feel, *talk!*

The result is interesting but undeniably stagey. Perhaps a more high-powered score would have helped, but, again, we are presented with a hodgepodge of abilities on various levels in composer-lyricist Sam Coslow, composer Richard A. Whiting, and lyricist Leo Robin, billed as a fixed threesome on every number. So who wrote what? How do three men write a song? Which reminds us of Cole Porter's immortal remark, upon hearing the insanely dreary "Cossack Love Song" from *Song of the Flame* (1925), whose score was similarly billed, inseparably, to composers George Gershwin and Herbert Stothart and lyricists Oscar Hammerstein and Otto Harbach. Said Porter, "It took four men to write *that*?"

The Dance of Life is a Plot B backstager, following the marriage, separation, and reunion of performers Skid (Skelly) and Bonny (Carroll) when he

3. According to *Photoplay* magazine, Paramount changed the title because "burlesque" was thought confusing, as the form had changed so since its origins in the 1870s: from a spoof of a literary or dramatic work to a cheap variety show to a lowdown smutty cheap variety show that municipal authorities often closed down on the theory of Sex = Freedom. The burlesque of the play is the middle of these three formats, something like vaudeville with a stock cast made entirely of women and a few male comics.

goes on the rise without her, ruins his career with drink, and at last finds redemption through love. But you'd never know much of that from Coslow, Whiting, and Robin's "King of Jazzmania," "Mightiest Matador," or "The Flippety Flop." Yet one number, though a performance piece like the others, does serve the action. In fact, it essentializes it: "True Blue Lou," the sad tale of a woman who stuck by her man no matter what he did to her. Again, the first line tells us what kind of number it is: "She was a dame," the chorus begins, "in love with a guy," and the A strains are based on a melodic cell repeated over shifting harmony and a stepwise descending bass line, a standard genre of the day. (The Gershwins' "The Man I Love" is the most famous example.) Skelly sings it in his characteristic outfit, a clown's tramp attire, lying prone on the stage, smoking and more or less talking his way through the music while the violins play the tune for him.

It's a strange way to put over a number, but it's a part of the intimacy that is *The Dance of Life*'s salient quality. John Cromwell must have known how to talk to actors, because this saga of a True Blue Lou is quite touching and believable. It's also full of that ripsnorting repartee of putdown and patois that so enlivens *The Broadway Melody*. Al Jolson is one reason silent film had to die, but wisecrack humor is another: we can't *hear* the character interaction of warring personalities on title cards.

Thus, early on, two minor players ramp up to a fight in their dressing room. Gussie, a heavy woman in a tutu, is getting aggressive with Mazie just as Nancy Carroll's Bonny enters:

BONNY: You better beat it, Gussie. You'll be late for the Fairy Number.
MAZIE: What is it, an elephant act?
GUSSIE: When I come back, I'm going to chase you till you find six new streets!

Still, it's the sincerity of the playing that makes the film, and the way in which Cromwell and Sutherland amplified the stage script's feelings—at that, often using the silent optics that were just then turning into ancient history. On stage, *Burlesque*'s first-act curtain comes down as the crowd of well-wishers takes the hero to the train that will carry him to the big time, leaving faithful Bonny behind. As the gang goes careering off, Bonny drags herself to the doorway to watch them. Says the script, "She remains looking after all is silent," and at length the curtain falls.

Good enough. But *The Dance of Life* doesn't stop there. As Bonny sits, bereft and worried, she is called to the stage for the "Swanee" number. Somehow, Carroll conveys her anxiety in an expressionless face, and the camera follows her as she trudges toward the stage. The "Swanee" number,

Stephen Foster's "Old Folks at Home," has been established (in both play and movie) as a prize duet in Skid and Bonny's act together, a token of their love. Now Bonny must dance alone, listlessly smiling, almost in tears at this sour variation on The Show Must Go On. And the camera keeps on taking her in, letting everyone in the movie audience move close to her in a way a theatre audience never could.

Later, Bonny writes Skid, telling him they're through; now he, too, must go onstage in despair, and we watch him make up in his dressing-room mirror. The black + on his eyes. The mouth extension lines. That lurid fake nose. Skelly plays the entire scene in a daze, the absurd cosmetics at war with what is happening in the story: the ripping open of a Plot B torso to reveal its broken heart.

One important difference between Broadway and Hollywood backstagers lies in the genre of play-within-a-play they feel comfortable with. New York producers Florenz Ziegfeld and George White plugged their own revue franchises in, respectively, *Sally* (1920) and *Manhattan Mary* (1927), in which the heroine scores a hit in Ziegfeld's *Follies* and White's *Scandals*. But Broadway more commonly treated companies putting on *story* shows, which in effect gave these shows two narratives to juggle. And that can be confusing.

So perhaps Hollywood was right to stick to backstagers about putting on a revue, a usefully plotless format that allows a film to slot in any song, dance, or comic sketch in the onstage scenes. Whether in smalltown burlesque (as in *The Dance of Life*) or on Broadway with all the trimmings (as in *The Broadway Melody*), each number begins with parting curtains and finishes with closing curtains, making each episode an insert, independent of the rest of the program.

Thus, *The Broadway Melody* could present "The Wedding of the Painted Doll" as a self-contained sequence: an unseen tenor (James Burroughs) sings of the fairyland nuptials, attended by such folk as Red Ridinghood, Buster Brown, and the Jumping Jack while rows of girls glide into view through trap doors and others cavort about, not so much dancing as carrying on. It's fun-filled yet eerie, in a tone of deadpan fantasy totally at war with the high-pitched realism of the rest of the film.

The revue format particularly suited Hollywood's Tin Pan Alleymen, as they could pull songs out of the air rather than have to give them story-and-character content in the manner of the Harms group. So it was inevitable that Hollywood would film full-length revues; each studio tried one in 1929–30, with very variable results. Generally, the aim was to let the stars cut loose, showing off hidden talents or going goofy, as when, in MGM's *The Hollywood Revue of 1929*, John Gilbert and Norma Shearer run through *Romeo and Juliet*'s Balcony Scene, first in Shakespearean text and then in

Jazz Age jive. (GILBERT: Julie, baby, I'm gaga about you!) At a time when actors were known by their work only, it's a bit precious, and we sympathize with tough guy George Bancroft when, trapped in white tie and tails at a too-too soirée in *Paramount on Parade* (1930), he turns right to the audience (you could do this at Paramount) and says, "I know no parlor tricks."

The scores for these early Hollywood revues generally favored easy content—dating songs, comic specialties, songs about the movies, what we might call "whatever songs": whatever the audience will enjoy. On Broadway, revues pitched numbers to an au courant public—songs about the latest political rumble, the newest hit show, "If a Table at Rector's Could Talk" (at the restaurant notorious for extramarital rendezvous), or "You Must Come Over" (after the tumultuous drag comic Bert Savoy's signature command, in anticipation of Mae West, "You musssst come over").

Hollywood, however, needed to reach a broader public, one that never heard of Rector's and wasn't up on New York's calendar of first nights. In the movies, revue songs were just songs. So Warner Bros.' revue, *The Show of Shows* (1929), gives us "Li-Po-Li," about a dangerous Asian bandit who'll "sneak around and peek around," not to mention "come a-creeping"; or "Dear Little Pup," which charmless emcee Frank Fay aims at an Alsatian he drags about, on the borderline of animal abuse; or "My Sister," in which eight pairs of supposed siblings (one couple was fake) sing about nothing in ever-changing sets and costumes depicting European countries; or simply "Lady Luck [don't give my hopes the razz]," in the emptiest lyric premise imaginable.

Who wrote such numbers? A typical songwriter of the first years of the Hollywood musical might be Con Conrad, a composer and sometime lyricist, and clever enough to have written the music for the Oscars' first Best Song, "The Continental." Conrad typifies as well the Tin Pan Alleyman in the late 1910s and early 1920s, when he was turning out one-off pop hits: "My Little Sunshine," "Sheeksa, The Queen of Araby," "Margie," "The Co-Ed," "Barney Google" (after a famous comic-strip figure), or "Ma! [he's making eyes at me]," originally published with the single word spanning virtually all the sheet's cover space.

Yet Conrad did write for Broadway. One hears a kind of wrench in his style as he moves out of the simple demands of the pop tune into the rigor of a stage score in *Kitty's Kisses*, to Gus Kahn's lyrics. A hit of Broadway's 1925–26 season, *Kitty's Kisses* relied on one of those absurdly farcical plots that Didn't Matter the way the songs, dances, jokes, and performing talent did, and these songs are not only tuneful but imaginative. "Thinking of You" runs on descending chromatic lines in its A *and* B strains, "I Don't Want Him" is a dizzy argument for three, "Choo Choo Love" boasts a charleston in its verse, and "Step on the Blues" (this one by Conrad and co-composer Will Donaldson, with lyrics by Otto Harbach) is so syncopated that the vocal careens past bar lines as if drunk on dance.

So this question of how much content a movie musical's score needs, and who is equipped to write these scores, is complex. I oppose Tin Pan Alley to the Harms group—the often simplistic Nacio Herb Brown and Arthur Freed to, for instance, Jerome Kern and Oscar Hammerstein writing at genius level on *Show Boat*. This comparison helps us to understand an essential difference between what Hollywood wanted (which was songs created to appeal to a very wide public) and what Broadway wanted (and that was, often though not invariably, songs engrossed in the development of plot and character).

These dueling policies can be encapsulated in the use of one specific number, another easy-listen Brown-Freed title, "Singin' in the Rain." It first appeared in MGM's aforementioned *Hollywood Revue of 1929*, with the cast in slickers standing in front of Noah's Ark. They were singin' and it was raining; that's all.

But consider how much more the studio got out of the same number in *Singin' in the Rain* (1952) itself, for there the song reveals how Gene Kelly's character feels about life. He's young and talented and he has just realized that he's in love. Stomping and splashing around in the wet, he shows us what an enlightened heart looks like. A downpour and even a suspicious cop can't faze him, and this is one of the American musical's elemental lessons: love makes us independent. Liberated. But note that this teaching moment is not really inherent in the song as it was written—only in how it was re-used twenty-three years after it first appeared.

On the other hand, Tin Pan Alleymen could prove surprisingly resourceful even when writing those easy-listen pieces, as in *King of Jazz* (1930). This was Universal's revue. However, as the studio lacked music-ready contractees, it was decided to build the event around an outsider: bandleader Paul Whiteman, along with the kind of music he played in the style in which he played it.

Actually, Whiteman played a wide variety of music, from Victor Herbert to George Gershwin—it was Whiteman who commissioned and premiered the *Rhapsody in Blue*, in 1924. His style, however, was unique, a re-invention of the "jazz band" as an orchestra working in an above all smooth texture; Whiteman's orchestrator, Ferde Grofé, would introduce instrumental solos to complement the overall sound rather than jump out of it. Whiteman was famously known as the "king of jazz"—but it was your father's jazz, the opposite of the erotic chaos that mayors and police chiefs heard in the work of the real jazzmen.

This suggests a demure little movie, but *King of Jazz* is not only the best of the revues but one of the best of the early Hollywood musicals. And that's because Universal brought in a New Yorker to direct the film, John Murray Anderson. One of the artier sorts of director on Broadway, Anderson had established himself in the revue in versions intimate (the *Greenwich Village Follies*) and grandiose (*The Music Box Revue*). Anderson had done several stage shows with composer Milton Ager and lyricist Jack Yellen, Alleymen at heart, and Anderson brought them out to California to create the *King of Jazz* score.

It's a fine one, tuneful if not especially original in its subject matter. Anyway, it's really Anderson's unifying vision that makes the picture (along with the $2,000,000 budget and all-Technicolor cinematography). This really is the Paul Whiteman Show (with a few short comedy sketches here and there), with the band freely participating in the action. That includes the Rhythm Boys—Al Rinker, Harry Barris, and Bing Crosby. It's Crosby who opens the film, singing "Music Has Charms" over the credits.[4]

Like other numbers in *King of Jazz*, the song makes a paradox out of the tonic and tonic minor, playfully slipping back and forth. The score has its bold moments, too, as when, in the generally simple "Song of the Dawn," Ager closes the first A strain in the submediant minor, then the subdominant, the dominant seventh, and the tonic but resolves the second A, hair-raisingly, in the leading-note minor seventh (with the melody on the sixth), then the submediant major with a minor seventh and a major ninth, and a flatted submediant with a natural sixth and a sharpened second (!) before the dominant seventh and the tonic. That's *bold*.

Still, again, it is Anderson who makes all of this special in his stagings, for instance in a guide visual for "A Bench in the Park" in the use of small set pieces seen from the rear and then revolved to present the performers. The color display is part of the bonding, emphasizing pink, white, and blue. (Early, "two-strip" Technicolor famously had trouble reproducing blue, but certain shades of it, now of a white tinge and now of a green, did turn up now and again till the improved three-strip process was adopted for features, from 1935 on.)

With almost all of *King of Jazz* devoted to music-making, one might assume that the score was recorded live during shooting, as was common at

---

4. Crosby sings "hath" instead of has, probably thinking, as many do, of the famous line "Music hath charms to soothe the savage beast." It's not only famous, but wholly incorrect. The actual words, the very first to be heard in William Congreve's play *The Mourning Bride*, are: "Musick has Charms to sooth a savage Breast, To soften Rocks, or bend a knotted Oak." *Breast*, not *beast*.

the time. In his autobiography, Richard Rodgers says, "Every time someone sang, the entire studio orchestra had to be on the set"—and Rodgers didn't get to Hollywood till 1930. However, when he was interviewed for an advance piece on *King of Jazz* in *Photoplay* by Harry Lang, John Murray Anderson described an innovation: "We made the sound-tracks [*sic*] . . . separately from the picture, just as we'd make phonograph records."

Was Anderson the first to do so? Certainly, by the time of *42nd Street*, in 1933, lip-synching to pre-recording was routine. But no one knows exactly when the practice began, especially as the on-set orchestra, playing away just behind the camera, was still—as Rodgers recalled—in vogue in 1930.

Hollywood's revues were not successful enough overall to survive their first two years (except in altered form as the storyline-*cum*-revue, which lasted into the 1940s). Revue's songs, however—self-contained and independent of character and situation—became essential to Hollywood's *story* musicals even as they were losing traction on Broadway in favor of scores more concerned with plot and character.

True, even the Gershwins, on *Girl Crazy*, a Broadway hit of 1930, filled the evening with revue-ish numbers.[5] The love plot did maintain story songs—"Could You Use Me?," "Embraceable You," "But Not For Me." But everything else was local color or specialties. "I Got Rhythm" sounds like a song delineating personality, especially as it was introduced by the dynamic Ethel Merman—yet it's simply a floor number, put over in a nightclub setting. Or surely "Treat Me Rough" is a character song, one thinks. No: it's a shrimpy-Second-Couple-male-flirts-with-the-girls bit for William Kent, as Merman's always-true-to-you-in-my-fashion husband.

As we'll see, the irruption into Hollywood of the Harms writers will reorient the movie musical—in part—toward the integrated score. But the movies' backstagers remained devoted to the notion that all Broadway shows are revues with songs run up in Tin Pan Alley style, like "The Wedding of the Painted Doll" or "True Blue Lou." This is what Hollywood loved about these numbers: the Broadway curtains part, the singers and dancers entertain, the Broadway curtains close, the Broadway theatregoers, dressed to the nines, clap, and the live public in the cinemas across the country do not have to know anything to enjoy what they saw. It's only lyrics and music. The woods are just trees, the trees are just wood. There's none of that . . . that

---

5. A popular misconception assumes that musicals weren't integrated till *Show Boat* (1927) or even *Oklahoma!* (1943). In fact, the musical as a form has been integrated since *The Beggar's Opera* (1728), an English "ballad opera," and the American musical fell into line with, for example, *Evangeline* (1874), a "burlesque"; *Robin Hood* (1891), a "comic opera"; and *The Belle of New York* (1897), a musical comedy with operetta flavoring.

New York sophistication to trouble the moviegoer with thoughts of who a character is or what he or she needs.

Nevertheless, 1929 brought us an exceptional backstager in which the show being produced is not a revue but a story show with story songs. It's a favorite of historians because it's so screwy that writers always enjoy an excuse to rescreen, take notes on, and write about it: Warner Bros.' *On With the Show!*.

Based on Humphrey Pearson's apparently unproduced play *Shoestring*, *On With the Show!* follows the real lives of the cast and crew of a musical called *The Phantom Sweetheart* during its out-of-town tryout. The 104-minute running time takes place backstage and onstage during a single performance, which may be its last, as the producer has run out of money. Worse, the box office has been robbed, the scenery wrangler wants his sets back, the leading lady is going to pull a sitdown (enabling a Plot C resolution when the theatre's hat-check girl goes on in her place), and everyone is generally on everyone else's case.

There is no protagonist. This is the ultimate ensemble cast—producer Sam Hardy, leading juvenile (and future B-movie Dagwood) Arthur Lake, prima donna Betty Compson, comic Joe E. Brown, surprise artiste Ethel Waters, sweethearts William Bakewell and Sally O'Neil (the hat-check girl who goes on for the star), and many more. What fascinates is less *On With the Show!* than *The Phantom Sweetheart* itself, because it's not only a story musical but so idiotic it borders on the thrilling. Sample dialogue:

LAKE: (striking a pose) Engaged to one girl, madly in love with another! But! Is she real, or just a phantom sweetheart?

Sample ensemble number:

LAKE'S BARITONE FATHER: (leading off in hoptoad tempo) Aren't we happily, very happily, gathered here today?

and the chorus, raising prop glasses, replies, "We certainly are!" as they proceed toward the refrain of "Lift the Juleps To Your Two Lips."

Is this supposed to be a spoof, or were some stage shows or the 1920s this loony? Because, in every respect, *The Phantom Sweetheart* observes the conventions, from the spectacularly unimaginative ensemble choreography (by Larry Ceballos, a Broadway veteran of unimposing titles) through the solo dancers who stroll on after somebody else's vocal and start moving to the melody and on to the massed finale, with its recitatives and reprises as Lake spurns his fiancée during the wedding to claim instead his beguiling spook.

This is a musical comedy, however, so Joe E. Brown pairs off with the bride without a word, and there's your happy ending. Even the *Phantom*

Sweetheart scenery is strictly Broadway-compatible, with an arriving-boat effect (and we see the stagehands pushing it on from the wings) and garden hedges that part for a set change.

Once again, we have the resourceful Alan Crosland directing, and he really gets into the backstage atmosphere. Silly or not, this film oozes greasepaint. And the eight Harry Akst and Grant Clarke songs are truly of the Broadway type, even if mostly third division in quality. True, Ethel Waters' numbers, "Am I Blue?" and "Birmingham Bertha," are first-rate, but they serve as insert numbers, bearing no connection to the *Phantom Sweetheart* milieu. In fact, Waters' entire role is an insert, as she is the only player absent from the backstage continuity.

Still, whether *On With the Show!* is laughing at mediocrity or attaining to it, we have to note how much Hollywood depended on the arts of New York in the making of musicals: in the backstager format itself, in New York's patois and attitudes and prestige, and its guardians of the doorway to success (as music publishers, producers casting a show, and the like) as talented young people forever try to charge through that portal.

This brings us to Hollywood's most obvious emulation of Broadway: the adapting of hit stage musicals into movie musicals. Of course, there was still that problem of characters bursting into song outside a performing context— but one solution lay in operetta, because it was filled with sopranos and tenors, and somehow it doesn't feel odd if those hifalutin types suddenly start singing.

Hollywood's first direct-from-Broadway operetta was *The Desert Song* (1929). While *The Jazz Singer* was still drawing crowds, and before *The Singing Fool* was released, Warner Bros. decided to film one of Broadway's hit operettas, and Sigmund Romberg's *The Desert Song* was available. This one had the best story of all the standard operettas: as the French Foreign Legion fights the local Rif (called "Riffs" in the stage show), romantic Margot toys with mollycoddle Pierre but loves and fears the Riff leader...the Red Shadow! Will he overcome Margot and take her to his tent of forbidden love? Could that lame Pierre save her? But only the villainous Azuri and the audience know the show's secret: Pierre and the Red Shadow are the same man.

Eager to retain the show's content, the studio had scenarist Harvey Gates do very little actual writing; he simply cut down the original stage dialogue with some altered wording here and there. Parts of the score went missing, as stage shows of the day could span nearly three hours while the movie is almost exactly two hours flat.[6] Thus, the celluloid *Desert Song* is essentially the stage show

---

6. Only two major numbers were dropped, the heroine's "Romance" and the comics' duet, "It." Even so, we hear a bit of the former in the spot where it was reprised on stage, and a few of "It"'s lyrics are used as spoken dialogue in *its* reprise spot.

abridged, with a few cut-in shots of men riding horses in the desert, along with a view of stunt doubles for the two comics struggling over the dunes on a donkey. Further, to make the storyline intelligible to all, the movie departs from Broadway in showing Pierre changing into the Red Shadow's mask and cape (and vice versa) in a near-simulacrum of Clark Kent and his telephone booth.

The Desert Song is our first example of Hollywood's boldly using the sound of Broadway without adulteration. The Romberg music and its lyrics, by Oscar Hammerstein and Otto Harbach, are the opposite of Tin Pan Alley in every possible way, for all of the numbers—even "It," meant to capitalize on Hollywood knowitall Elinor Glyn's term for "sexual magnetism"—are plot- or character-driven. Uniforms and sand and the Riffs and even prostitution (in "Song of the Brass Key," included in the film) run through the lyrics because they run through the story.

Faithful to the stage text though it was, the Warners' *Desert Song* cast from scratch, with John Boles, a Broadway jeune premier in the mid-1920s; Carlotta King, whom studio PR handouts billed as "a graduate of stage operetta," though she had never played Broadway; and Johnny Arthur, who gave the comic exactly the air of hetero swish the authors had in mind. Douglas Carter Beane's play *The Nance* (2013) recently revived this once ubiquitous character, usually a nervous little pantywaist bullied by men and chased by women. His weapon is repartee, as here when he is about to depart from North Africa:

HIS ALLEGED GIRL FRIEND, WHOM HE INVARIABLY
REBUFFS: You're not going away without me?
ARTHUR: That's one of the big features of the trip.

. . .

GIRL FRIEND: What about our engagement?
ARTHUR: Oh, I forgot to tell you about that—that's off!
GIRL FRIEND: Off? Bennie, don't you love me?
ARTHUR: Don't get technical.[7]

The girl friend was Louise Fazenda, famed for her expertly trilling laugh (it's a running gag in *On With the Show!*). Further, for a special treat, the villainess is Myrna Loy in her exotic-conniver phase that preceded her graduation into sophisticated comedy. "Where is Pierre?" she ironically asks the French general—who is Pierre's father and who fears that Pierre has been killed—for, again, only Loy knows the secret. "*Where is Pierre?*" she growls into his face, mocking and taunting. All she needs is a top hat and a mustache and she'd be Snidely Whiplash.

7. This is the scene in the play script, carried over in the film with the addition of only two words.

"With all its Original Stage Enchantment," Warners' ads cried. "Love's heart beat set to the golden notes of the most famous music-play of our generation." Made without superstar salaries like Jolson's and on only two good-sized sets, *The Desert Song* cost a bit more than $350,000, and grossed over $3,000,000. Clearly, New York was valuable not only for the back-stager and its smarty talk but also as a source of ready-made smash-hit subjects. So Warners decided to branch out and invent its own Broadway operetta, using Romberg and Hammerstein to write four films from scratch.

The first was *Viennese Nights* (1930), which gave the two authors a chance to create a traditional 1920s operetta in an unconventional staging: on film. With none of the physical limitations of the playhouse and its cumbersome set changes, Romberg and Hammerstein could venture anywhere in their tale's geography at any time, yet they chose to work with the content of a typical Romberg-Hammerstein Broadway piece. *Viennese Nights* takes the form of the three-generation love story in which the first generation suffers but the grandchildren redeem all sorrow with a happy resolution; Romberg himself had contributed one of the exhibition works in the genre, *Maytime* (1917).

One of the charms of the format is the way the music is updated in each act, from nostalgia to the hot new rhythms. And of course there must be a Theme Song to center the program.

Viennese Nights' Theme Song—the published vocal score specifically identifies it as such—is "I Bring a Love Song." It belongs to unhappy sweethearts (Alexander Gray, Vivienne Segal) in Vienna in 1879, torn apart because her father manipulates her into marrying not struggling musician Gray but a baron (Walter Pidgeon). As if defying Segal's cruel father, "I Bring a Love Song" haunts *Viennese Nights*, almost trying to enmusic Gray and Segal into a unit.

It's hopeless, as we see in the first-act finaletto, a blend of song, arioso, and dialogue that all but invariably brought down a stage musical's first-act curtain. (Operetta essentialized it, in a historical line going back at least to Mozart's *The Magic Flute*, but musical comedy had its finalettos as well.) *Viennese Night's* finaletto takes place in a basement tavern, where Gray, Segal, and Pidgeon are thrust together just as she accepts Pidgeon's proposal. At first scornful, Gray suddenly grabs a violin from a handy gypsy band, fiddles a bit as if unable to articulate his feelings, then suddenly bursts into the final A of "I Bring a Love Song," becoming so upset on the high-lying last phrase that his voice cracks. It's a brutal moment, so intensely brought off that we can't tell if Gray is acting or has lost the notes for real.

In all, *Viennese Nights* is infinitely more absorbing than that tidy little *Desert Song*, and it was filmed entirely in two-strip Technicolor, albeit in subdued tones when the process freely unleashed fire-engine reds, brick-road yellows, and greens suitable for a rite of spring. And it does have one arresting touch completely untypical of the stage musical—a shrewish wife. Not a comically shrewish wife: someone mean and destructive. True, *Show Boat* has one, sort of, but Parthy Ann Hawks, though truly evil in Edna Ferber's *Show Boat* novel, was gentled down in the musical into a sort of tetchy busybody. *Viennese Night*'s shrew turns up in the second "act," set in New York in 1890, for the heartbroken Gray has left Europe to seek his destiny as a composer, and he fails. Why he married this baleful creature is a mystery, and as actress Virginia Sales catches very well the character's utter lack of sympathy and understanding, we are truly appalled. Gray lives for music, yet Sales insists he get a job with an old friend in the pickle business, nagging away from the bedroom while he entertains their little boy by playing and singing at the keyboard:

> SALES: Nobody wants to listen to [your] kind of music, [but] people will always eat pickles. That music ain't no good—it ain't popular. Otto! Are you listening?

Gray dies young, but Segal lives on, ending as a slightly grumpy "at my age I hate everything" widow. But wait: *her* granddaughter loves the new classical music and *his* grandson composes it, and the film climaxes at the premiere of his "Poem Symphonic," whose main strain is…"I Bring a Love Song." Segal has left the concert hall during the performance, yet when she hears "their" melody of true yet thwarted love, she returns to her box, transfixed. Here, again, we see the movie musical effortlessly out-narrating the stage, showing us all these locations and, above all, Segal rapt in her memories, an effect lost without the camera's close-up.

There remains only for the authors to bring Segal back to the park bench where she and Gray used to meet. "He didn't die," she says, to the group helping her to settle herself:

> SEGAL: (pointing to Gray's grandson) There—there he is! That's Otto, and (pointing to her own granddaughter) that's me.… We all live on, all part of one thing. Beauty. Beauty becomes more beautiful as the years go on.

The others leave her to her memory, and, as a solo viola and chorus intone the theme song, Gray appears, in double exposure, as a ghost. He starts the vocal, and Segal, as a second double-exposure ghost, joins him. As they move together, the real-life Segal drops her cane and loses consciousness. She has been graduated into operetta's higher plane of existence, amid the beauty that lives forever. I bring a love song. And there the movie ends.

Now for the bad news: *Viennese Nights* has an almost terrible score. There is one superb number, "You Will Remember Vienna," a Johann

Straussian waltz with an irresistible swing. And that theme song is what Italian opera critics would call "correct," meaning it does what it's supposed to do without being in any way special. And there is a relatively sprightly march of the sort without which no operetta would feel complete. But the rest of the music is dull, and Hammerstein—with *Show Boat* behind him, remember—fails to produce more than a handful of interesting lines.

At least Warner Bros. let the two authors write whatever they wanted, creating numerous musical scenes—conversations in music, rather like an intimate version of the finaletto. But that Poem Symphonic is a massive dud, consisting entirely of ramp-up passages till it finally bangs out the theme song. And, lo, it gets an ovation instead of rotten fruit.

As for the cast, they were not Hollywood names, which is what most moviegoers wanted to see. One reason for the flash success of RKO's *Rio Rita* (1929), an operetta-*cum*-musical comedy drawn with great fidelity from a Ziegfeld stage show, was its heroine, Bebe Daniels, already famous from her work in silents. The revelation that she could sing soprano was rather secondary. *Viennese Nights'* heroine, Vivienne Segal, was important on Broadway but a nobody on screen, though she was a "natural" performer rather than one of the operetta school, with their elocutionary diction and hollow acting.

Alexander Gray, unfortunately, was of the school, with that famously wooden quality that afflicted many operetta baritones when they weren't singing, that look of "I have to act, too?" on their face. As his rival, Walter Pidgeon was much more screenable, though he actually started as a would-be opera singer. Today, he is remembered as an old clunkabunk, for instance as a schoolmarmish Ziegfeld in the *Funny Girl* movie. But he was quite the hunk in his youth, and he has the advantage over Gray, who is stuck with an unflattering blond dye job to distinguish him from the dark-haired Pidgeon.

Viennese Nights was released in the late fall of 1930, when the public's boycott of musicals was in full swing, and Warners' plan to make Romberg-Hammerstein operettas an annual treat proved worse than a failure: a catastrophe. The studio had contracted to pay the authors $100,000 apiece for each of those four movies; the second, *Children of Dreams* (1931), was less released than thrown out—even today it has been seen by few—and Warners paid the men off and closed the operetta file.

Nevertheless, while this early operetta cycle was on, it was *really* on. MGM went right to the top for another all-Technicolor feature, *The Rogue Song* (1930). This time, the production had a star, albeit a new one, the Metropolitan Opera baritone Lawrence Tibbett. If the general public thought opera a place where the fat lady finally sings and everybody's glad to go home, Tibbett came from a different sort of opera altogether. "A personality like none other," *Photoplay* caroled. "His complete abandon, his lavish, mad acting and his glorious voice [make him] unique." Tibbett was even better than that, with a truly spectacular vocal style and a larger-than-life bravado that filled the screen. He wasn't merely a singing actor; he was an *actor* actor, reading lines with a gutsy naturalism that operetta had never possessed before.

The Rogue Song is supposedly based on Franz Lehár's *Zigeunerliebe* (Gypsy Love), one of his darker pieces, but by the time the usual crew of rewriters was through with the screenplay only the dimmest outline of the Lehár remained: a highborn lady is attracted to a man well out of her milieu, but Alas My Darling We Must Part. There are two main links with the stage work, the heroine's coquettish friend, who makes a play for the dangerous hero; and a storm scene (which very unconventionally opens the operetta but is used later in the film's action). Certainly, nothing in the Lehár anticipates the use of Stan Laurel and Oliver Hardy as tribal cutups. There is one famous bit, when the storm forces them to shelter in a cave. The camera simply stares at the cave's opening while we hear what's going on inside:

HARDY: Say. Where'd you get that fur coat?
LAUREL: What fur coat?
HARDY: Haven't you got a fur coat on?
LAUREL: Why, I got no fur coat.
HARDY: Well, it feels like a fur coat.
(Something roars: a bear! Crying out in their usual panic, the boys reappear, dashing out of the cave.)

That scene is one of the few we can see today. *The Rogue Song* was long thought lost except for its sound discs, but in recent years a few scenes have turned up, giving us a look at Tibbett in his magnificent blood-red uniform hung with long gold thingamabobs on either side of his torso and hair roughened into curly spikes. The rest of the cast names mean nothing to even the connoisseur, including that of Tibbett's vis-à-vis, Catherine Dale Owen, which makes her sound like an English novelist of the 1910s who specialized in romantic picaresque.

A few matters are of interest to us concerning *The Rogue Song*'s music. One is that, except for a tiny bit of choral work, Tibbett does literally all the singing, a strange way to run a musical of any kind. Don't operettas emphasize the Love Duet? The military march of the stouthearted men? The ladies' Gossip Chorus? A bit of Lehár's *Gypsy Love* found its way into the film, but the score as such is by composer Herbert Stothart and lyricist Clifford Grey. Stothart must have liked MGM; he stayed on to run the music department. But Grey was just visiting—and he has an arrestingly unusual backstory for a Hollywood songwriter, one useful to our look at how the movies developed a model for the use of music in musicals.

An Englishman, Grey worked as librettist and lyricist in the West End for some ten years before making New York his base of operations (partnering with Jerome Kern, Vincent Youmans, Rudolf Friml, and Sigmund Romberg) in the 1920s. Though he never gets credit for it, he would appear to have been instrumental in transforming the staid post–Gilbert and Sullivan British musical with a liberal use of the zany roughness that had long reigned in English music halls. Thus, the high point of Grey's first show, to Nat D. Ayer's music, *The Bing Boys Are Here* (1916), is a goofy trio called "Another Little Drink." It's simplicity itself: a verse about anything at all is interrupted by repeated calls for "another little drink":

SOLO: In Parliament today, when they get into a stew,
    And they're all mixed up, and they don't know what to do,
    Mr. [Prime Minister H. H.] Asquith says, in a manner sweet and calm—
ALL THREE: And another little drink wouldn't do us any harm!

So Grey unquestionably had the popular touch, but he was also prestigious (simply by being English). It was a Hollywood dream come true. But how "popular" could operetta be? Wasn't it terminally prestigious in the same way that opera was? And prestige, Hollywood knew, could backfire on you.

This is because there were, generally speaking, three different moviegoing audiences in America at the time. One was the more sophisticated audience of the theatre capitals—New York, Chicago, Seattle, and cities along the coastlines.

The second audience dwelled in the towns of the interior: less sophisticated but occasionally adventurous.

The third audience was that of the American village, with antique taste and a limited appetite for novelty.

Now, a movie made on the cheap could succeed by appealing to any one of these groups. But most musicals were big-budget items, and one needed enthusiasm from at least two of the groups in order to see a profit. One might, of course, attract portions of all three audiences, but village folk were hard to please, with their wariness of anything foreign or highly spiced—all of which operetta was. Nor was the urban population of the nation's interior—the second audience—eager to partake of the affairs of singing bandits and the princesses who love them. Operetta turned out to be a luxury item. In 1929, *The Desert Song* could soar to success on the sheer wonder of the singing film. By 1930, however, the movie musical had lost its wonder—and operettas were flopping on Broadway by then as well.

Yet Tibbett's debut was so electrifying that MGM would not give up. More neatly packaged now, to look the proper romantic hero, he was paired with Grace Moore—an opera soprano who had also sung on Broadway—in

New Moon (1930), from the Romberg-Hammerstein show of 1928 (with a *The* in its title). MGM kept the four hit songs and the use of a sea voyage from the original piece but otherwise changed everything, moving the action from Louisiana and the Caribbean to Russia. Even so, the two leads are still, as on Broadway, a dissenting member of society and a haughty lady of the ancien régime. This was standard operetta practice, adopted by Hollywood. In MGM's *Devil-May-Care* (1929), he was a Bonapartist and she a royalist. In Warner Bros.' *Song of the Flame* (1930), he was a Cossack prince and she more or less leading the Russian Revolution. In RKO's *Dixiana* (1930), he was a southern gentleman and she the star of a cheesy circus.

In *New Moon*, Tibbett played an army officer—an irreverent one—and Moore was the usual operetta princess, promised to another. (It's really *The Rogue Song* all over again, down to the inserted ballet and the Russian setting.) For plot interest, he insults her with a party piece, "What Is Your Price, Madame?," and is sent to a suicide post in a galaxy far, far away. But all ends well.

Anyway, the main thing is the music. Like Tibbett, Moore was one of the most passionate singers of the era, and when the orchestra isn't right in front of the camera it's right behind it, because lip-synching to playback (whether or not it was in use by this time) would not have worked for singers this outgoing, this vital. The two are tremendous in "Wanting You" especially, although Moore hadn't quite got the hang of moviemaking in her MGM period. She looks matronly at only twenty-eight and was not to master movie charisma till her comeback in Columbia's *One Night Of Love*, four years later.

Now, what about Clifford Grey and Herbert Stothart? They supplied *New Moon*'s two new songs, and we wonder how well these stage technicians work in the Hollywood milieu. "What Is Your Price, Madame?" is less a song than an aria; Tibbett is too angry at that point in the action to make music. But the other new number is an interesting addition to the Romberg-Hammerstein pieces, as it covers one of the most basic functions in the musical's storytelling apparatus, the Boy Meets Girl. Grey and Stothart constructed an extended scene using music and dialogue, as Moore hears Tibbett singing, in dialect, a ditty beginning, "Once there was a farmer's daughter," set to the g minor Allegretto choral movement from the second act of *The Merry Widow*. (MGM had bought the rights to the Lehár to film it as a silent, so the music was theirs to use.) Sparring over the song's meaning, the two bond. But more: this is a mating of artists bigger than their roles, as if Grey knew how beautifully Tibbett and Moore would accommodate this mixture of sex-skirmishing and song. Then Moore's uncle (the eternally tut-tutting Roland Young) gets in a double meaning a lot naughtier than the "farmer's daughter" number. A court busybody asks after the princess—is she in bed?

YOUNG: (chuckling) Not yet.

Grey's most important assignment, now for Paramount, was one great double meaning, Ernst Lubitsch's *The Love Parade* (1929), an insinuatingly sexy romp about a queen (Jeanette MacDonald) who takes a husband (Maurice Chevalier) the way a man takes a wife: as the boss. This was the movie musical's first original story that was not a backstager. True, there was a source, a French comedy by Leon Xanrof and Jules Chancel that had been done on Broadway in 1905 as *The Prince Consort*. But Lubitsch had a fond habit of basing his Hollywood movies on European originals to use only the plot premise, filling in the details in his own merry way. Ernst Vajda and Guy Bolton wrote *The Love Parade*'s screenplay, avoiding both operetta's mouthy poesy and the wisecrack-laden patois of the urban farces, thereby emphasizing this film's unique format. It's a musical comedy, but it toys with the talking points of operetta—the Ruritanian setting (actually Sylvania; in the Xanrof-Chancel play it was Corconia), the uniforms, the ladies-in-waiting, the waltz, and the march.

Then there is the odd pairing of Broadway lyricist Grey with Hollywood composer Victor Schertzinger, classically trained (in fact a child prodigy on the violin) and drawn to Hollywood to write scores in silent days. Somehow or other, Schertzinger fell into directing, and he became one of the movies' dependable journeymen. As songwriters, Grey is clever and Schertzinger elite, yet they blend well, contriving for *The Love Parade* a score that hits musical-comedy marks while respecting the needs of operetta.

Take for example the Heroine's Wanting Song, for which operetta requires something expansive—not merely wanting but ecstatic. MacDonald's "Dream Lover" pays the bill in full, in the three-quarter time that dance bands of the day would render as a Boston (also known as the "hesitation waltz" because of little pauses in mid-phrase). In the film, an awakening MacDonald sings the number *en negligée*, her handmaidens taking the tune in the second chorus while she sings a descant over them in the old-fashioned manner. And her "March Of the Grenadiers" is also rather dated, as MacDonald, uniformed (but in a dress below her tunic) like her soldiers, carols away as they parade. The lyrics to so generic a number might embarrass even the nimble Grey if we could hear them, but through the ancient sonics and MacDonald's notoriously Turkish diction, we have no idea what she's singing.

This much suggests an old-hat score. On the contrary, most of it has such modern oomph that the traditional numbers seem merely picturesque, Lubitsch's private joke to himself while he fills the screen with risqué capers. Certainly, Chevalier's songs bring operetta down to earth, in "Paris,

Stay the Same" and—in Grey's best invention—"Nobody's Using It Now," his complaint that he isn't getting any, because he isn't the top man in the royal relationship. MacDonald's dream lover, it seems, is someone she can keep in a cage, taking him out when she wants to play.

Note that he doesn't act the number as a soliloquy. Rather, he puts it over in the style of the French music hall, whence he came to the screen in the first place. In France, singers are either *réaliste*, like Édith Piaf, emoting from within a song's dramatic context, or they are *fantaisiste*, goofing on the words and notes, flirting with the public in their own persona, gesturing and stamping. "Tam *tam!*" Chevalier sings at the song's end, throwing his knees out on the first syllable and pulling them back on the second, as if "Nobody's Using It Now" were not his role's character song but his own show-off piece.

Character songs are the American musical's glory, from *The Red Mill*'s "Every Day Is Ladies' Day With Me" (over a century old as I write) to *Wicked*'s "Popular." But Hollywood feared the genre. Once again: people shouldn't be singing in forests, living rooms, on city streets. People sing only on stage in theatres or nightclubs—and not about themselves, not really. It was a housekeeping problem: those plot and character numbers posed a difficulty in credibility.

Yet these two genres are the very content of the Broadway score. The character number cues us into the principals' emotions, reasonings, existence. Typical character numbers: "I Get a Kick Out Of You," "Oh, What a Beautiful Mornin'," "Wouldn't It Be Loverly?," "Tomorrow." The plot number musicalizes a situation. Something is happening, but instead of speaking about it, everybody sings. Typical plot numbers: "The Rain In Spain," "Normal American Boy," "She's a Nut."

Contrary to what we sometimes hear, the plot number doesn't necessarily advance the narrative. There are such numbers, yes, but they are few, and they often depend on a certain amount of dialogue between the sung passages. Typical advance-the-narrative plot numbers: "You Did It," "Guenevere," "A Weekend in the Country."

Actually, the typical plot number does little or no advancing. Rather, it simply relates to the action in some pointed way. Thus, in *The Music Man*, "Marian the Librarian" is a plot number in that we see the hero woo the heroine. But there isn't a lot of narrative in the vocal, and the ensuing dance is just an excuse for the town kids to cut up in the library (till, at the very end, there's a bit more plot when the heroine tries to slap the hero and hits a schoolboy instead). Rather, "Marian" treats a certain transaction between two characters. It isn't "plot" per se, perhaps, but it does take them from Zone A to Zone B in their relationship. Thus, the plot number is really more of a *situation* number.

One thing that sets *The Love Parade* apart from coeval movie musicals is its insistent use of plot and character songs. Not a single number is presented in a nightclub, or on stage, or in rehearsal for something: this film is suffused with music. Thus, Chevalier's valet (Lupino Lane) lays the dining table for an assignation in "Champagne" (also known as "Ooh, La La"), gets off the old "grabbing the tablecloth out from under the dinnerware" stunt, and pulls the door shut behind himself on the orchestra's very last chord. Or, as MacDonald studies Chevalier's curriculum vitae, the soundtrack merges "Dream Lover" (is he her beau ideal?) with "Champagne" (but he's so frisky!). Or MacDonald and Chevalier's duet "Anything To Please the Queen" is a conversation more than a song, and the two get so into the information they're conveying that they talk as much as sing.

In all, *The Love Parade* is very, very unlike *The Broadway Melody* or *The Dance Of Life*, not only in its elegantly bawdy tone (as opposed to their hard-knocks slang) but in its genre. Those two are films mostly just tolerating songs. *The Love Parade* is a *musicalized* film, to the point that, without the numbers, the story would implode. Character numbers. Plot numbers. There's even one plot number played as a character number—"My Love Parade," wherein Chevalier names his favorite girls, whose charms are combined and idealized in MacDonald: "Lips of Lucille" and "Beauty of Camille." It's another Chevalier identity piece, but it's also his courtship rite, ending with a *long* kiss—so long she faints, then grabs him for another.

The Love Parade was a hit, but one wonders how well it did with that third audience of the small towns. It's a naughty piece: sinful. Didn't southern Bible towns reject it? Certainly, when it came to a truly integrated musical—that is, one dependent on character and plot numbers—far more attractive to the less worldly taste would be the Goldwyn studio's *Whoopee!* (1930), "a Musical Comedy of the Great Wide West" (as the title card bills it), released during the public's resistance to musicals yet still a huge hit.

The credit belongs not to Goldwyn but to Florenz Ziegfeld, for it was he who first put the material together, as a Broadway show built around the idiosyncrasies of Eddie Cantor. Ziegfeld was a doyen of the American melting pot, combining the "Aryan" beauty of his showgirls with comics drawn from the ethnic neighborhoods—black Bert Williams, rustic Oklahoman Will Rogers, Jewish Fanny Brice, and so on. Cantor worked in the Jewish vein, and it is doubtful that the general audience got all of his jokes—at one point, in Indian garb, he calls himself "Big Chief Izzy Horowitz"—but the Cantor fun came so fast and variously that if you missed one jest you caught the next, two seconds later.

The central premise of the piece is Cantor among the cowboys of southern California, now outsmarting them and now cringing in fear. They're bullies, but they're dopes. As a hypochondriac, Cantor ran one of those aforementioned hetero-gay romances with his nurse (Ethel Shutta, who was to achieve apotheosis introducing "Broadway Baby" in Stephen Sondheim's *Follies*), but Cantor really drove the plot by helping the ingenue (Frances Upton) escape from her mean-sheriff fiancé (John Rutherford), because she loves the half-Indian Wanenis (Paul Gregory).

That's the core of the plot, but of course the typical stage musical of the 1920s was about not the narrative but its decorations—Ziegfeld's patented showgirls in their fabulous costumes; his star vocalist (Ruth Etting) and dancer (Tamara Geva); and assorted doodads. *Whoopee* (without the exclamation point, on Broadway) was the musical smash of the 1928–29 season. Then the stock market crashed, Ziegfeld was wiped out, and, when Goldwyn offered to buy the production, Ziegfeld sold it, cast and all.

Now the movie. Goldwyn dropped Etting, Geva, and the doodads, because they had nothing to do with the story and, as I've said, the typical *movie* musical of the talkie era was all about the narrative. Further, Goldwyn let director Thornton Freeland open up the action with a few vistas; brought Busby Berkeley in for new choreography designed for the screen and the camera's eye; omitted from the script a few "special" passages (for example, Cantor's plea for tolerance in noting that such prominent Americans as Will Rogers and Herbert Hoover's vice-president, Charles Curtis, were part-Indian); and sharpened the stage show's scene climaxes (as in the end of the first act, which, on Broadway, featured Cantor setting off a gun and everyone else running for his life but, for Hollywood, moved on to Cantor escaping with the ingenue in their roadster). And Goldwyn filmed in Technicolor. And added an exclamation point to the title. And he even gave Ziegfeld first placement in their co-producer billing.

Whoopee! is, above all, the anti–*Love Parade*. Lubitsch's musical is subtle and elegant. It even has a theme, asking what kind of dream lover a woman can accommodate if she's a monarch. But *Whoopee!* has no theme. It's corny and irrational, a giddy explosion of coincidental meetings and pointless subterfuges: anything for a laugh. Thus, near the film's end, Cantor runs in pursued by Shutta, attacking him with an ax:

CANTOR: Why don't you bury the hatchet?
SHUTTA: That's what I'm trying to do!

And that, really, is the extent of the erotic in *Whoopee!*: Wanenis' chaste love of the white ingenue (and he turns out to be all-white, fostered in infancy by Indians) and the comic scuffles between Cantor and his demanding nurse.

Compare that with the first dialogue scene in *The Love Parade*, spoken partially in French, which already makes it borderline sexy. One of Chevalier's ladyloves is fighting with him:

CHEVALIER: (as so often looking right at us) She's terribly jealous.

Now we see a woman's garter. It's not hers, so *whose?* She threatens Chevalier with a pistol. Noise outside.

CHEVALIER: Her husband!

Uh-oh. To guilt her spouse into forgiveness, she shoots herself and falls, and her bereft widower now shoots Chevalier. Hmmm. There's no wound. Oh—the pistol was empty. Chevalier deposits it in a drawer filled with pistols. This must be his day job.

Lubitsch gives us one more comment on Chevalier and women. The wife needs the back of her gown fastened, but her husband is a fumbler. She impatiently strides over to Chevalier:

THE WIFE: *S'il vous plaît.*

Chevalier obliges, and the married couple leave, fighting.

These two films are utterly unalike as well in their use of songs. *The Love Parade* was conceived to flow musically, but, back on Broadway, *Whoopee* had a score that is only vaguely integrated. Walter Donaldson and Gus Kahn were the composer and lyricist, and their work is tuneful but not always appropriate. For instance, Wanenis sang "Here's To the Girl Of My Heart" after he learned that the girl of his heart was pledged to another. But the song isn't ironic or plaintive; it's absurdly positive. "Here's [hoping] that we may never part," he sings. You may never part? She's marrying Sheriff Bob that afternoon!

Or: as the gang heads for the mission to attend the nuptials, Cantor stops six lovelies so they can flank him looking fabulous while he sings the show's hit, "Makin' Whopee!." A comic look at marriage, it isn't exactly excrescent—but it isn't necessary, either.

Of course there was Cantor's blackface specialty spot, always by Tin Pan Alleymen and changed from time to time at Cantor's whim (and to give the show talkabout if any of the titles caught on as a hit). Now it was "Hungry Women," now "I Faw Down and Go Boom!," and so on.

Most egregiously irrelevant of all was "Love Me Or Leave Me," which Etting sang in a poppy field to cover a set change. It's a wonderful character song for no character, in the minor, with the vocal line dropping down an octave, then rising stepwise, a kind of methodical blues. However, Etting took virtually no part in the action. Nor did she have a boy friend to love or leave her. So it was easy for Goldwyn to eliminate her and her songs from the film.

Indeed, it was easy for Goldwyn to eliminate almost all of *Whoopee*'s stage score and commission four new songs from Donaldson and Kahn (along with a ballad for Wanenis to sing to his girl, which for some reason was by Nacio Herb Brown and Edward Eliscu). Amusingly, the new Donaldson-Kahn songs are just as irrelevant as the old ones—but they're sharper as sheer music-making. On Broadway, *Whoopee* began with the cowboys and bridesmaids singing "It's a Beautiful Day Today," another "merry villagers" curtain-raiser, the Genuine Imitation Leatherette of show tunes. The film, however, starts in a whirl of excitement, with a long-distance shot of two posses of wedding guests riding on horseback on separate trails that meet at the southern end of a Y-joint, then dismounting to run onto a sound stage. They're the chorus kids, who drop off two lines of exposition, leading an unbilled Betty Grable—incredibly, only fourteen years old at the time of filming—to launch a Cowboy Number, in which she lassos a buckaroo in a spoof of gender war.

Note that the chorus kids are costumed identically, just as they would be on Broadway, the boys in white shirts, pink ties, and black hats over black and white chaps, the girls in pink skirts, white shirts and hats, and light blue ties (yes, blue, despite two-strip Technicolor's supposed difficulty in realizing the color). Yet Berkeley does slip in an arresting novelty to close the number, directing some of the extras to walk off "upstage" while the dancers use the right edge of the screen as a kind of exit into the "wings." While this is happening, the actors for the next dialogue scene are coming onto the set *simultaneously*, thus sustaining a visual continuity that Broadway shows themselves were not to adopt till the 1940s, in *Around the World*, *Allegro*, and *South Pacific*.

As for Cantor's own personal *aria d'obbligo*, the Blackface Number, Donaldson and Kahn wrote a superior example in "My Baby Just Cares For Me," an irresistible rave-up with charleston pulsing in the release. "My baby don't care for Lawrence Tibbetts," Cantor explains, strutting back and forth as the rest of the cast just stands there and drinks him in. "She'd rather have me around to kibbitz."

This, presumably, is one of the many lines that those out in the regions didn't get. However, anyone could enjoy a Big Ziegfeld Showgirl Parade, unaltered from the stage show, "The Song of the Setting Sun." Again, the storyline doesn't need it. But if there's a Cowboy Number, why not an Indian Number? This one starts with the tribe's leader, played by a baritone billed as Chief Caupolican, mournfully intoning Kahn's lyric about the passing of the great days of the red man. Chorus women dressed as squaws take over for a dance to a pounding rhythm, and then come the Girls, first wrapped in ponchos to reveal the latest in teepee chic when they get "downstage," then led in on horseback by shirtless braves. In 1930, this gave American villagers a taste of Broadway at its zenith, for Ziegfeld was the land's prestige producer, a Name so celebrated that none of his attractions— not even *Show Boat*—was as famous as he himself was at the time.

Besides "The Song of the Setting Sun" and "Makin' Whoopee," the other holdover from Broadway was "Stetson," an example of how Busby Berkeley—a veteran, mind you, of over a dozen Broadway outings—created unique art for Hollywood. The number starts as the cutest of the cowboys tells Ethel Shutta they don't have the clothes to attend her coming wedding to Cantor. "Why, you can be high-hat in a Stetson," she tells him, gently flicking his hat and talk-singing her way into the verse: "I had an uncle by the name of Jerry, and he was a cowboy, too..." By the chorus, however, Shutta is singing full out, and she follows the vocal with a solo dance in a singular strut-and-kick style while the boys wave their hats and shout encouragement. Then they all go into a standard formation, a kind of flying wedge of musical-comedy hoopla, celebrating the joy of being young and physically attractive in a world where the mean sheriff never wins. It's the First Law of the Golden Age musical: Boy gets Girl and the bad guy gets nothing.

Interestingly, just as the number seems about to end, when Shutta and the cowboys dance "offstage" into the limbo to the right of the screen, Berkeley gives it a restart with the dancing girls. Now the number really *is* "Stetson," as the girls toy with their headgear, each one doffing hers and slapping it on the next girl, passing them around at waist level, and cresting with those overhead shots.

Thus, while *Whoopee!* is the most faithful of Hollywood's early Broadway adaptations, it is also the most cinematic. Yes, it retains a load of stagey mannerisms, from gag lines delivered in scare quotes— Audience, laugh here—to that procession of Indian maids down a papier-mâché hillside with the camera frozen at about Row G of the New Amsterdam Theatre. Nevertheless, the zesty playing tempo, the crazy music that somehow hits all the right marks in the story even when it isn't trying to, and Berkeley's bizarre combination of old-time hoofing and visual inventions make *Whoopee!* much more *movie* than all those *Desert Songs* and *Dance of Lifes* were.

All together, this chapter's representative sampling of Hollywood's use of songs emphasizes two trends paramount in the movie musical's first few years. One trend favors "performance" numbers. The other trend held the Harms group of Broadway's style setters in suspicion. They were experimental to a fault—and a generation's experience had taught Hollywood that experiments tend to fail. Not always, no. But often, and big time: *Intolerance, Greed, The Crowd*. That other group of songwriters, the composers and lyricists of Tin Pan Alley, were so much more agreeable. They had the common touch. True, every so often they took their little quirks out for an airing and slipped some vinegar into the syrup. But they caught the national ear, from the jaded first audience in the cultural capitals to the third audience in the small towns, suspicious of any attempt to change their lives by artistic means. Isn't music supposed to free us, expand our understanding? "Music," says Jamie Foxx in the *Dreamgirls* movie (2006), "is supposed to sell."

All the same, such Harms group chieftains as Jerome Kern, the Gershwins, and Rodgers and Hart did a lot of work in Hollywood. Even the ultra-sophisticated Cole Porter was writing for the movies as early as 1929: two numbers in *The Battle of Paris* (1929). But another *Paris* (1929), this one from Porter's stage show, included only one Porter number along with a horde of Alley inserts, and *Fifty Million Frenchmen* (1931) used Porter only as soundtrack accompaniment. And when RKO filmed Porter's *Gay Divorce*, it retained the story and some of the stage cast, but *The Gay Divorcée* (1934), primly retitled to avoid endorsing the shattering of marriage vows, dropped all of Porter save "Night and Day." At that, the film would have been unthinkable without it, as this was one of America's first global song hits, a phenomenon from Kalamazoo to Krakatoa.

Nevertheless, Hollywood would soon hire Porter to fashion a full-scale new score, just as it hired virtually every major songwriting talent Broadway produced. What the movies wanted was music with the class and distinction of the Harms group but the populist appeal of Tin Pan Alley: catchy and not "too" clever, yet imaginative enough to stimulate all three of the publics.

So they sent for De Sylva, Brown, and Henderson.

CHAPTER 2

✧

De Sylva, Brown, and Henderson

Once again, we ask: how do three men write a song? Ray Henderson was the composer, but De Sylva and Brown were both lyricists. So who wrote what section of the verses? The unusual teaming occurred by accident: George Gershwin and De Sylva had been supplying the scores for George White's annual revue, the *Scandals*, from 1920 through 1924. Then Gershwin abandoned variety shows to partner with his brother Ira on book shows, and White, who had the keenest musical ear of all the revue producers, sought to pair De Sylva with composer Ray Henderson. But Henderson was already paired: with lyricist Lew Brown.

No problem: White bunched the three together, and their *Scandals* numbers were better than those De Sylva had written with Gershwin. But the team lasted for only six years, from 1925 into 1931, and apparently broke up because Lew Brown got into a fistfight with George White at the premiere of the *Scandals* of 1931, infuriating De Sylva, a White loyalist.

Still, in their prime, this trio (from now on DBH) had an uncanny ability to bridge the gulf between Tin Pan Alley commercial savvy and the higher art of the Harms group. (In fact, though the trio founded its own music-publishing firm, it aligned De Sylva, Brown & Henderson, Inc. with Harms' distribution facilities, as if creating a bond with the Kern-Gershwin-Rodgers circle.) DBH were ideal for White's *Scandals* in giving him the self-contained numbers that revue needed—"The Birth of the Blues," "The Girl Is You and the Boy Is Me," the touristy march "Sevilla," "I Want a Loveable Baby," "[Kiss me, dear] What D'Ya Say?." Such titles tell us all we have to know about each song's content—a hallmark of the Alley song, which is static rather than dramatic.

That is, it states a basic concept and simply repeats it. DBH did this even in their book shows, such as *Good News!* (1927), in which the sweethearts' numbers—"Lucky in Love," "The Best Things in Life Are Free"—are cute and catchy but devoid of narrative energy. The heroine's "Just Imagine [that he loves me dearly]" starts its refrain on the sixth tone of the scale, which does give it a dreamy character. But the other two titles really could be sung by any young lovers—and therein lies their power as hit tunes: they appeal as easily outside their storytelling context as they do within it.

There is this as well: somewhere in this agglomeration of two lyricists and one composer lay a sharp ear for sudden harmonic caprices as well as a rhythmic spark that, once ignited, fires up an excitement. The 1920s was the great decade of the New Dance Sensation on Broadway: the ensemble promises to teach the audience how to do it, offers idiotically vague directions, then goes into a series of choreographic "combinations" that would be beyond us, anyway. A few of the first film musicals partook of the genre, as with *The Dance of Life*'s "The Flippety Flop." ("Snappily wobble and wiggle, happily hobble and hop.") DBH contributed several titles in this line, but another *Good News!* number, "The Varsity Drag," stands out for its avid power. The verse starts on the dominant seventh chord with an accompaniment of three descending quarter notes in $\frac{4}{4}$, repeated so that a different note of the three is accented each time. It creates a pleasurable anxiety in a genre that by 1927 was a hopeless cliché, and, when the chorus cuts in, scarcely a bar lacks syncopation. The thing simply takes off on wings of youth and joy and goofing off—a combination of the Alley's populist ease and Harms ingenuity.

The odd thing about DBH is their lack of a sound autograph. We recognize the pure melody of Kern, the wicked wit of Porter. But while DBH have a style, it's an all but invisible one, a "standard" style, anonymously all-American.

But that makes them perfect for Hollywood's wish to corral all three of its audiences onto a profit platform. After some work in shorts, the trio broke into the movie songwriting elite with the aforementioned super-hit in *The Singing Fool*, "Sonny Boy." A famous tale shadows the song, introduced in an article by Jerry Hoffman in the September 1929 issue of *Photoplay*, "Westward the Course of Tin Pan Alley." Hoffman tells us that Al Jolson was unhappy with the number he was to sing to little Davey Lee, supposedly by Irving Berlin, and decided to send out an S. O. S. for a replacement. Though Hoffman doesn't mention it, Jolson used to count on interpolations by De Sylva to stick into Jolson's Winter Garden shows for the Shuberts—"California, Here I Come" (to Joseph Meyer's music), "April Showers" (to Louis Silvers' music), and so on. Not surprisingly, Jolson turned to De Sylva once more—from which we can infer the reason George White was determined to hang onto De Sylva when Gershwin left the *Scandals*: he could put a hit tune together virtually on demand, with Meyer, Silvers...and now Lew Brown and Ray Henderson.

So Jolson makes a phone call and, says Hoffman, four hours later De Sylva is singing "Sonny Boy" to Jolson over the wire. Jolson sings it in the film. And, within a year, Hoffman concludes, "Sonny Boy" has sold "one and a quarter million copies of sheet music" and "two million records."

As to the song itself, it's a blatantly sentimental piece, as called for. One might even see it as an unhappily ideal match for the obsessive relationship that Jolson has with his son—and Hoffman's anecdote later took on the idea that DBH wrote "Sonny Boy" in exasperation, spoofing its bathos, though this is not in the original tale. Perhaps some writers can't believe that DBH would have meant this music as anything but rebellious satire.

In any case, "Sonny Boy" served as *The Singing Fool*'s Theme Song. We met up with this genre in *Viennese Nights*, but it was ubiquitous in the years of the silent-with-music-track, the part-talkie, and the early full talkie: a song whose directness and simplicity would enchant the world—and provide free advertising for the movie it "themed." Better yet, it made fortunes for the studios, which had been buying full or part-ownership in New York publishing houses. Warner Bros. lost out on a net profit of something like $250,000 when "Sonny Boy" came out under the DBH imprint instead of a Warners' outfit: which may be why, shortly after, the studio bought Harms outright.

With their popular touch, DBH were born to create theme songs. Fox gave them terrific billing on *In Old Arizona* (1928), in big lettering on the third title card: "Words and Music of 'My Tonia' by DeSylva [sic],[1] Brown and Henderson." This was only the fourth full talkie ever, after Warner Bros.' *Lights of New York* and *The Terror* and Paramount's *Interference*, all in the second half of 1928. Still praised today for its advanced sound technology in a primitive age—when a cowpoke rides off, the hoofbeats actually diminish in volume—*In Old Arizona* is made entirely on the triangle among the Mexican bandit known as the Cisco Kid (Warner Baxter), the army sergeant chasing him (Edmund Lowe), and the tempestuous señorita they both love (Dorothy Burgess). Like most of the first dialogue films, this one is marred by a slow delivery of the script. Burgess, who had been on the stage and was making her Hollywood debut, picks up her cues with speed. But the two men take forever to reply to anything. Again, they were too

---

1. De Sylva's name is frequently misspelled thus, but it's "De Sylva" in the trio's publishing insigne and also on his tombstone.

used to silent acting, when you "mimed" your reactions, and it didn't matter when you finally spoke because the audience couldn't hear you in the first place.

Now, what of "My Tonia?" DBH did their work well, casting the music in a tango verse and an expansive fox-trot chorus. Fox uses it here and there in the continuity (especially as a real-life song, on a 78 played on a Victrola), but "My Tonia" is mainly heard as prelude and finale, first before the credits, sung by an operatic baritone, and last by a tenor with a mini-glee backup. It's an appealing tune, vague enough ("My Tonia, with your dark eyes dancing...") to charm every ear.

So far, so good. Fox now positioned DBH as their musical-comedy men, paying them an advance of $150,000 to write both the script and score for *Sunnyside Up* (1929). This was to be the full-talkie debut of Janet Gaynor and Charles Farrell, one of the most popular teams of the era—but what's notable here is that $150,000 advance, because nowhere on Broadway could *any* songwriter get anything like that amount of money up front. As we'll see, it was why New York songwriters went Hollywood—that and the magnificent exposure their work would enjoy, making them truly national figures. Before sound came to Hollywood, only one theatre writer permeated the culture, as ubiquitous as the parlor piano and the summer bandshell: Victor Herbert. Recordings and radio then gave him a rival: Irving Berlin. And now the movie musical seemed about to democratize the entire field.

Sunnyside Up offers yet another New York-based narrative, confronting the tony Long Island set (Farrell's community) with urban havenots (Gaynor's). And Farrell has a mean-girl fiancée to get between the two stars. But the film sympathizes with Gaynor's crowd by opening on their turf. Director David Butler was a slow pacer generally, but his first sequence is a historians' favorite: a pan-and-crane tour of Yorkville (centered on Eighty-Sixth Street in Manhattan) and its denizens. Without ever cutting away for breath, Butler shows us kids romping at a sprinkler and playing stickball, strolling sweethearts, nosy views of apartment life including a husband hiding under the bed from his rolling-pin-wielding wife, a mannish woman (1929 code for "socially progressive") offering the "Birth Control Review" to an Irish mother sitting on a stoop with her seven children. "This is a foine time to be tellin' me!" she cries.

Thereafter, the camera work is routine, and, besides, DBH didn't write a movie. They wrote a Broadway musical comedy which Fox then filmed: with a First Couple (for the romance) and a Second Couple (for laughs), a star comic (Gaynor's avuncular confidant), and a shortish score of seven numbers alternating the plaintive ballad, the rouser, the Second Couple's joshing duet, and the rhythm number. In *Good News!*, these are, respectively, "The Girl of the Pi Beta Phi," "Good News," "Baby! What?," and "The Varsity Drag." To sample another DBH show, *Flying High*, these are, respectively, "Without Love," "Happy Landing," "Good For You—Bad For Me," and "Red Hot Chicago."

See? It's the same score in every show. But DBH wrote in genre as if giving bullet points to theatre music. It's banality with imagination, a seemingly artless art. And it needs personality players to put it over. Commentators fault Gaynor for her babyish voice—she has been compared to Minnie Mouse, especially when she sings—but she attacks her role with honesty and charm. She sings the plaintive ballad, "I'm a Dreamer (Aren't We All)" while accompanying herself on the autoharp, and takes the rouser, "Keep Your Sunny Side Up," with surprising confidence, going on to a dance with hat-and-cane tricks. In his *Encyclopedia of the Musical Film*, Stanley Green called Gaynor "something of a transitional figure between Mary Pickford and Shirley Temple"—that is, a girl of the people who can cajole or defy oppressive authority as required. It's not too much to call her talentless but adorable, and if Farrell was little more than tall and handsome, he went very well with Gaynor. "We need someone wonderful like you," he tells her. He's speaking of a charity show he wants her to appear in, but he really means that the hoity-toity of his world hungers for the lovable energy of hers.

The Second Couple, Frank Richardson and Marjorie White, are typical DBH characters, eccentrics who date and scorn each other:

HE: You never encourage me!
SHE: Well, you never offer to jump out of a window!

Almost everything about them is absurd, just as it would be in the shows DBH wrote for Broadway. Thus, he makes a running gag out of getting inane ideas for songs he wants to write. Or their joshing duet, "You've Got Me Pickin' Petals Off Of Daisies," comes with the risible dance expected of comics, at the climax of which they fall backward over a low embankment. Nevertheless, White can also keep it real when consulted about the love plot. Of course Gaynor loves Farrell—but he has a snooty mother to overcome. And when love finally triumphs:

GAYNOR: (trembly, unsure, can this be true?) He...asked me...to marry him...
WHITE: Well, what the hell are you crying about?

Another Broadway touch: the mean fiancée (Sharon Lynn), an all but inevitably non-singing role in movie musicals, gets into the score, as she would in a stage show, delivering the starting vocal for the rhythm number, "Turn On the Heat," at the charity show. This is *Sunnyside Up*'s other notably cinematic moment (besides the opening street episode), in which an icy set magically becomes tropical and Eskimo girls strip to two-piece bathing togs as trees shoot up and flames erupt.

But now we reach the film's comedian, El Brendel, arguably the most irritating performer in the early-talkie period. His was a dumb-and-dippy act, with a grin so vacant it was a featurette in itself, and he managed to play entire roles without a single funny line or a funny inflection. What did he have? A Swede, Brendel commanded some devotion from that second audience in the north midwest, where many Scandinavians dwelled—and we should add that most comics of this time were divisive talents, counting legions of fans and hate-watchers alike—Bobby Clark, Joe Cook, Jimmy Durante, Willie Howard, Leon Errol...and we've got Billy Gilbert and Jules Munshin yet to come.

Sunnyside Up was a huge hit, earning over four times its negative cost. It embedded DBH in Hollywood as contenders, but movies were different from plays in their production power structure: studio heads, showrunners, stars, and directors shared authority, while writers were no more than hirelings, even orderlies. Thus, when DBH wrote most of the numbers for Warners' Jolson vehicle *Say It With Songs* (1929), the trio was utterly overwhelmed by the Jolson meme, the bathos meme, even the "Davey Lee back as Sonny Boy" (renamed "Little Pal") meme.

DBH of course wrote a "Sonny Boy" knockoff, "Little Pal," and three other tunes, but their art really belonged to carefree musical comedy, and *Say It With Songs* was a serious tale that happened to have music in it. A backstager Plot B, it told of a singer who decks his love rival and kills him, is convicted of manslaughter, and attacks his wife verbally so she can divorce him and be free of a jailbird. It's Jolson as Job—where is there room in this for a Second Couple joshing duet? One almost imagines studio officials discussing how to add to Jolson's misfortunes. One says, "Couldn't Little Pal be hit by a truck?"

And WHAM!

The child recovers this time, but, clearly, this was no place for DBH. Luckily, Fox wanted another musical comedy in DBH style, and this time the boys came up with something wild: a tale set fifty years in the future, when folks bear such names as Z-4 and MT-3, marriages are arranged by the authorities, newborns come out of vending machines, telephone conversations are televised, in anticipation of Skype, and air travel is so habilitated that the narrative builds to a voyage to Mars.

This is *Just Imagine* (1930), using the title of one of the *Good News!* numbers, and the film starts well, with an amazing view of an evolved New York (using a miniature), as countless autos run along highways in the air and searchlights attack the skies. That may suggest a comparable visual in Fritz Lang's *Metropolis* (1927), but Lang's futurism is a mad dystopian fantasy while DBH (and director David Butler again) just want to have a good time. That opening shot of space-age New York, though seen for only a few seconds, cost $168,000, according to *Photoplay*.[2] "It took 205 engineers and craftsmen five months to build it," the magazine reported, and the model was so big it was erected "in a balloon hangar at a former Army flying field twenty miles from Hollywood."

Alas, after that smashing start-up *Just Imagine* crashes into banality. Unlike *Sunnyside Up*, this second all-DBH project lacks the energy and tang of a DBH stage show. True, it has Broadway's typical First Couple (operetta baritone John Garrick and Maureen O'Sullivan) and Second Couple (Frank Albertson and *Sunnyside Up*'s Marjorie White), but the former are pallid and the latter dull and noisy. Worse, El Brendel has returned, now as a 1930 corpse reanimated by science in 1980, and just as obnoxious as ever. Further, as the good and evil queens of Mars (everyone on that planet is twins), there is the inveigling yet strangely unnerving Joyzelle, who sometimes had a last name (Joyner) and sometimes didn't.

Actually, Joyzelle is the sole amusing element in the whole film. First of all, when seen close-up, the future is austere and spartan, like a high-school principal's office. And let's take a sample of El Brendel's humor (albeit duplicating the Irish mother's line from *Sunnyside Up*), when he thinks the ship he's on is headed for "Ma's":

GARRICK: It's the planet Mars.
BRENDEL: (collapsing on floor and fanning himself with his stupid hat)
    Oh, for heaven's sake. This is a fine time to tell me.

The worst thing about *Just Imagine* is its score, for DBH utterly failed to justify their signature genres here. The plaintive ballad, "I Am Only the Words, You Are the Melody," is less plaintive than dreary, though the Second Couple's joshing duet, "Never Swat a Fly," has minor merit. (It was thought snappy enough to be included in the currently licensed revisal of *Good News!*.) But the film lacks both the rouser and the rhythm number, those ultra-characteristic DBH moments when music and dancing take over the scene.

2. Edwin M. Bradley, in *The First Hollywood Musicals*, notes that Fox itself gave the figure as $250,000: more than half what a big movie musical of 1930 cost in toto.

By then, the trio was heading for its break-up. They gave Hollywood a few more songs, but no full scores, and the remaining DBH titles were simply movies of their stage shows, with scores adulterated by others: *Good News* (1930), *Follow Thru* (1930), and *Flying High* (1931).

If Hollywood had made only one early talkie based on a Broadway musical, it would have been MGM's *Good News!*, because its waif-enchants-football-hero plot hits a sentimental nerve unusual in college musicals. We see this in the primitive poetry of "The Best Things in Life Are Free," with its "sunbeams that shine," whereupon "They're yours" is answered by "They're mine." The words alone seem lame, but the way they fall on the melody lifts them into a virtual philosophy of musical comedy: life is about neither wealth nor ambition but happiness, because it's so much more fun.

Like *Good News!*, *Follow Thru* and *Flying High* were huge hits on stage. Of course, Hollywood would want them as well, but all three came out during the boycott of movie musicals, when studios were desperately trying to turn the genre into a sort of Land Without Song. On Broadway, *Good News!* scored five hit tunes, extremely rare for the day (even the phenomenal *Show Boat* has only six). But two went missing, and "The Best Things in Life Are Free" was almost a throwaway.

Yet Hollywood was careful to use original-cast members in all three cases, as if seeking authenticity. Bert Lahr won tremendous notice in *Flying High*, so he was essential to MGM's version, not least because Hollywood's established star comics were used to mime, not dialogue. But Paramount's *Follow Thru* is a strange mixture of movie-industry sweethearts (Charles "Buddy" Rogers and Nancy Carroll) and stage people (the show's Second Couple, Jack Haley and Zelma O'Neal). And Paramount retained also the show's Third Couple, Don Tompkins and Margaret Lee, who do almost nothing but repeat their joshing duet, "Then I'll Have Time For You." You lugged them all the way to California for *that*?

Some of *Good News*' casting is questionable as well. Heroine Mary Lawlor (in her Broadway role) is charming enough, if in a "When is some guy going to take me away from all this?" manner, but comic Gus Shy (also from Broadway) is, at thirty-six,[3] too old to matriculate in a college musical. (His vis-à-vis, Bessie Love, was thirty-two but looked younger.) Shy does work well with Love, though, especially in an interpolation by Larry Shay, George Ward, and Reggie Montgomery, "Gee, But I'd Like To Make You Happy." It's no better than the joshing duets the Second Couple got to sing

3. Shy's official bio gives his birth year as 1903, but Edwin Bradley and other sources place it much earlier, in 1893 or 1894.

in the stage original, but it dips into meta-cinema at the end, when Love and Shy try to button the number with can-can kicks and an "arms outstretched" freeze while the orchestra keeps playing. So they keep on kicking and freezing till Love's right leg faints and Shy simply drags her out of frame. *End.*

That zany bit suits the DBH worldview in general. Even the sheet music of the movie's interpolated numbers has a "mad twenties" air, with a splendid John Held Jr. cartoon of dancing co-eds, a football hero (with a black eye), a male cheerleader, and a campus cut-up in one of those crazy twenties overcoats lettered with dumb sayings. It was the energy of DBH that made their shows the ultimate musical comedies, and, even while molesting the score, MGM clearly wanted to adhere very closely to the stage original, at least in the script. It crackles with the best lines from the Broadway book almost from moment to moment. (There's a nifty new one, as sports trainer Cliff Edwards dryly disparages an athlete with "He plays good football...and so does Baby Peggy.")

Further, while Hollywood veteran Nick Grinde angled the camera, it was Edgar J. MacGregor—*Good News!*'s Broadway director—who controlled the action, in the aforementioned "one film, two directors" plan typical of the early talkie. So the comedy scenes have the explosive vivacity that the sound revolution was all about, a mixture of Broadway smarts and Hollywood technology, like that seminal burst of Jolson's "Blue Skies" in *The Jazz Singer*.

MGM's *Good News* really excels in the two DBH rhythm numbers. For the "Drag," the girls are in striped jackets over white blouses and gray skirts and the boys are in sweaters and ties—a kind of musical-comedy uniform, as if they intended to launch a production number the moment the professor left the room. He does. And, sure enough, they all get into it, led by Dorothy McNulty, one of the most spirited of the era's musical personalities, more an acrobat than a dancer. This being a Latin class, three chalked outlines of Roman soldiers on the blackboard take up the drag as well: a runaround with the arms pulling up and down and the slapping of both hands on one knee, charleston-style. The band that was almost certainly playing away just behind the camera goes utterly wild as the ensemble pounds the floor with the abandon of primitive folk rousing their gods.

For the other rhythm number, "Good News," the cast is again in matching outfits, and this one boasts what used to be called a "specialty": everyone runs off and Al Norman solos in "rubberlegs" style, in which the torso is more or less immobile and the bottom half defies biological physics with science-fiction footwork. Interestingly, Norman's accompaniment is the song's verse, which doesn't get a vocal. True, McNulty starts the "Good News" refrain so suddenly that MGM might have filmed her singing the verse and then cut it to appease musical-weary moviegoers. At a few other moments in the feature, we hear stray bits of the stage score (the opening chorus, for instance, used as accompaniment to a dance) that suggest that the studio had intended to give the show a more thorough musicalization than it ended with.

The *Good News* movie everyone knows is MGM's remake of 1947, with Peter Lawford and June Allyson and, as the Second Couple, Ray McDonald and Joan McCracken. As in 1930, the score on offer mixed a handful of the Broadway numbers with inserts. The new scenarists, Betty Comden and Adolph Green, completely rewrote the continuity, adhering faithfully to the storyline while dropping the self-contained sketches the twenties stage musical was full of and which the first film retained—Bessie Love "innocently" taking over a dice game or playing hide-and-seek in the men's dormitory.

Still, we are less interested in Comden and Green's script changes than in their changes in the score, for they entirely revamped its relationship to the narrative. Indeed, they had to, for, after DBH's heyday, the musical as a form had renegotiated its contract with its songwriters. They could no longer write *fun*; they had to write *story*. By 1947, the musical was living in a post-*Show Boat* world, a post-*Jubilee*, -*Knickerbocker Holiday*, -*Oklahoma!*, and -*Bloomer Girl* world. Scores had to explain the characters and follow the plot, and Comden and Green needed to bring *Good News!* up to speed.

For instance, "He's a Ladies' Man," on stage in 1927, was a throwaway number, a girls' chorus praising the football hero. As "Be a Ladies' Man," it now became (with new lyrics credited to Kay Thompson and the chief of MGM's music department, Roger Edens) the hero's character number, his worldview on how conquering the co-eds gives a man prestige. Then, too, as a smallish ensemble piece for the boys, it grounded Peter Lawford in the campus setting as an alpha male among a set of buddies, thus taming his classy English accent and naturalizing him in a culture in which the guys major in Football and the gals in Marriage Plans.

Again, "Ladies' Man" is just a throwaway bit in the stage show (in the 1930 film, we hear it for exactly seven seconds). Comden and Green's redeployment of the *Good News!* elements makes it a major number. It starts in the locker room, where Lawford and McDonald have been dressing after football practice, Lawford almost neon in red and gray. "Tommy," McDonald asks Lawford, "how do you do it?," and Lawford, after considering for a bit, decides to sing his response. In 1927, the lyrics ran, "There he goes, the modern knight." Now, on screen, the message is personal and direct. "It's a cinch," he reveals, "and it's a snap..."

Now director Charles Walters takes over, as Lawford and McDonald roam the campus with three other guys (one of them Mel Tormé in a sweatshirt decorated with those crazy twenties catch-phrases we just noted on the 1930 sheet music). It's a dance staged as a march of young Tait College stallions, which emphasizes another difference between *Good News!* the stage show and *Good News* the 1947 movie: the show was partly about football. The film is completely about romance.

Therefore, Comden and Green needed to place a duet for Lawford and Allyson, to bring them together. Not, as in the stage show, in "Lucky in Love," which is just a DBH charm number. Rather, something that bonds them in the way the story bonds them. She's coaching him, smartening him up to pass an exam so he can play in the Big Game. That is, she is empowering him. In the stage show, his subject is Astronomy. But that's so...factual. Let's change it: to sexy. So Comden and Green wrote, to Roger Edens' music, "The French Lesson," because you know the French and their appetites. Better, Comden and Green created a reprise of "The Best Things in Life Are Free" for Lawford to sing in French, showing us that love doesn't just make us happy: it makes us smart.

Even the Second Couple's joshing duet was transformed. This item is often the least imaginative in the DBH calendar (though it did produce a standard in "Button Up Your Overcoat," from *Follow Thru*). However, for McDonald and McCracken the spot was repointed as an ensemble dance in the local soda shop, and someone—possibly the film's producer, Arthur Freed, who, we remember, was a musician as well as a former lyricist and very attuned to the way songs function in musicals—had the idea of bringing in an unused song from another MGM production, Roger Edens and Hugh Martin's "Pass That Peace Pipe."[4]

This is no mere bickering caper, but a rhythm number promoting the unique McCracken, who did important work on Broadway for Agnes de Mille and Jerome Robbins but made only one full-scale musical feature, this one. Thus, the scene stands out as McCracken's legacy, yet it so suits the saucy DBH outlook that it fits in with the authentic *Good News!* songs. Stanley Green tells us it was intended for Fred Astaire and Gene Kelly in *Ziegfeld Follies* (1946), where it would have come off in a vastly different performing style. So perhaps director Walters—one of Hollywood's most underrated artists, by the way—is as responsible as Comden and Green for the overall consistency of this repurposed *Good News*.

Indeed, they even got a plot number out of "Lucky in Love," which DBH wrote back in 1927 simply to connect the two sweethearts on an up note. "The Best Things in Life Are Free" scores love's soulful pas de deux; "Lucky in Love" sounds the merrier steps of the courtship dance, and by the time MGM's crew

---

4. Martin's official collaborator, Ralph Blane, is also credited, but only because of their contract with MGM. In his memoir, *The Boy Next Door*, Martin says that, after *Best Foot Forward* (1941; filmed 1943), for which Martin wrote half the numbers—words and music alike—and Blane the other half, all "their" work was Martin's alone.

were finished adapting it, it had turned into a juicy ensemble involving all the principals in a slew of new lyrics. Lawford's soon-to-be ex, Patricia Marshall, cozies up to a moneyed student (making it easier for us to want her to lose Lawford). The Second Couple fights off the attentions of McCracken's stalker, the aptly named Beef (Lon Tindall). June Allyson slaves away in the kitchen (because she is unmoneyed, which gives her democracy control). And, finally, Marshall calls Lawford, in French, *"incorrigible."* All in all, it's a big number, set against a load of lovey-dovey couples—and, amusingly, only Mel Tormé sings the original DBH lyrics: everyone else has been rewritten.

That might have been the last of De Sylva, Brown, and Henderson but for the popularity of the biographical musical, which gave Hollywood a chance to run through songwriters' catalogues while concocting a more or less science-fiction version of their life events. The bios came in two varieties, one with star cameos for flashy song spots and the other on the modest scale. Fox gave DBH something between the two styles, for *The Best Things in Life Are Free* (1956) isn't really modest yet could use a few star cameos. "John O'Hara's flaming portrait of the Jazz Age," the posters cried, "and the guys and gals who made it zing!" Unfortunately, zing! is exactly what this movie lacks. O'Hara's name was a dog whistle to the literary crowd, but not a single line of dialogue reflects his amazing ear for colloquial American—and his name in the credits sat below the nominal scenarists, William Bowers and Phoebe Ephron.

This is strictly by-the-numbers bio-izing. De Sylva (Gordon MacRae) is the opportunist deserting his pals for Hollywood. Henderson (Dan Dailey) is the mild family man. Brown (Ernest Borgnine) is the hothead. "De Sylva may hire 'em," he snarls, "but Lew Brown fires 'em." Sheree North is their pet performer, in love with MacRae.

And that's all there is as far as the story goes, and the tale of how the trio joined up is completely false even by Hollywood-bio standards. Fox poses De Sylva as the composer of Brown's lyrics, Henderson magically turning up during the inevitable show-in-trouble-in-Atlantic-City rehearsal scene.

No. As I've said, Henderson and Brown were the established team, and it was George White, not magic, who hooked them up with *lyricist* De Sylva. White, DBH's regular producer, isn't even in the movie, and the Brown-White fistfight becomes MacRae's shoving Borgnine onto the floor and stomping off as Dailey holds Borgnine back.

It's the only dramatic moment in the film. We do at least hear all the aspects of the DBH canon, from plaintive ballad to rhythm number. But they aren't well presented. The integration of ballet in the musical, inaugurated in the 1920s, developed in the 1930s, and perfected in the 1940s in such shows as *Oklahoma!*, *On the Town*, and *Brigadoon*, was by 1956 a major

Hollywood thing, and Rod Alexander choreographed two Big Ballets for *Best Things*. The first is a twenties study, with a gang war, speakeasy, and charleston to "Black Bottom"—and it even revives the little known "Red Hot Chicago" (from *Flying High*) for the gangsters. Georges Balanchine acolyte Jacques d'Amboise, as the gangster chief, is wasted, but he dominates the second ballet, to "The Birth of the Blues," as an escaped jailbird who enjoys an erotic pas de deux with North before being apprehended.

This is only the first of the many bios we shall encounter in these pages. Ironically, Hollywood never got around to the life saga of the one song-writer with the longest parade of hits, including two of the most popular songs of all time. Further, his was a great American success story, even an American epic, as he published his first titles when De Sylva was running around in a propeller beanie and his last show opened after De Sylva had died. The little-known Gus Kahn got a bio, and Cole Porter got two. Yet Irving Berlin didn't, and there's a reason for that.

CHAPTER 3

✧

Irving Berlin

His early songs, starting in 1907, were often collaborations, as Berlin began as a lyricist more than a composer; not till about 1914 was he almost exclusively the composer-lyricist of every title bearing his name. "Alexander's Ragtime Band," his first huge hit (and all his own in words and music), came out in 1911, which makes Berlin the senior of all the writers discussed in this book.

There's another distinction. Those others wrote primarily for stage and screen; the very ID of the Harms group was their fascination with song as an element of the narrative form. Berlin was known primarily as a pop tunesmith. When he did write a show or movie, however, it tended to have impact. Berlin's *Watch Your Step* (1914) was the first major Broadway musical to use dance as a cultural signifier, "integrating" choreography into the whole long before it became trendy. Berlin's *Music Box Revues* (1921–1924) were the only variety-show series to compete with Ziegfeld's *Follies* in imagination and glamor. On screen, Berlin's *Top Hat* (1935), the fourth teaming of Fred Astaire and Ginger Rogers, crystallized their genre so luxuriously that it seemed, to many at the time, the ultimate Hollywood musical. And back on Broadway, Berlin's *Annie Get Your Gun* (1946) developed musical comedy's alternative to Rodgers and Hammerstein's musical play even while working within their format of period Americana (after *Oklahoma!* and *Carousel*) using an exclusively narrative-based score.

There is this, too, often overlooked. Berlin began by using the clichés of ethnic-stereotype numbers—"Cohen Owes Me Ninety-Seven Dollars," "Sweet Italian Love," "Colored Romeo." Yet he was the first major voice on Tin Pan Alley to write beyond genre. The Alley was obsessed with standard memes, from the Moon Song and the New Dance Sensation to anthems of

Dixie and Mother, because they were easy to concoct, drawing on images from the public domain. As De Sylva, Brown, and Henderson tell us, "The moon belongs to everyone."

But Berlin began to dramatize odd corners of real life—"How Do You Do It, Mabel, on Twenty Dollars a Week?," "My Wife's Gone To the Country, Hurrah! Hurrah!"—and did so in idiomatic wording, to articulate what many people would say in the way they said it, if only they thought a bit more poetically.

Thus, in "You'd Be Surprised," from 1919, Berlin explains why Mary loves quiet little Johnny:

> He doesn't look like much of a lover,
> But don't judge a book by its cover.

It seems that Johnny has hidden talents. "On a streetcar or in a train," the lyric continues, "you'd think he was born without any brain." Yes, okay, "but in a taxicab":

> You'd be surprised!

Berlin's coevals in the Alley tended to phrase in a kind of stilted pop English, but Berlin's lyrics flow naturally, prefiguring the revolution in Broadway versification that began with Harms men P. G. Wodehouse and B. G. De Sylva in the late 1910s and exploded in the 1920s with the appearance of such as Oscar Hammerstein, Lorenz Hart, and Ira Gershwin.

Berlin was not a Harms member except culturally, because his strong business sense led him to become his own publisher. We have seen De Sylva, Brown, and Henderson do the same thing, but, as I've said, they were all the same contractually aligned with T. B. Harms. Irving Berlin, Inc. stood apart. Nevertheless, by the time Berlin made his first association with Hollywood, he could boast of a Harms-like influence, as no longer just a writer of (countless) song hits but a maker of musicals. And he took an active interest in every aspect of production, from the concept to the casting, a quality we associate with not the Alley man but the Harms writer.

Here's an example of how acute Berlin's show-biz instincts were: in the early-middle 1920s, he was offered a project built around Vivian and Rosetta Duncan, playing what they were: one sweet and one feisty sister. The script was no more than functional, but the Duncans—unique for the loving chemistry we noted in *It's a Great Life*—could put anything over. Berlin was interested till the Duncans proved unavailable; without them, he reasoned, their roles would be cast with anybodys, making the show a sister act without the sisters. Berlin pulled out, and, indeed, *Sitting Pretty* (1924) had a terrible time casting the two leads. Even with a wonderful score by Jerome Kern and P. G. Wodehouse, the show failed.

Berlin was smart enough also to see the immense possibilities in Hollywood once sound came in. As Jack Warner famously expressed it, "Who the hell wants to hear actors talk?" The music-publishing profits alone could be phenomenal—and, remember, Berlin was one writer whose songs addressed all three moviegoing audiences. So Berlin went Hollywood very early, in the Theme Song. "Marie," the Theme of a Vilma Banky romance called *The Awakening* (1928), runs its refrain through the most modest of chord changes—four measures in the subdominant, four in the tonic, back to the subdominant, then the dominant seventh, and so on, with just a hint of chromatic harmony and a bit more chromatic languor in the melody. This is music made, quite simply, to please. By the time the film was over and the tune thoroughly plugged as only Theme Songs were, the public could have formed "Marie" glee clubs and headlined the land in concert.

If Berlin had ever codified his approach to making music theatre, it would have run thus: one, cast the leads with smash personalities, at least some of whom are smash singers; two, write songs good enough to chart; and three, be the showrunner. True, one had at times to compromise if one wanted to work with the best. Rodgers and Hammerstein were *Annie Get Your Gun's* showrunners, because they produced it. *Miss Liberty* (1949) lacked smash personalities and vocal tone. *Mr. President* (1962) suffered a score that couldn't have charted.

Nevertheless, the program was working till Berlin got past the Theme Song era into full-scale movie musicals, because Hollywood played by a rule unknown to Broadway: the producer (and certain directors, only to an extent) held the power, not the songwriter. Paramount's *The Cocoanuts* (1929) was to have been a faithful preservation of Berlin's 1925 stage show starring the Marx Brothers, and the studio seemed eager to give the score wide exposure. As the star quartet were just then playing Broadway in *Animal Crackers*, Paramount filmed *The Cocoanuts* on the Marxes' off-hours at Paramount East, their "other" studio, in Astoria, Queens. Paramount even retained the two key non-Marx players of the original cast, eternal grande dame Margaret Dumont and, as a suspicious but ever-defeated hotel detective, Basil Ruysdael.

And then, says Allen Eyles in *The Marx Brothers*, the film "ran as much as 140 minutes at a preview but was cut back to 96 minutes for release." Forty-five minutes is missing—and it was apparently mostly music. The casualties included the main ballad, "A Little Bungalow [an hour or so from any-where]," a beguiling little tune with a secret: the entire refrain, complete with coda, is made of a single strain or a variation of it—a bit of technical wizardry that reminds us that, while Berlin could not notate music, his level of composition was anything but primitive.

Presumably stifling his outrage at the way Paramount had stripped *The Cocoanuts* of almost all its music, Berlin headed out to California for two big projects for release in 1930, *Mammy* (for Warner Bros.) and *Puttin' On the Ritz* (for United Artists). But he found himself caught up in shoving matches with tin-eared producers, unwritten laws, the star system, and various mysterious forces that kept him from executing whatever vision he might have nurtured for the finished film.

Mammy was an Al Jolson project, so everything in the film is Jolson and nothing is Berlin, or anyone else. Still, Berlin did create a generic Jolson Number, "Let Me Sing and I'm Happy"; not till Judy Garland appeared was a performer to rival Jolson in making the sheer outgoing verve of singing the very substance of his or her ego projection. But *Mammy*'s importance—if any—lies in its rather authentic depiction of a minstrel troupe (with some of the onstage scenes in Technicolor). Lois Moran, the original woman lead on Broadway in *Of Thee I Sing* is on hand, and, in the title role, we get Louise Dresser, far more vivacious than the helplessly accommo-dating Eugenie Besserer of *The Jazz Singer*. Even so, Jolson is so busy ob-scuring melodies with his eccentric singing style, getting in touch with his inner ham, being framed for murder, and generally tilting the room that, in the end, there is neither mammy nor Berlin on offer, just Jolson.

Puttin' On the Ritz gave Berlin more of a showcase, though he contributed only three numbers and had to contend with another egocentric star, the "second Jolson," Harry Richman. In fact, Jolson and Richman were compa-rable in limited ways at best. Both represented the so to say "ethnicity" of New York and commanded a vocal style to put over a number with a fierce address of the audience. The new "crooning" vocalism created by the inven-tion of the microphone, epitomized by Bing Crosby, Russ Columbo, Nick Lucas, and, obviously, "Whispering" Jack Smith, was a half-measure to Jolson and Richman. A quarter-measure. A nothing. These two sang to fill the house.

Otherwise, however, the pair were quite different. Jolson was a come-dian and singer: his roles onstage in the Shuberts' Winter Garden shows were written in the wisenheimer mode used by the likes of Bobby Clark, Jimmy Durante, and Bert Lahr (albeit after Jolson, and each in his unique tone). Richman was no comedian; he was barely an actor. He just sang. Further, Richman performed his numbers as written, while Jolson fiddled with them. And Jolson, like him or not, was magnetic on screen despite off-kilter looks while Richman was not a screen natural in any sense.

But Richman could indeed justify Berlin's music, slipping in endearing little portamentos and making the most of his terrific high notes. Richman sang two of Berlin's numbers, the bathetic ballad "With You" and the title cut, an onstage production number telling how the fashion-makers of Harlem enjoy a night out on Lenox Avenue. (Years later, to neutralize the racial content, Berlin rewrote the lyric, now to tell of the white trendsetters of Park Avenue.) "Puttin On the Ritz" is the movie's high point, made of A strains effervescent with syncopation and a bridge built on trick rhymes ("Every Lulu Belle goes" mates with "her swell beaus" and "rubbin' elbows")[1] while white and then black ensembles dance before a skyline of expression-istically grinning houses. For his part, Richman struts about, introducing the number and then soaring into a wild high descant over the vocal of the chorus. Then the two ensembles appear in long shot but separated (as the unwritten racial law of the day demanded), the whites on the deck and the blacks on an upper level, while the background houses join in the dance themselves.

If there's an onstage number, then this has to be a backstager—and it's a Plot A type, as Richman deserts his friends (James Gleason, Lilyan Tashman) and sweetheart (a very young Joan Bennett) because success and the patronage of bigwigs have swollen his head. At a tony party, Bennett angrily confronts him. He has traded the loyalty of true camara-derie for the flattery of knaves:

BENNETT: You've turned into a vain, impossible fool. A blind fool!

Fatal words! Richman then drinks a bad flask of Prohibition liquor and loses his sight. Nor does he regain it, in the forgiving Hollywood manner, though he does reconnect with Bennett, who has become a Broadway star in—of course—a revue. Bennett's big spot is "Alice in Wonderland," and the audience gives her an ovation for nothing: an offstage tenor sings the vocal, and it's the dancers (in Wonderland outfits) who do all the work, while Bennett simply walks around the checkerboard stage. Every so often, director Edward Sloman effects a close-up of Bennett looking thrilled.

---

1. *Lulu Belle*, a smash Broadway melodrama of 1926 by Edward Sheldon and Charles MacArthur, was a modern-dress version of *Carmen*, re-set in Harlem and Paris (and played in blackface). For a generation, "Lulu Belle" was a summoning term for a siren, usually though not invariably black. Berlin's use of the specific character reference was somewhat unusual for him, more typical of Lorenz Hart or Cole Porter.

It's a wonderful number all the same, originally in Technicolor,[2] and rather imaginatively staged (by Maurice Kusell) to be as much a pageant as a dance. One wonders why Berlin didn't insist on creating *Ritz*'s entire score, but the three non-Berlin pieces, mainly by unknowns and Richman himself and built around Richman's exhibitionistic address, are genuine tailor-mades.[3] Jolson's key numbers generally treated concepts (as in "April Showers") or other people ("Where Did Robinson Crusoe Go With Friday on Saturday Night?"). Even his "I" songs tended to focus on something outside himself ("California, Here I Come"). But Richman sang of Richman, explored Richman, explained Richman. Thus, one of the non-Berlin *Ritz* numbers, the proudly marching "Singing a Vagabond Song," is utter Richmania, as he describes his roguish, independent personality. A wanderer is he, it appears, scornful of "your fashions, your passions," not to mention "your fool'ry, your jew'lry," as he treads life's highway. The song's meaning anticipates Rodgers and Hart's "The Lady Is a Tramp" (from *Babes in Arms*), but the music is stentorian and the lyrics bear none of Hart's site-specific allusions ("I follow Winchell and read ev'ry line"). In fact, it's hard to imagine even the very versatile Berlin writing in this vein; it's almost like an American "On the Road To Mandalay."

At only sixty-eight minutes and very modest-looking except for the two production numbers, *Puttin' On the Ritz* did not come off as the major project that Berlin had had in mind. The movie starts well, in the inevitable New York music-publisher's office. Bennett is a would-be songwriter who has come in off the street; Gleason works in the office. Richman, a song plugger, has a star's surprise entrance: Gleason and a co-worker are listening to an unseen Richman singing "I'll Get By," yet another of the non-Berlin numbers. But where *is* Richman? Down the hall? On a phonograph record? No: he pops up from behind a piano. And note this odd bit of New York lingo when the boss, a Mr. Wagner, comes in:

---

2. The storybook-fantasy sequence, shot in color within a black-and-white feature, was a genre at the time, as in *The Broadway Melody*'s aforementioned "The Wedding of the Painted Doll" or *Lord Byron of Broadway*'s "The Woman in the Shoe," during which the titular item is transformed from a rundown clodhopper into a palatial high-heeled slipper of dazzling silver. Berlin's "Alice" was actually a save, originally used in the fourth *Music Box* revue; Berlin had written a completely different "Alice in Wonderland" for a revue co-produced by Florenz Ziegfeld and Charles Dillingham, *The Century Girl* (1916).

3. Irving Berlin, Inc. published two of them, so perhaps Berlin was content in seeing his business get a lift during the first days of the Depression. The third number was brought out by the little-known Santly Bros., Inc. "Sing Santly songs," its sheet-music cover indicia urged.

GLEASON: (to the others, quietly) Ixnay, the pansy!

"Ixnay," pig Latin for "Nix," means "Stop, no more!"—but why the "pansy?" Wagner is not played as gay—there were no gay music publishers in Holly- wood backstagers, only gay costume designers—but rather as a no-nonsense businessman who has had it with the imploring Richman:

RICHMAN: Mr. Wagner, did you hear the last song I wrote?
WAGNER: I hope so.

This opening segment runs fourteen minutes—about one-fifth of the whole film—which proves how pervasive the "New York atmosphere" was in the backstager. Moreover, it sets up the story well, as Richman and Bennett unite in creating a song hit and Mr. Wagner does some firing so the pair can join Gleason in initiating the camaraderie that Richman will destroy in his egocentric rise to the top. But the rest of the action is fits and starts, and Richman himself is a trial: brash and full of himself, and I don't mean his character. I mean him. Worse, he keeps appearing in black lip stick, as if preparing for a second career as Maria Montez's stand-in. At that, the big reveal of the first movie musicals was that moviegoers pre- ferred established stars even in the privileged world of song and dance. Richman's name meant nothing to the second and third audiences, even after he managed a publicity-rich affair with Clara Bow.

And then came *Reaching For the Moon* (1931), Berlin's worst experience in the movies. This time he wanted auteur status, not only writing a full score but co-authoring the script and co-producing. Further, the concept was en- tirely his, although there was nothing especially innovative in his tale of a Wall Street tycoon chasing a glamorous woman on a transatlantic cruise, with a drink that causes wild personality changes stirred in to pepper the pot.

Now we reach the first problem. A lawyer acquaintance of mine, Paul Epstein, likes to quote his mother: "With everything comes aggravation." That could read as a warning over Hollywood's portal, because back on Broadway, a musical could be planned, cast, and written inside of two months, whereupon it went right into rehearsal and tryouts and reached the New York premiere some six to eight weeks later. But in Hollywood, very often, delay provoked delay as casting hit snags, as scripting became layered with editors and add-on writers, as other features on a studio's re- lease calendar were accommodated.

Lucky Break, the film's original title, needed above all a charismatic male (thinking in 1930 Broadway terms, a Fred Astaire or Dennis King); a leading lady with pizzazz (Vivienne Segal? Gertrude Lawrence?); an "eccentric butler" type, possibly Leon Errol; a soubrette, also with pizzazz. In *A Song in the Dark*, Richard Barrios tells us that Lawrence Gray and Jack Whiting were at least considered for the protagonist (though Gray was not a big enough name and Whiting, a first-choice leading man on Broadway, was unknown to moviegoers) and Ginger Rogers succeeded Ruby Keeler in line for the soubrette part. Then June MacCloy succeeded Rogers.

All this Hollywood dithering. But Bebe Daniels was to play opposite whoever got the central role, and Busby Berkeley was to stage the dances.... No. Berkeley was out—and the film's director, Edmund Goulding, didn't like musicals. We can imagine Berlin's exasperation: why does it take so long? In New York, we cast it and we write it and we *put on the show*!

Then came the second problem: Douglas Fairbanks as the Wall Streeter. Like *Puttin' On the Ritz*, *Lucky Break* was a United Artists project, and Fairbanks (with his wife, Mary Pickford, D. W. Griffith, and Charlie Chaplin) was a founding owner of the studio. So there was logic in the casting—and Fairbanks was eager to rejuvenate his costume-swashbuckler brand with something hip and snazzy. But Fairbanks was wrong for this part; he was wrong for talkies, period. For one thing, his voice was unattractive, and, for another, the restlessly athletic devil-may-care that had served him so well as D'Artagnan or Robin Hood or the Thief of Bagdad in silents seemed grotesque amid the more composed naturalism of sound films. When speaking, he seems abrupt and off-key, unable to "place" his lines in relation to those he's conversing with. And, strange to say, Fairbanks suddenly turned out to be short: he is clearly a full notch below all his co-players, a flaw that was somehow kept from us in his preceding titles. At least he was still in great physical shape; Goulding gave him a few shirtless scenes to prove it.

Then, too, Fairbanks commanded a faithful following among the third audience in the small towns; he (and Pickford) symbolized for rural America a nobility, a merriment, a morality in the movies. And, at United Artists, he was everybody's boss in the first place. But Fairbanks couldn't sing. Berlin had to reconfigure the score to work around Fairbanks' character, though *Reaching For the Moon* finally previewed with, Barrios tells us, a full complement of six songs, even one for Fairbanks. (He may have talked his way through it; this was not uncommon even on Broadway at the time.)

And now the third problem, already known to us: the public was tired of musicals. When *Reaching For the Moon* was released, the entire score had been cut, save one number, "When the Folks High Up Do the Mean Low Down."

But it's a doozy, at any rate. It starts on shipboard, just after Bebe Daniels has had a taste of that crazy drink, which leads her to stalk through the public areas getting into mischief. She reaches the bar, and, lo, Bing Crosby erupts out of nowhere. He has taken no part in the action to this point, but someone calls out, "It's Bing!," and Crosby slides right into the number, Berlin in his jazzy mode. Daniels also gets into the vocal, as does MacCloy (for a tiny bit), and suddenly the entire salon goes wild with dancing. We see what Berlin is driving at—music makes people step out of their skin even more than that alchemical drink does. One dowager slaps her daughter—you *dare* to *shimmy* in *public*, Miss Reckless? For these five minutes, we can visualize the musical Berlin had hoped to show us.

Otherwise, *Reaching For the Moon* is a dud. It had been designed to run on the rhythmic and emotional drive that lifts a silly storyline because music is a high. Without the songs, all we get is bum fluff. "Musicals were the rage out there," Berlin told the *New York Times* much later, "and then they weren't." He was so offended by the experience that, when he published the title number (supposedly heard in the soundtrack underscoring, though no melody stands out as a Theme Song), he issued it in a standard edition rather than with Hollywood poster art or, indeed, any mention that the number belonged to a movie at all. With everything comes aggravation.

Finished with Hollywood, Berlin returned to Broadway for two splendid hits, *Face the Music* (1932) and *As Thousands Cheer* (1933). But after *42nd Street*'s flash success brought musicals back into vogue, Hollywood needed Berlin; he had the populist address of De Sylva, Brown, and Henderson but greater range, and he was probably the most famous songwriter of the time. Then, too, the new RKO studio, organized specifically to make talkies, was New York-centric in tone, boasting a producers' circle very aware of the talents of the theatre world. Here was a place for the "theatrical" sensibility of Katharine Hepburn or George Cukor, the home of Fred Astaire and Ginger Rogers, whose producer, Pandro S. Berman, was keen to hire Broadway masters for their teamings.

Berlin was to write three Astaire-Rogers films: *Top Hat* (1935), *Follow the Fleet* (1936), and *Carefree* (1938), and the business deal that started it all is one of the most famous in Hollywood history. Stanley Green's *Encyclopedia of the Hollywood Musical* outlines the terms: Berlin wanted $100,000 for *Top Hat*, but Berman couldn't pay more upfront than $75,000. How about this, then? Let Berlin take the lower fee—but if the picture grosses over $1,250,000, he gets 10 percent of every penny the movie makes. Berlin "accepted reluctantly," says Green, "since few films grossed over a million." (Of course, Berlin would in any case get all the profits of the song sheets.) In the end, *Top Hat* took in over $3,000,000, giving Berlin a stunning windfall: $300,000 for just five numbers (plus another three or four that weren't used).

The Astaire and Rogers RKOs bring us to the series format, a business-as-usual platform offering another instance of the difference between

Hollywood and Broadway. There were series book musicals on stage in the nineteenth and very early twentieth centuries—the *Mulligan Guard* farces of Edward Harrigan and Tony Hart or the *Letty* shows built around Charlotte Greenwood. And variety annuals were extremely prominent in the 1910s and 1920s. By about 1930, however, the theatre had largely discarded the series model; the death of Florenz Ziegfeld, in 1932, was a termination point, even if his *Follies* made sporadic appearances in other hands through the 1950s.

But Hollywood reveled in the series, then as now, whether in detective procedurals, westerns, or specialty items such as *The Cohens and Kellys*. Each series nurtured its own genre, the RKOs so densely that *Top Hat* is often called a remake of the second Astaire-Rogers outing, *The Gay Divorcee* (1934), with the dressy European setting; the mooing sidekick, Edward Everett Horton; the vainglorious Other Man, Erik Rhodes; the fastidiously mouthy butler, Eric Blore; and the sarcastic lady, Alice Brady earlier and Helen Broderick here. *Top Hat* even had the same scenarist as *The Gay Divorcee*—almost. Dwight Taylor, son of the celebrated actress Laurette Taylor, had written the unproduced script that *Gay Divorce* (the stage show's title) was based on, and RKO hired Taylor to write *Top Hat*, with co-author Allan Scott (though the usual helpfully unknown Hungarian play was the film's official source).

Business as usual. Yet *Top Hat* feels unique. Generally regarded as the best of the nine Astaire-Rogers RKOs, it has a secret weapon: Irving Berlin. This, the fourth entry in the series, was the first to attune its music precisely to its stars' zany charm; the songs sound the way Astaire and Rogers act, and, like them, bear highly inflected profiles, genuine character content. "Isn't This a Lovely Day (To Be Caught in the Rain?)" is a beguiling piece, certainly. But, more important, its blithely dancey rhythm and air of making the best of misfortune (a sudden storm: so let's fall in love) pours out a Depression tonic and tells us why these two performers so suited the 1930s.

Or consider "The Piccolino." This is not a New Dance Sensation, even if it does inspire a production number, as the two stars, in Arlene Croce's words, "literally kick up their heels . . . in a scintillating, dipsy-doodle affair." Rather, "The Piccolino" salutes the latest Venetian hit tune, written by a gondolier . . . in Brooklyn. Berlin sometimes amused himself by giving a song unusually sturdy construction—the refrain of *Top Hat*'s "Cheek To Cheek" sports *two* releases—and "The Piccolino" is something like a rondo. Better, its harmony is astonishing, starting with a vamp that repeatedly moves from the tonic to the tonic flatted seventh. That's amusing enough, except Berlin patches in a chord from an entirely different key where that seventh is "supposed" to be, giving the vamp a bizarre clomping effect, as if a giant was executing a bourrée. Using the published sheet as a guide, this vamp veers from D Major to a suspended C Major over D Major, probably a first in the history of pop music, and the rondo's first episode's harmonic footprint, in F Sharp Major, runs through a chromatic bass line to reach b minor, then g sharp minor, and somehow slithers back into the tonic D Major in a kind of harmonic double-talk in which F Sharp Major uses g sharp minor diminished seventh to establish an A Major seventh for the return to D Major. It's quite an excursion for a composer who could hear the chords in his head but lacked the training to notate them himself.

Finally, "The Piccolino" gives us yet more of the irreplaceable silliness of Astaire and Rogers, the "dipsy-doodle" that Croce mentioned. There were comparable numbers in their earlier films; one thinks at once of "The Continental" in *The Gay Divorcee*. But that isn't an Astaire-Rogers number. It's an all-purpose New Dance Sensation that anyone might have danced to, especially given its mysterious intro and its "dangerous rhythm." Astaire and Rogers aren't mysterious or dangerous. They're morale boosters who democratize elegance.

And note that they move freely in the elegant world but are never inhabitants of it. *Top Hat* opens in London at the Thackeray Club, where silence is rigorously observed. This is the salon of the one per cent in Depression uprics: the leisure class at its worst, reading newspapers in greedy armchairs and going into tizzies if one dare speak a word. Parasites. Idiots. Why do they dude up in evening clothes just to read the papers? And why the silence? Astaire shows his opinion of all this by breaking into a clacking tap statement as he exits the place.

Later films brought Astaire and his partner into less elite precincts. *Follow the Fleet* is working-class—dance-hall girls and sailors—and *Carefree* is country-club bourgeois. The former returns us to the movie star meme, for the film's Second Couple is Randolph Scott and Harriet Hilliard (later Ozzie Nelson's wife with his band and then on fifties television), and Scott doesn't dance or sing. He's an important figure in the movie, not least because of his imposing looks and height, because when he and his buddy Astaire stand next to each other in their sailor blues, Scott is embarrassingly taller, with much broader shoulders. He even has a huge head. This is Hollywood casting: there was literally no one like Scott in the Broadway musical at this time.

Again, only a movie musical could get away with a leading man who didn't make at least a token appearance in the score. And the Scott-Hilliard romance drives *Follow the Fleet*'s plot far more than anything between Astaire and Rogers, who rather take each other for granted; their only emotional point of contact, "Let's Face the Music and Dance," is a performance piece, not a story number.

So it's Hilliard and Scott who must interest us, especially as Hilliard (as Rogers' sister) is supposed to be a wallflower. The charismatic Scott would appear to be out of her reach:

> HILLIARD: There's a sailor I want to meet. How do I go about it?
> LUCILLE BALL: (staggered at her naiveté) Are you kidding?

Yes, Ball is on site, knocking around RKO in minor roles because nobody realized that she was more arresting as a clown than as a showgirl. It's Ball who helps Hilliard attract Scott, using Hollywood's patented method: lose the glasses and jazz up the hairdo.

Of course it works, giving Berlin the opportunity for "Get Thee Behind Me Satan," Hilliard's "thrilled but scared" solo as she awaits his arrival for their night out. There's something wonderful in the number's structure, for while it accords with a more or less conventional AA^1BA^2, the final A sweeps in in the orchestra while Hilliard is still singing the last words of the B section. That's dramatic enough—but to cap it, director Mark Sandrich brings the approaching Scott, with a grin you can see from outer space, into the background of the frame during that last A. This occurs just as Hilliard reaches the climax of the vocal, on "Satan, he's at my gate," thus placing the lyrics into visual italics. It's another of the usages of film that Broadway had no access to, employing the concentrated geography of the camera to highlight a narrative point—Hilliard's fear of engulfment by Scott's well-routined charm—that would be lost on the expanse of a stage.

By this point, Berlin felt so comfortable writing for the movies that he temporarily gave up on Broadway, offering nothing between the "newspaper headline" revue *As Thousands Cheer* (1933) and *Louisiana Purchase* (1940). Fox's *On the Avenue* (1937) brought in another non-musical movie star, Madeleine Carroll, as a Society beauty offended at being spoofed onstage by Dick Powell and Alice Faye. The film's opening shots are newsprint, especially gossip columns—Ed Sullivan, Mark Hellinger (and, later, Walter Winchell). So this will be another of those New York-centric stories, this time a backstager merged with a screwball comedy. Will Carroll and her wealthy father sue over the offending sketch—in, of course, Dick Powell's revue? His producer, played by Walter Catlett, knows all about it:

> CATLETT: When people are that rich, they'll do anything for money!

But Powell and Carroll are dating, which gives us screwball's indispensable "Manhattan sophisticates goofing around in humble places to prove they're regular guys" sequence. Unfortunately, this particular sequence is set in a Greek diner run by Billy Gilbert, whose ridiculous accent and slow-burn impatience with these madcap mischief-makers make one long for the uninflected wit of El Brendel.

In all, *On the Avenue* occupies the other side of the Hollywood musical, the side Astaire and Rogers never heard of, where the music consists almost entirely of insert numbers (on stage or in rehearsal) that impede the narrative rather than animate it. *On the Avenue's* six songs are wonderful, from the dynamic "He Ain't Got Rhythm" (with its enticing biographical detail about a professor who "attracted some attention, when he found the fourth dimension") to the suave "I've Got My Love To Keep Me Warm," which, come to think of it, would have been perfect for Fred Astaire. And the movie opened at Radio City Music Hall, the greatest booking available at the time.

But there's a reason why *Top Hat* stands on the short list and *On the Avenue* is forgotten: it doesn't care about its music the way the RKOs do. Even though Madeleine Carroll actually sings two lines (in a reprise of "Slumming On Park Avenue"), it is all the same difficult to perfect a musical with a romantic lead who ain't got rhythm. True, it worked for Randolph Scott in *Follow the Fleet*. But we expect more emotional give from a heroine—especially in the 1930s, before Rodgers and Hammerstein revealed the vulnerable male (on Broadway in the 1940s) in *Carousel's* "Soliloquy" and *South Pacific's* "Some Enchanted Evening."

Nevertheless, Fox must have been pleased with *On the Avenue*, for Berlin was asked to write the score for a Sonja Henie vehicle, *Second Fiddle* (1939), the sole title in the Fox Henie series with songs by a Broadway name rather than one of the studio's house teams. One of the many spoofs of David O. Selznick's search for a Scarlett O'Hara in a certain southern film, *Second Fiddle* supposes that Henie is up for the part of Violet Jansen in *Girl of the North*. Amoral PR man Tyrone Power is her love interest, Rudy Vallee and Mary Healy complicate the romance, and Henie's tart-tongued aunt, Edna May Oliver, keeps the joint jumping. It's a trite setup, brightened only by Oliver and Power's sleazily irresistible hustler; these roles wrote themselves. "If [fading star Vallee] were to die tonight," says Power, "I couldn't get his name in the obituary column."

So *Second Fiddle* is minor Fox. It's even minor Berlin. Worse, it's minor Henie. She's a schoolteacher, so we first see her leading her class in "The Song of the Metronome," which then provides the music for a skating interlude with those same children. It's amusing enough. But a Henie ice number usually took in a host of triple-axel pros, not kids from the neighborhood.

Berlin did find room for another of his salutes to yesteryear, in "An Old-Fashioned Tune Is Always New," with Vallee and showgirls perched on a set made of sheet music. And "[Dancing] Back To Back," a production number, allows Oliver to cut loose with Power. It's capable fun, as is Healy's "I'm Sorry For Myself," built into a showy sequence for swing combo, black solo, and girls' quartet. And Henie's third and last skating scene finally shows off her superb icy poetry, a solo flight zooming through turns and jumps with a perfect single-blade freeze-finish.

Moving to Paramount, Berlin embarked on a trio of films teaming Fred Astaire and Bing Crosby, generally with second-division women: *Holiday Inn* (1942), *Blue Skies* (1946), and *White Christmas* (1954), though in the last title Danny Kaye substituted for an ailing Astaire and the women are Rosemary Clooney and Vera-Ellen, who add to the fun because the former didn't dance and the latter didn't sing.[4]

Unfortunately, these films take the tone of the later Crosby, a singer of imagination and verve in the 1930s but by the 1940s so mild he's almost sleeping. Some of Crosby's thirties roles find him in danger or at least in ironic situations, and one title, which will be along presently, casts him as the dueling terror of the Old South. By the 1940s, however, Bing is ambling through life—and that really doesn't suit Irving Berlin, always at his best when he has a puzzle to solve, as in the smooth-versus-hairy quodlibet of "[Won't you play a] Simple Melody," a honeyed fox trot set into conflict with a snazzy rag. Or in "The Lord Done Fixed Up My Soul," a gospel rave-up for Broadway that can't get too gospel because Broadway prefers pastiche to the heavy stuff. Or in "You Can't Get a Man With a Gun," because the singer's own forte is her nemesis.

Or even in "Puttin' On the Ritz," built on the paradox of the working class en grande toilette. To move from such pointed drollery to *Holiday Inn* is a humiliation. Remember, Berlin was more than a songwriter: he actively collaborated on projects, sometimes earning a "based on an idea by" credit in the title cards. Berlin's idea behind *Holiday Inn*, however, is feeble, perhaps too closely molded on Crosby, who runs a hostel that doubles as a cabaret, the songs chiming in on holidays—"Let's Say It With Firecrackers," "White Christmas," "Let's Start the New Year Right." But Crosby's squishy persona can't support a narrative with any real story in it—and what's so exciting about a holiday inn

---

4. Though dubbed in all her movie numbers by a succession of specialists from Carol Richards to Trudy Stevens, Vera-Ellen sang on Broadway before she went Hollywood. The curious can hear her on the original cast of the 1943 revival of Rodgers and Hart's *A Connecticut Yankee* (on CD on Decca Broadway). The voice is rough-and-tumble, but valid for the character, a hoyden of the Excalibur era.

in the first place? There was much more going on—albeit melodramatically—when Jolson fled a murder rap and when Richman went blind.

Crosby's somnolence drags Astaire down as well. *Blue Skies* has only his solo backed by eight miniature Astaires, each mirroring what he does, to recommend it. (There's a nifty trick, too, when his cane, lying on the floor, flies up into his hand.) This number, as it happens, is "Puttin' On the Ritz" again, now in its neutralized lyrics. But then, this trio of films as a whole is neutralized. Berlin did give *White Christmas* a largely new score—*Blue Skies* drew mainly on pre-existing numbers—and he happily reclaimed the melody of "Free," dropped from *Call Me Madam* on Broadway and now re-lyricked as "Snow." But the songs are more useful than delightful.

Meanwhile, Hollywood had opened a sub-office in filming Berlin's more recent stage shows, in faithful versions that used some Broadway cast members—*Louisiana Purchase* (1941), *Annie Get Your Gun* (1950), *Call Me Madam* (1953). Considerable adjustment was necessary on *This Is the Army* (1943), for the original was a revue and Warner Bros. wanted a storyline to hold it together. The show, now forgotten, was a phenomenon of its time, created entirely by soldiers (and Berlin himself was a World War I veteran) in the jingoistic spirit so basic to the war years. The optics of the presenta tion, with row upon row of uniformed men ranged on bleachers before a spread-winged eagle, was the wallpaper of the day. The musical did turn-away business at every stop in a world tour, and the event inspired such immense talkabout that it led Jack Kapp, of Decca Records, to take down ten 78 sides of the score in 1942 in the very first American original-cast album in the modern sense, with all the Broadway performers in their original roles and the pit orchestra playing the original arrangements.[5]

Warner Bros. went all out with *This Is the Army*, using Technicolor and almost all of the score, with the essential addition of Kate Smith's "God Bless America," complete with a belter's high D (the ninth above middle C) of immense power. And, yes, the film included the famous view of the chorus men ranged on their bleachers and Berlin to encore his "Oh, How I Hate To Get Up in the Morning." True, the added narrative is awfully corny, starting in 1917, when doughboy George Murphy puts on the soldier revue *Yip Yip Yaphank* (as Berlin had done, in 1918) and moving up to 1943, when

5. Certain earlier albums with original-cast elements—Brunswick's 1932 *Show Boat* and 1933 *Blackbirds of 1928* (both also produced by Jack Kapp), Victor's 1935 *Porgy and Bess*, Musicraft's 1938 *The Cradle Will Rock*, and Decca's 1940 and 1942 *Porgy and Besses*—all fail my definition above for various reasons. The popular belief that Decca's *Oklahoma!* is the first original-cast set (when it was in fact the second) shows how fully *This Is the Army* has slipped out of common memory.

Ronald Reagan is Murphy's son, putting on another soldier revue. This one. There's some spoofing of army life, as when Charles Butterworth shows up at a rehearsal, eager to join the show:

MURPHY: What do you do?
BUTTERWORTH: I'm the bugler [who plays reveille].

So of course the other soldiers immediately attack him:

MURPHY: Whoa, men! Hold it, it's no use, they'll [just] find another one.

The film's pleasures reside entirely in the songs, which take in war anthems, unusual inventions in that "American Eagles" and "With My Head in the Clouds" (a combination of love song and paean to bombing runs) sound like Berlin in their music yet bring him into subject matter he isn't associated with to public knowledge. These aren't comic numbers, like "The Army's Made a Man Out of Me," but genuine war cries. Berlin was patriotic, but not, till this score, notably combative.

No, what the nation knew about Berlin was all those hit ballads and specialty numbers. And that's why Berlin never got a bio movie with a song cavalcade: Hollywood had been exploiting Berlin's catalogue before he had enough life story to film. Nowadays, Broadway obsessively produces "jukebox musicals," rebooting pre-existing songs in a new scenario. But Hollywood invented the genre in four Berlin movies aggregating his old titles with a few new ones: *Alexander's Ragtime Band* (1938), the aforementioned *Blue Skies*, *Easter Parade* (1948), and *There's No Business Like Show Business* (1954).

One of Fox's major exhibits of the late 1930s (albeit in black and white), *Alexander's Ragtime Band* gives us another non-musical movie star in Tyrone Power as a classical lad who turns to pop to make his fortune. Symphony or ragtime? High-concept or demotic? Leopold Stokowski or Benny Goodman? The question was the preoccupation of the day, and the answer seemed to be that America needs its democratic bedrock to support its elitist outcroppings.

But there's always a price to be paid, isn't there? So a soap-opera plot carries bandleader Power; his singer, Alice Faye; his pianist, Don Ameche; his drummer, Jack Haley; and his "other woman" singer, Ethel Merman (who makes her entrance about an hour into the 105-minute running time) from rag into the swing era and from San Francsico dives to Carnegie Hall. A backstager Plot B with musicmakers instead of a show, and with the woman (instead of the man) as the one who betrays her colleagues for show-biz stardom, *Alexander's Ragtime Band* uses Berlin's music to map the passing of time. Thus, we move from the amusingly antique "Ragtime

Violin" to one of the film's two new numbers, "My Walking Stick," which sounds exactly like the kind of thing songwriters would create for Fred Astaire in his RKO period. In fact, it isn't a man's song: Merman introduces it, adding to the air of *now*, for her delivery, with its precise respect for the written notes and words, and her even intonation marked a complete break with the eccentric mannerisms of the Al Jolsons who preceded her.

As so often, all the numbers served as performance pieces, though a few functioned simultaneously as character songs, as when an unhappy, Tyrone Power-less Faye sang "All Alone" in a café. The film makes a splendid meal out of the other new number, "Now It Can Be Told," in a sequence in which Don Ameche, unrequitedly in love with Faye, performs this valentine for her when they're alone together. He wrote it for her, but it's about him. "Imagine you having that in you," she says, getting it and not getting it at the same time.

But we're not done yet. Ameche now shows the song to the whole band, and Power has the trombone and clarinet come up to the piano, the former taking the melody and the latter improvising a middle voice using the harmony in a descending line. It's precisely how such musicians might "discover" a piece, working off a lead sheet,[6] and while Power never persuades us that he is a musician, the actors playing the band members are extremely convincing. All this leads up to Faye's presenting the number publicly, in a feathery white gown, constantly throwing looks at Power. And he gets it. Capping the episode, the two move off into the moonlight for a kiss.

Indeed, this movie is made of music, counting three or four times as many song-and-dance spots as the average film musical of the time. And the stagings are exhilarating. "Everybody's Doin' It Now" is one of the great cuts of the day, as Dixie Dunbar and Wally Vernon put it over in a deliberately mismatched coupling of svelte girl and heavy guy (though he can execute a flip). Faye sings this one, too, in her typical one-tone-fits-all approach that is so noncommittal that you wonder if she knows what the song is about. (Sex. Or no: dancing. But Berlin's lyrics always equate the two.) True, Faye emotes during the torch songs. But in up tunes like this one she navigates around the music rather than the words. It is Dunbar and Vernon who make the number theirs.

And if you can't justify the music in a film like this one, you become story-bound in a world beyond story: because the narrative is silly. It gets in the way of all those wonderful songs. And then the plot becomes truly eerie, as Fox needs to bring Faye and Power together after a long separation.

---

6. This denotes a skeleton score, with the melody notated in a single staff and the chords cited above, leaving the performer to develop his own arrangement: something like a modern pop equivalent of the seventeenth-century figured bass.

The studio actually resorts to a deus ex machina figure, a spooky cab driver (John Carradine) whose job it is to deposit Faye at Carnegie Hall just in time to rush onstage to rejoin Power's band, now a symphony orchestra of pop. Even his old music-snob aunt and professor admire him. As thirties and forties movies loved to tell us, Benny Goodman *is* Stokowski.

MGM's *Easter Parade* is the best of the Berlin-catalogue films, because of the chemistry in the teaming of Fred Astaire and Judy Garland, as she keeps him lively in the way the Crosby alignments failed to. It's partly because Garland is so vivid herself—so emotional yet so playful—but also because she really throws herself into her numbers. And she can keep up with Astaire's footwork. *Easter Parade* shows them auditioning for Ziegfeld with "When That Midnight Choo-Choo Leaves For Alabam'," in Hollywood's typical imaginary Broadway: extras hanging out motion-lessly in the background in semi-focus while the movie's stars slather the stage with their act. Sometimes they're in poor form, as when the Mahoney Sisters audition for "Francis Zanfield" in *The Broadway Melody*. Usually they're fine.

But Astaire and Garland are terrific, which creates a logical paradox: they're too expert to have to audition, even as a new act. Again, this is Hollywood's Broadway, not Broadway's—because, back east, Ziegfeld would have been tipped off to their talent, caught them in full true with costumes and lights onstage somewhere, and signed them up in their dressing room.

Ironically, Garland told interviewer Jerry Mason of the *Los Angeles Times* (at the time of a different film, *Girl Crazy*), "I am the world's number one dance faker"—ironically because no faker keeps up with Astaire. But Garland did know her worth, at least as a vocalist. When she and Berlin were going over one of her *Easter Parade* numbers and he ventured a suggestion, she told him, in the mock-diva tone she sometimes put on, "Listen, buster, you write 'em. *I* sing 'em."

Easter Parade as a whole is rather grandly brought off, in the carefully musicalized production typical of MGM's self-contained outfit run by Arthur Freed. A songwriter himself, he understood as few producers did—RKO's Pandro Berman was of course another exception—the needs of the song-writer, the polish of the vocal arranger, the fizz of the orchestrator. Further, *Easter Parade* boasts almost as many new songs as old ones in a very big score; one imagines Freed urging Berlin to outdo his ancient hits "I Love a Piano" and "Shaking the Blues Away" with the debut items. One was "Let's Take an Old-Fashioned Walk," an irresistible waltz cut from the film but re-booted in the stage show *Miss Liberty* the very next year, but the classic was "A Couple of Swells." It presents the two stars as tramps in music suggestive of a quiet, measured walk but then, in a bit about the two proceeding "up the avenue," Berlin pumps air into the piece in a melody that now sounds like a fancy stroll up the high street on a festival day.

Fox's *There's No Business Like Show Business*, about a show-biz family, the Five Donahues, is much less amusing. The senior Donahues, Dan Dailey and Ethel Merman, are so *embourgeoisés* that we hardly recognize them, son Donald O'Connor is overparted with a very dramatic role, and other son Johnnie Ray becomes a priest, which is if nothing else a novelty in the musical genre. Mitzi Gaynor, the Donahue daughter, gives the action some color, but it's Marilyn Monroe who animates the event, after a very late entrance, as O'Connor's love interest and the bane of Merman's life. Eventually, in that direst of show-biz geographies, a dressing room, the two women make peace.

Except for Ray's vocation, the film is as much a cavalcade of clichés as of Berlin's songs, as father Dailey is always the last to understand anything, mother Merman worries, true-blue Gaynor is…true-blue. And so on. Worse, the music is unimaginatively used. "Alexander's Ragtime Band" is typical, an overproduced onstage number in which each of the Donahues gets a chance at the refrain. The two seniors go Tyrolian, O'Connor heads to Scotland, complete with the inevitable "Hoot, man" (has anyone living ever heard a Scot say, "Hoot, man"?), Gaynor is *gaie en France*…but the less assimilable Ray sings alone at the piano. He accompanies himself in a slow, expansive reading, then picks up speed and tears emotionally into a melody that, till this film's release, had always seemed merrily contented.

In the end, *There's No Business Like Show Business* is at once unimportant and inflated. It does preserve something of what Merman was like on stage, but its best element is Monroe. Here is another of those "non-musical" movie stars, but a most underrated one, possibly because some viewers can't quite place the most beautiful woman on earth as a resourceful actress and marvelous musical-comedy worker as well. She so rejuvenates "After You Get What You Want You Don't Want It," a ditty left over from 1920 complete with the oxymoronic title that Tin Pan Alley loved (cf., "She's a New Kind of Old-Fashioned Girl" or "There's No Place Like Home, Boys, When Your Wife Has Gone Away"), that Berlin might have written it for the film.

He did well by Hollywood, Berlin, despite his frustration at losing the creative control he exercised on Broadway. Indeed, a pattern will emerge in these pages in which a member of the stage musical's leadership class finds his art compromised in Hollywood one way or another. Here's one way: Berlin's most popular movie score, to *Top Hat*, contains just five songs. His most popular stage score, to *Annie Get Your Gun*, consists (in its original version) of fifteen. You get an awful lot of story development in fifteen numbers.

CHAPTER 4

✣

George and Ira Gershwin

The second reason Hollywood needed Broadway songwriters was that there were few of their kind in Los Angeles in the 1920s, and literally none of the major ones.

The first reason was prestige. The movie industry had not yet risen above its origins as a cheap amusement made by and for "society's riffraff," and the theatre, culturally imposing, gave Hollywood cachet. After all, its founding father — more or less — was William Shakespeare.

There was something else. In some scarcely palpable way, American popular music began a kind of re-emergence in the 1920s as something not always "easy"—at times, in fact, "artistic." The defining event was a concert that Paul Whiteman produced at New York's Aeolian Hall in 1924, entitled "An Experiment in Modern Music." Le tout Manhattan turned out for it, led by "patrons and patronesses," from stars of opera and instrumental music to columnists and critics: Rachmaninof, Kreisler, Galli-Curci, stage director and professional genius Max Reinhardt, arts philanthropist Otto Kahn. The "modern" referred to jazz (which, to repeat, was simply the twenties term for the newest work in popular music, as opposed to "After the Ball," Scott Joplin's ragtime, and "Mary's a Grand Old Name"), and this obviously trendy concert was Appointment Jazz, in which the popular merged with the elite: in samples of songs played straight and "modern"; in "classy" show tunes (some by Kern and Berlin, the two outstanding progenitors of the "modern" in the 1910s); in piano virtuosity by Zez Confrey, in not Chopin or Brahms but his own "Kitten on the Keys"; in a new Victor Herbert piece, "A Suite of Serenades" (in four movements, from Spanish and Chinese to Cuban and "Oriental"). Herbert was the ultimate name in the notion of elite pop, but the center of the program—the very latest in "modern" and the reason history was made that day—was George Gershwin playing *his* new piece, billed as "A Rhapsody in Blue." The event's fusion of concerto form with Confrey's playing style and Herbert's sense of structure[1] altered the course of American music.

It got Gershwin the cover of *Time* magazine, bundling eminence with commercial power: so Hollywood must have Gershwin. But RKO's *Girl Crazy*, released in musical-hating 1932, was less an adaptation of a Gershwin show than a Wheeler and Woolsey comedy; MGM gave the music more respect in its 1943 remake, retaining nine of the Broadway numbers. (There was even a little-known third go-round, in 1965, again by MGM, *When the Boys Meet the Girls*, with Connie Francis, Harve Presnell, and drop-in specialties by those Gershwin specialists Liberace, Louis Armstrong, and Herman's Hermits.) Not till Fox signed George and brother Ira for a wholly original movie score did the nation get an idea of what a Gershwin movie would be like: *Delicious* (1931).

With Janet Gaynor and Charles Farrell starring, this was very much a knockoff of *Sunnyside Up*. He's Society again, but this time she's a Scots lass emigrating to America; they meet on shipboard, first class charmed by steerage. That ghastly El Brendel is back, along with another Society debutante to try to rout the romance. And this one has an unscrupulous mother.

There's a wonderful scenelet early on, aboard the ocean liner, wherein the whole thing is clarified for us during a musical number, the near-title song, "[You're so] Delishious." Fellow steerage passenger Raul Roulien, a composer, woos Gaynor with his latest tune, accompanying himself at the keyboard while Farrell looks on. We expect the orchestra to sneak into the soundtrack after the verse or perhaps the first A, but director David Butler is going for naturalism, and the entire sequence is rendered on piano only. Watch how the movies, once again, can set plot development into a number: a tray-bearing steward, passing by, stops to listen, appreciates Roulien's melody, and starts off, with the camera following him. He offers sandwiches to two women—the mother and daughter, by hap—as Roulien continues to play on the soundtrack. Mother is peeved that daughter rebuffed Farrell's marriage proposal. When a rich boy asks, the answer is yes:

MOTHER: You're never sure of a man until you're sitting in the bridal suite brushing the rice out of your hair.

---

1. This was, admittedly, slightly on the free side, especially regarding key relationships. Herbert himself famously said that he could have made much more of the Rhapsody's E Major Andantino Moderato—the score's "ballad" section—than Gershwin did, and Herbert suggested a change in the section's introductory bars that Gershwin incorporated.

Now Butler glides back to the piano, where Farrell and Gaynor are exerting their wonderful chemistry together. We can see why two less than fabulous actors, neither of whom can sing or dance, were top names in early Fox musicals: they simply go well as a pair in the silly-happy format of American musical comedy. They're so likably insubstantial that their lack of talent doesn't matter. And look what Butler sneaks into the rear of the shot: mother and daughter, professional matrimony racketeers.

Thus Butler shows us the action in a few glances. Roulien, we see, hasn't a chance against the far more engaging Farrell. He likes Gaynor. She likes him. And mother is going to interfere.

"With George Gershwin Music," the title cards boasted. Yet the four songs George and Ira contributed are third division; historians brush past these to consider two extended musical sequences. The first is Gaynor's dream of welcome to America on the eve of her arrival at Ellis Island. The brothers created for this a miniature opera, using cinema technique to jump from visual to visual: cops and paparazzi; four reporters, each of whom magically materializes as he starts to sing ("I'm from the Journal...the Wahrheit...the Telegram...the Times"); a troop of Uncle Sams; "Mr. Ellis" (in Gaynor's naive imagining, because it's his island); the Mayor with a Marine Guard; and the Statue of Liberty raining greenbacks on everyone.

Alas, a legal technicality blocks Gaynor from entering America, and an aggressive cop named O'Flynn moves *Delicious* into satire, for his brogue tells us that he, too, is an immigrant, yet he's anti-immigration:

O'FLYNN: If I had me way, I'd keep all ye pesterin' furriners out of our country.

He even calls El Brendel a "squarehead," the old derogation for a Swede.

All the rest of *Delicious* sees poor Gaynor trying to escape from O'Flynn and his minions while being blocked from resolving her romance with Farrell by the manipulative debutante-and-mother team. Gaynor even, finally, agrees to marry Roulien. Of course all ends well—but only after the second of the extended musical sequences, the "New York Rhapsody." This nine-and-a-half-minute pantomime (with a bit of dialogue) follows Gaynor distractedly wandering through the city at night, scared and desperate and even contemplating suicide till she at last spots a police station and walks inside to give herself up.

The music belongs to a genre unique to the 1920s (and, somewhat, the 1930s as well), in which composers devised an indigenous American style using "jazz" and the urban landscape in settings for band or full orchestra that, imitating *Rhapsody in Blue*, adapted classical technique. Note these titles' emphasis on what had become the City of Cities, the modern Rome: Louis Alter's *Manhattan Serenade*, Werner Janssen's *New Year's Eve in New York*, and, especially, John Alden Carpenter's ballet *Skyscrapers*, clanging with traffic and construction noises and haunted by groans from the brass as if the earth were sinking beneath the weight of the Manhattan skyline.

There was a hint in all this of expressionism, the defining mode of the 1920s—some of Eugene O'Neill's early plays popularized the style—and the filming of *Delicious'* "New York Rhapsody" is partly expressionistic, with inhuman crowds and near-anthropomorphic buildings, leaning in as if spying on Gaynor. The entire sequence was photographed in almost total darkness and is difficult to view, but the point is that Fox understood that "George Gershwin Music" was a commercial asset, even in a movie whose only apparent purpose was to reteam Gaynor and Farrell. Later, this "New York Rhapsody," extended to twice its length, entered the concert repertory as (in its full title) the *Second Rhapsody For Orchestra With Piano*, even as all four of *Delicious'* songs melted away.

True, we occasionally hear El Brendel's solo, "Blah, Blah, Blah," Ira's takeoff on Tin Pan Alley lyric clichés. The melody was originally intended for the unproduced *Ming Toy*, and there is a trace of Asian je ne sais quoi about it, and while George mirrors his brother in using harmonic clichés, he impishly goes for a supertonic seventh with a flatted sixth and a submediant nine-seven chord for Ira's "cottage for two." The music then retreats to a sedate dominant seventh and tonic close for "darling, with you."

Speaking of Ira, this wise and clever writer meshed wonderfully with his brother's jangly music in a marriage of smooth and rough. *Girl Crazy's* "I Got Rhythm" melody drives assertively, but Ira playfully plucks up clichés fit for "Blah, Blah, Blah" to soften the message—"starlight," "sweet dreams," "daisies in green pastures." The *Delicious* assignment must have stumped them, because their next Hollywood score, for *Shall We Dance* (1937), is one of the glories of thirties cinema.

Just as *Top Hat* presents the first realization of what Irving Berlin could do in film, *Shall We Dance* is the Gershwin showcase, and it must be due to the alchemy RKO mixed for their Astaire-Rogers series. At first, the two stars were supporting players in stories that didn't need music; *Flying Down To Rio* could lose its four numbers and remain perfectly coherent. But from *Top Hat* on, the Astaire-Rogers platform seems to navigate from number to number with a greed for song and dance, and RKO kept using Allan Scott as a scenarist while tending to pair him with Broadway people such as Dwight Taylor and Howard Lindsay.

Best of all, *Shall We Dance* was the first Astaire-Rogers teaming (the seventh of the nine RKOs; a reunion at MGM came much later) built around a truly Gershwinesque theme: pop vs. classical. "JAZZ–BALLET MERGE" is a headline the film shows us at one point, because Astaire plays the pseudo-Russian Petrov of the dance world and Rogers is a musical-comedy star. So it's a challenge film in the line of the Rodgers and Hart stage show of the year before, *On Your Toes*: sweet or hot, elite or popular, art or fun.

Some of the film's dance music suggests those symphonic jazz pieces mentioned above. The vocals, however, occupy a unique niche in Gershwin's output, as they are definitely popular yet highly innovative—not as grandly evolved as *Porgy and Bess* but more advanced than anything in George's Broadway musical comedies. Astaire sings his first number, "Slap That Bass," in an ocean liner's engine room with black workers on hand; the music naturally takes on jazz (and swing) inflections, with some of George's trickiest harmony. "Zoom, zoom," runs a little meme in the lyric—is that to represent the twang of a bass fiddle, the hum of the ship's engine, or the loony eructations of jive?

Just after that, "Walking the Dog," a non-vocal accompaniment to Astaire's courting of Rogers as they promenade the liner's deck with Fidoes, has the flavor of the British Billy Mayerl's sophisticated piano solos, comparable to Zez Confrey's yet more eloquent, even Lisztian. Marked Allegretto in $\frac{4}{4}$, "Walking the Dog" takes off on an amiably insolent vamp using footfalls made by one bass note answered by one chord, over and over, while the harmony moves from C^{maj7} to a^7 to d^7 to an astonishing $G^{\flat\frac{9}{7}}_{\natural\frac{7}{6}}$. When the melody arrives, it is one of those lazily busy figures with a lot of snazzy-flirty half-step *appoggiature*. If *Delicious'* "New York Rhapsody" was Gershwin the jazz symphonist, "Walking the Dog" is Gershwin the party pianist, so famous for taking over the keyboard at Manhattan's soirées that Cole Porter dropped a joke about it in the stage musical *Jubilee* (1935). An upcoming party will be so chic and special, "Gershwin's promised not to play."

In contrast to the harmony, the number's structure is a simple ABA; all interest lies in the way the tune never quite fits its bass line—a phrase in c minor will sit on that C^{maj7} chord, for instance, all but defying it—and in a devious use of dotted eighth notes and triplets. It's like a box made of curves. Oddly, the piece wasn't published at first, though there was a huge market for playful piano solos with thematic titles: the slithery march "Toy Town Topics," "Jumping Jack," "China Doll Parade," all in the style of "Kitten On the Keys" but really looking back to, most famously, "Jimbo's Lullaby" (for a baby elephant), "Golliwog's Cake-Walk," and the rest of Debussy's *Children's Corner* suite (1908). Decades after *Shall We Dance* released its song sheets, "Walking the Dog" finally came out in print, as "Promenade."

Returning now to *Shall We Dance*'s vocal spots, we find that Rogers' solo, "They All Laughed," leads to a dance duet promoting the "challenge" effect: he ballets, she taps, he ballets, and so on. But then he taps, too, and suddenly, but very naturally, they dance together, and she starts to melt. She had been cold to him, but there's no courtship like the dance of Fred Astaire. Katharine Hepburn's by now cliché remark that "He gives her class and she gives him sex" misses the point. His tails give her class. But his dancing gives her warmth. After he throws Rogers up onto a handy piano a few times, he joins her, and there the two of them sit, grinning at the way music has bonded them.

"Let's Call the Whole Thing Off" (the "you say *ee*ther and I say *ai*ther" song) isn't especially innovative, but "They Can't Take That Away From Me," Astaire's solo, is masterly in the way the melody smoothes its way over startling harmonic changes. This is Harms creativity at its height, as far from Tin Pan Alley as a composer can get while respecting the limits of pop. Yet George does it so suavely that a Hollywood producer, by nature wary of too much New York "cleverness," would be not dubious but entranced. Then, too, Astaire's way with a song is as artless as his dancing is elaborated. This is pop music experimenting while pretending it isn't.

Another Astaire solo, "(I've Got) Beginner's Luck," is even richer. It's a simple situation: Boy tells Girl he loves her. But the tone is jaunty and rest-less—so much so that (in the published key) a verse in D Major slithers into G Major for the chorus, and the latter's first note is an extremely un-likely F sharp. In a single measure, on a throwaway line ("Gosh, I'm lucky!"), George uses a different chord on each of the four syllables, and the secre-tary who notated the sheet had to move from "G$^+$" through "F$^{\#7}$" and "B^{6}mi.^{6}" to "Ami.^{6}"—simplifying at that, because three of those notations are harmonically incomplete.

It's as if *Shall We Dance*'s very premise had intoxicated George, the up-start elitist who wrote a piano concerto for jazz band in B Flat Major but billed it as a Rhapsody in Blue: free and jazzy, overthrowing the rule of fa-thers—in this case the WASP guardians of Euro-American culture—to write as well a black opera in blue, *Porgy and Bess. Shall We Dance* is what happens next: a movie musical unified by the union of pop and classical.

Yet the film doesn't take itself seriously, as when Astaire and Rogers arrange their union in New Jersey though the plot demands they separate:

ROGERS: What are grounds for divorce in this state?
COUNTY CLERK: Marriage.

Then the newlyweds take the boat back to town. As Astaire sings "They Can't Take That Away From Me" to a misty-eyed Rogers with the Manhattan skyline in the background and George's all-mixed-up notes tooting sadly in our ear, we realize how dependent the Hollywood musical is on New York in all its issue: its talent, its attitudes, its symbolism.

Though cordial with each other, neither Astaire nor Rogers enjoyed being typed as a team. The series gave them career insurance, but each longed for other things to do. Rogers wanted to act in serious stories and Astaire wanted new partners. So the next Astaire-Rogers film was made without Rogers—without a romantic dancing partner at all. And while Berman retained the Gershwins, he infused the movie with an entirely new cast of helpers. The chief comics were now George Burns and Gracie Allen, a far cry from Edward Everett Horton and Eric Blore, with their moues and hysteria. Horton and Blore inhabit the dressy world (albeit as master and servant types) while Burns and Allen are middle class and goofy in an entirely different way, as when secretary Gracie strolls late into Burns' office:

> BURNS: [You] should've been in two hours ago.
> GRACIE: Why? What happened?

or when Burns threatens to get another stenographer:

> GRACIE: Another stenographer? Do you think there's work enough for the two of us?

This is *A Damsel in Distress* (1937), set in the P. G. Wodehouse world of the English country manor with the Sleeping Beauty heroine and the lord (Montagu Love) who potters about in his beloved garden dressed like a ragman. And of course the heroine's micro-managing dragon-lady aunt (Constance Collier), a Wodehouse fixture in countless novels. Add in a weaselly butler (Reginald Gardiner), the dauntless little footman (Harry Watson) who aids Astaire's courtship of the heroine, and the dragon lady's son (bandleader Ray Noble), who, to her outrage, wants to play swing, not Chopin. Finally, there is Leonard's Leap, a balcony high up in the manor house, from which a young swain once jumped "to avoid compromising the beautiful Countess of Marshmoreton"—an act Astaire is faced with having to replicate when he, too, nearly compromises the Sleeping Beauty.

The movie's nominal source, Wodehouse's eponymous novel of 1919, contains very little of this, though it does include the all-important "meet cute" scene in which Boy Meets Girl in a snafu in a taxicab. In fact, the screenplay, credited to Wodehouse, Ernest Pagano, and S. K. Lauren, has the Wodehouse flavor but not his wording. And, lo, we learn that Pandro Berman's recurring Astaire-Rogers scenarist, Allan Scott, was brought in, unbilled, to revise the script, and Scott found Wodehouse doing virtually nothing as a collaborator beyond picking up his weekly check. In a talk with Pat McGilligan in *Backstory: Interviews With Screenwriters of Hollywood's Golden Age*, Scott said, Wodehouse "used to drive Berman crazy. . . . When I had finished the script, [Wodehouse] said . . . 'Amazing, old boy, simply amazing—what you did to my little story!'" Then, presumably to justify his $60,000 salary, Wodehouse asked to edit the script and changed, Scott recalled, a single line. Very slightly.

Even so, it's a fine script, and working for Pan Berman once again inspired the Gershwins. The RKOs are about music—its joy, its healing power, its wonder, its enlightenment. We don't want to get too grandiose, but there's Shakespeare, there's Goethe, and there's the RKO dance musical of the 1930s, and George and Ira responded to the opportunity even though the film's heroine was not stimulatingly lyrical. Not only couldn't she sing or dance but, at this early stage in her career, she couldn't act. Worse, "The poor girl couldn't even walk" (or so said the film's co-choreographer, Hermes Pan, to John Kobal in *People Will Talk*).

But she was Joan Fontaine, so at least she looks terrific. And it could be argued that, in a film loaded with Wodehousian eccentrics, someone has to be normal—and not Astaire normal. *Normal* normal. Still, if Astaire and Rogers were a happy collision of dancer and movie star, Astaire and Fontaine don't collide at all. They have a sort of dance duet after he sings "Things Are Looking Up," but in trying to hide her lack of musical-comedy sympatico the scene exposes it. Burns and Allen weren't known for their dancing, yet they can keep up with Astaire in a little number with whisk brooms (which, at one point, each flips into the air and neatly catches) and a dance adventure in a funhouse. This only makes poor Joan Fontaine look all the more incorrect. Again, it's fine for Randolph Scott not to connect with the score in *Follow the Fleet*; his character is unsingably stolid. But the vis-à-vis in an Astaire musical must meet him on his level, and his romance isn't dialogue. It's music.

Clearly, the Gershwins had to work around Fontaine: virtually the entire *Damsel in Distress* score is thrown to Astaire. His establishing number, "I Can't Be Bothered Now," could serve this performer in any part, any film, as the devil-may-care lyrics, tossed off in staccato, two-syllable segments (e.g., "Bad news . . . Go 'way!"), leads Astaire to go into his dance in the middle of a London street, then to leap onto one of those red double-decker buses for his exit. On the other hand, "The Jolly Tar and the Milkmaid," a lively glee for madrigal singers at the Wodehousian manor, finds Astaire forced to join them, in a genre of song utterly foreign to him. Of course, the fun lies in how eagerly he takes part once it gets going; to the Astaire figure, all good music is equal. "Nice Work If You Can Get It" is another set piece, this time with a girls' trio, but the film's hit, "A Foggy Day," is a situation number. Here, again, George experiments, not only harmonically but structurally, in an ABAB¹C layout. Interestingly, the piece's very wide vocal range gives Astaire no trouble; he was a much better vocalist than generally thought, not just personable but resourceful. And Ira gets off one of his most endearingly quixotic lines, in "The British Museum had lost its charm."

Gershwin produced one last score before his death, in 1937, but *The Goldwyn Follies* (1938) gave him an invalid farewell to art, for this leaden gumdrop of a movie fails to revel in music the way Pandro Berman's RKOs do. Producer Samuel Goldwyn's plan was to combine ballet and opera with low comedy in a tale of an "ordinary" girl (Andrea Leeds) advising a mogul (Adolphe Menjou) on how to give his next movie "ordinary" appeal, though the film's star (Vera Zorina) is a Russian prima donna, anything but ordinary. *The Goldwyn Folly* might be a better title for this mishmash, for besides the fastidiously designed Technicolor, everything is wrong. Andrea Leeds has the charisma of a half-eaten petit four, and the Ritz Brothers, whose comedy consists of running around and screaming, make El Brendel's Fox talkies seem like Restoration comedies. Radio ventriloquist Edgar Bergen (father of Candice) and his dummy Charlie McCarthy had an act-within-an-act, as on the air, unseen, there was no reason for Bergen to animate the manikin. It was as if Laurence Olivier and Sybil Thorndike had joined a mime troupe. Bergen and McCarthy had made appearances in shorts, but *The Goldwyn Follies*, their first feature, reveals how feeble their routines were, as when Zorina says, "Be seeing you" in Russian:

ZORINA: Do svidanya.
CHARLIE: Cucaracha.

The music comes off only a bit better. It's gratifying to hear from Vernon Duke, an all but luckless (though wonderful) Broadway composer, here to write two ballets. Gershwin came from pop to classical, Duke from classical to pop; it's arresting to see the era's two outstanding crossover artists on the same bill. But Helen Jepson, of the Metropolitan, is one of the duller sopranos to reach Hollywood. Goldwyn's obsession was prestige: why didn't he hire one of the Met's *big* stars not already going Hollywood—Marjorie Lawrence, Bidù Sayão, or even the just-retired (and still formidable) Rosa Ponselle?

Moving over to pop, Goldwyn gave George's last great ballads, "Love Walked In" and "[Our] Love Is Here To Stay," to Kenny Baker, pleasantly empty after what Fred Astaire can do with Gershwin. Most irritating is the use of "I Was Doing All Right." For this number, and to play Leeds' sidekick, Goldwyn hired jazz vocalist Ella Logan, later the very memorable heroine of *Finian's Rainbow* on Broadway, back phrasing and "song styling" in defiance of the unwritten law that, when appearing in musical comedy, even a jazz vocalist has to sing the music straight. Logan's Goldwyn solo is cut down to its last measures, at that drowned out by tedious dialogue between Menjou and Leeds. These two also manage to talk through Baker's "Love Is Here To Stay," though he does put over the verse without interference.

In short, *The Goldwyn Follies* did not make good use of the Gershwins, whereas *Shall We Dance* is unthinkable without them. Nor is there anything happy about the inevitable George bio, Warner Bros.' *Rhapsody in Blue* (1945). Pitched halfway between the humble retelling and the all-star fiesta, this one sabotages the record with silly fictions, but then even reasonably authentic bios finesse the tricky parts, as when the George M. Cohan story, *Yankee Doodle Dandy*, leaves out Cohan's first marriage and his difficult personality. *Rhapsody in Blue* gives Gershwin two fantasy girl friends—he had them, truly, but none like these—in Alexis Smith (for glamor) and Joan Leslie (for something from the neighborhood). Ira hardly turns up at all, though we do get a lot of that professional éminence grise Max Dreyfus, the chieftain of the Harms group himself; Charles Coburn gives him an avuncular feeling too soft for this Napoléon of the music industry. Still, with so many bios navigating from song to song, this one, at least, thinks it's recounting a tale. And it does present the real Al Jolson, in "Swanee," which he introduced, and Anne Brown, the original Bess, on stage in a reasonable likeness of the Catfish Row set, for "Summertime."

Brown appears also in the film's *bombe surprise*, a reenactment of a section of *Blue Monday Blues*, the short "Negro" opera, to a libretto by B. G. De Sylva, that played on the opening night of the 1922 edition of *George White's Scandals* and immediately disappeared after a chorus of scorn from the critics. The piece shows George's early affinity for not only "black" music but Gershwin music as sung by black performers. As a rehearsal for *Porgy and Bess*, it's an interesting bit of history, yet it was so forgotten by 1945 that Warner Bros.' resuscitation gives *Rhapsody in Blue* a novel authority. And topping that is the casting of Robert Alda (father of Alan) as George: for once in a bio, the star actually looks like the subject.

A tragic early death and a valedictory bio might have been the all of George Gershwin on screen. Yet there was a fresh Gershwin score yet to come, as Ira, working with composer and George intimate Kay Swift from odds and ends that George left behind, was able to give Twentieth Century-

Fox *The Shocking Miss Pilgrim* (1947). The adventures of a "typewriter" (meaning, in olden days, the operator of the new typing machines), the story was the brainchild of Frederica Sagor Maas and her husband, Ernest. This particular typewriter was a woman working in an all-male enclave—and thereby hangs a tale.

The Maases' story, "Miss Pilgrim's Progress," dates back to 1941. In the authors' view, a woman entering the business world of men in the late nineteenth century encountered not only genderist prejudice but sexual harassment, and, when Miss Pilgrim fights off the office masher, he loses his footing, falls downstairs, and dies. Miss Pilgrim is arrested for murder, and, says Frederica Maas, "Womanhood is on trial in the courtroom." Though acquitted, the heroine nevertheless has revealed a corruption in society, and the name of the corruption is Man.

In Frederica's bitter but spicy memoirs, *The Shocking Miss Pilgrim: A Writer in Early Hollywood*, she tells of a flurry of interest in filming the tale. MGM wanted it for Norma Shearer and RKO for Ginger Rogers, but Fox bought it and nothing happened for six years. Then Darryl Zanuck thought it would give Betty Grable something interesting to play after her passel of backstagers and travelogues in exotic climes. Frederica can't have been happy to learn that her feminist argument was to be musicalized, and, in the end, she doubted there was any Gershwin in the film at all, the music "obviously written by studio hacks" and the lyrics a ghost job.

That much is nonsense. The three ballads, "Changing My Tune," "For You, For Me, For Evermore," and "Aren't You Kind of Glad We Did?," bear the Gershwin autograph in both words and music (though Kay Swift, an inspired composer herself, was so conversant with George's sound that she might well have expanded mere sketches into full-out numbers). "Aren't You" uses the same slithery middle-voice harmony that keeps shifting chromatically within the set chording that we hear throughout *Shall We Dance*; and a line like "Wanted a permit to make me a hermit" (in "Changing My Tune") "to grumble and glare at the moon" is pure Ira whimsy.

In fact, besides shifting the setting from New York to Boston and dropping the violence, Fox respected the Maases' spirit. At that, Boston's stuffy and intolerant atmosphere (as popularly perceived) makes an effective background for the judgmental resistance Grable is up against. Even her love interest, boss Dick Haymes, refuses to hire her at first because... well, you know. Women do upset the established structures so.

The entire film pursues this notion that innovation—really, nonconformism—is good for everyone. Even Grable's boardinghouse is a nest of rebellion. "This is Miss Simmons," says Grable's landlady, showing Grable around. "She's rewriting the dictionary." And when Grable displays some anti-Boston cheek on meeting Haymes' mother, that lady is so for-giving that Grable weeps. "You expected to find a witch-burner," says this woman of the avant-garde, who agrees with those rude comments about Boston—she's going to use them "at the next D.A.R. meeting."

Unfortunately, the film feels a bit underpowered in every way. It is in Technicolor, at least, as most Fox musicals were in the 1940s, and Grable's giving personality goes nicely with just about anyone. Still, beyond the three ballads, the score lacks distinction. "The Back Bay Polka," a gavotte for the boardinghouse tenants, is awfully dainty; had George been alive, the music would have had more bite.

On the other hand, we notice a forties trend in a certain Broadwayization of the way the songs suit the continuity. This musical isn't just integrated: dialogue and music interact naturalistically. "Aren't You Kind of Glad We Did?" starts before we knew there was a song coming on, as Grable and Haymes, in a cab after dinner, consider the propriety of a young woman staying out late. And with her employer! "What will people say?" Grable worries. "We shouldn't have done it." Haymes replies, "Oh, it really wasn't my intention to disregard convention"—and of course he's singing, because the song's verse is simply more conversation.

These were the last new Gershwin songs (except for "Ask Me Again," reclaimed, from the sound of it, from the 1920s and slipped into the black-cast 1990 *Oh, Kay!* revival). However, as with the Irving Berlin catalogue, Hollywood wasn't done singing George while so many standards, semi-standards, and novelties could provision the jukebox format in concocted stories for brand-new movies, one about Gene Kelly in Paris and the other about Fred Astaire...in Paris. Kelly's would be the Paris of the great paint-ers and Astaire's the fashion-capital Paris, with some beatniks thrown in. Kelly's film, *An American in Paris* (1951), was pure Gershwin; Astaire's, *Funny Face* (1957), included new numbers by others. And both were Freed Unit projects, though MGM made only the former. Paramount, using Freed's staff, made the latter.

It is an article of faith among critics and buffs alike that *An American in Paris* is an official masterpiece. Yet a few writers have resisted its charms, feeling its story is humdrum, its "staircase of living women" for "I'll Build a Stairway To Paradise" Ziegfelds its beauties in quite the wrong way, and its huge ballet using Gershwin's eponymous tone poem is on the precious side. Its animations of art by Raoul Dufy, Toulouse-Lautrec, and others of the *belle époque* seem just too artful, even creepy—and the music is fiddled with. Some of it isn't even Gershwin proper, as it toys with his tunes.

The movie did at least revive a long-lost Gershwin number (to Ira's lyrics, first presented pseudonymously as by "Arthur Francis"), "Tra-La-La," from

For Goodness Sake (1922). Still, the singing in general lacks body—and *Funny Face* is worse. Yes, Kay Thompson draws on a sort of nightclub energy in her spots (mostly by Roger Edens and the film's scenarist, Leonard Gershe). But Audrey Hepburn unfortunately does her own singing and Fred Astaire sounds tired.

Then there's the *Porgy and Bess* (1959) problem. Samuel Goldwyn, the longtime independent mogul with a now-and-again interest in socially important (and, especially, Broadway-important) projects, decided to cap his output with this monumental work, so intrinsic to the Great American Conversation between classical and pop. The *Porgy* legend tells us that it failed on its 1935 premiere and was then heard only in desecrated editions till the Houston Grand Opera revival of 1976, but in fact that original production lasted 124 performances, an excellent run for an opera in 1935, the worst Depression year on Broadway. Every time the work came back, in whatever form, it generated excitement, so Goldwyn was less reclaiming a neglected work than celebrating a famous one.

However, the producer quarreled with his director, Rouben Mamoulian (who had staged the original play *Porgy* as well as Gershwin's opera), and, after likely replacements said no, Goldwyn ended up with Otto Preminger, a choice that can only be called erroneous, even if he did direct the *Carmen Jones* movie.

Actually, there was disaster all over the place. The sets and costumes burned to the ground, and, worse, the most appropriate performers were reluctant to take on a work they deemed race-problematic. In the end, neither Sidney Poitier nor Dorothy Dandridge, in the title roles, could handle the vocals, necessitating the dubbing that never looks right in opera. Trained singers don't make music the way Bing Crosby or Ann Miller do: they *produce* the voice, and you can see them producing it. Without that visual, it isn't opera.

As for the score, the film spoke the recitatives as plain dialogue, and the scoring was only partly faithful to what Gershwin had written. However, a surprising amount of the outright musical numbers turned up, even "Good Mornin', Sistuh!" and "I Hates Yo' Struttin' Style," almost invariably omitted on stage at the time. Alas, after the roadshow engagements, the print was cut for general release, losing much music, and it is this crippled version that circulates today (on bootleg DVDs from Europe, at that). This gives the impression that Goldwyn cut half the score, even "My Man's Gone Now," one of the opera's greatest scenes, present for the roadshows but missing from the DVDs.

Worst of all, the very use of music as dramatic continuity—the "is" of opera—befuddled Preminger. His camera often sits immobile for long periods of singing as if on auto-pilot, and the ecstatic finale, "I'm On My Way," goes for nothing as Poitier rides his goat-cart into the distance, an ever diminishing figure. On the contrary, this is the climax of his growth from a spectator of life to an adventurer in it. Preminger robs the character of the stature Gershwin gave him: this final minute of the score tells us that Porgy is heroic, extraordinary, but Preminger doesn't show us that.

The movie lost a ton of money, and the Gershwin family moved against it, which is why it has so seldom been shown. Yet as George Gershwin's magnum opus in a workspan cut short at eighteen years, the movie should have been a landmark, something to cherish and an immortalization. Instead, it ended as little more than a footnote in the saga of Catfish Row.

Thus we must say that, so far, none of our Broadway songwriters has been able to adopt Hollywood as a platform comparable to the support he enjoyed on Broadway. De Sylva, Brown, and Henderson simply broke up their act. Irving Berlin was seldom able to persuade Hollywood's commanders to let him in on planning or executing a project. "Shut up and write your ditties" sums up their attitude. And Gershwin got only *Shall We Dance* as a model of how songs perfect narration.

Our next writers, however, got the chance to experiment in the movies, even surpassing what they were doing on Broadway at the time. And one of their films stands on the short list of Hollywood's greatest musicals—even, perhaps, the greatest of all.

CHAPTER 5

⚙

Rodgers and Hart

"Studio moguls," Rodgers wrote in his autobiography, "always seemed to have a certain antipathy toward people from the Broadway theatre. They used us when they had to, but they were never really happy about our being there."

Even so, Rodgers nourished "a feeling of gratitude" that his and his partner's Hollywood experience was so disappointing—because if the pair had been appreciated they might have become Hollywood regulars, "and that would have been the end of Larry Hart and Dick Rodgers. I'm sure I would have ended up as a neurotic, a drunkard . . . or both."

Actually, a neurotic and drunkard is exactly how Rodgers ended up, by all accounts. But Hollywood had nothing to do with it. He and Hart arrived, as I've said, in 1930, and—with intervals to do shows in New York and London—worked for a number of studios into 1934. Thereafter, Rodgers and Hart repatriated themselves as New Yorkers, thus dividing their stage output into two halves, before the Hollywood stay and after the Hollywood stay. The first half, almost entirely in the 1920s, is less well known than the second, which stretches from 1935 to 1943 and contains most of their classic titles: *Jumbo*, *On Your Toes*, and *Babes in Arms* to *Pal Joey*, *By Jupiter*, and the revised new production of *A Connecticut Yankee* and Hart's death.

A bit of movie work is scattered throughout the second half, but in truth most of their films are all but unknown. *The Hot Heiress* (1930), *Fools For Scandal* (1938), and *They Met in Argentina* (1941) are the sort of fare Turner Classic Movies runs once a century at four o'clock in the morning. Then, too, films of their stage shows scant the scores. *Spring Is Here* (1930) retained three of the numbers, *Heads Up!* (1930) only two—and the movie of *Present Arms* lost its title, appearing as *Leathernecking* (1930).

Nor could Rodgers and Hart have been happy with the assignment of writing new songs for the movie versions of other men's shows. Producers "had the sneaky habit of comparison shopping," to quote more of Rodgers' memoirs. "They'd ask three or four [writing teams] for a song or two and then would choose the one they liked best." Rodgers said he was not aware of being used this way himself, but in fact on De Sylva, Brown, and Henderson's aforementioned *Follow Thru*, Paramount seems to have lined up contributions for an interpolation contest, and Rodgers and Hart's four numbers weren't used.

But then, Rodgers' imaginative compositional autograph and Hart's worldly teaching moments stood far from Hollywood's Tin Pan Alley ideal of pop music that was literally popular: available to even the dullest ears. Of those *Follow Thru* numbers, "Softer Than a Kitten" is a merely acceptable love song, with unengaged lyrics that suggest Hart was deliberately writing down. But "I'm Hard To Please," a jaunty quarrel duet (a favorite genre in the stage musical from the 1920s into the 1950s), strikes some nifty poses, and two ballads, "Because We're Young" and "It Never Happened Before," are vintage Rodgers and Hart, serene fox trots looking into the intensity of romance. The latter number even refers to golf, to suit *Follow Thru*'s country-club setting, and Hart, so often sorrowful, waxes positively radiant. "What makes it worth," he asks, "sun and moon and earth?"

However it happened, the team was set free to write as they pleased on Paramount's *Love Me Tonight*—even in 1932, at the height of the ban on musicals. True, Paramount had been grossing impressively on Ernst Lubitsch's musicals since 1929, ban or no ban, and *Love Me Tonight*, directed by Rouben Mamoulian, was very much in the Lubitsch style, with a fey storyline in a continental setting and starring Lubitsch stalwarts Maurice Chevalier and Jeanette MacDonald.

Nevertheless, it is astonishing to find a movie so filled with plot and character numbers. Further, where the Hollywood musical depended mainly on dialogue with music only as decoration, *Love Me Tonight* is suffused with music, to the point that, at times, the score is doing the narrating and the dialogue, in a supplementary status, is filling in a few details along the way. Some may be reminded of early continental talkies such as *Der Kongress Tanzt* and the comedies of René Clair, which are indeed musically organized. But they have very few actual vocal spots for their characters, while *Love Me Tonight* programs eight songs, including a few that seem to have seized control of dialogue scenes.

This is particularly evident when a doctor examines MacDonald. Both of them communicate in lyrics, with scan and rhyme—but they're talking, not singing, in what Rodgers in his memoirs specifically terms "rhythmic dialogue." True, the orchestra accompanies them, and in some of these rhythmic dialogues one discerns a melody. But it's always in the background. The "singers" themselves are talking.

Rodgers and Hart may have devised this procedure to seem like a musical number by other means, something otherworldly and piquant, because *Love Me Tonight* is a fairy tale. It's another *Sleeping Beauty,* in which Prince Charming is "a common tailor": Chevalier makes his way to the sleeping (i.e., romance-starved) princess in her château and temporarily disenchants all within (of their snobbish, fuddy-duddy noblesse) by sheer charisma, though his errand was actually to get payment for bills owed by Charlie Ruggles, another of the aristos in the enchanted castle.

Historians always make a port of call out of *Love Me Tonight's* exhibition number, one of the most ambitious ever filmed, as it anticipates Chevalier's visit to the castle by traveling there itself: a song that becomes almost a character in the movie. This is "Isn't It Romantic?" It starts in Chevalier's tailor shop in Paris, where, after some rhythmic dialogue (this time without orchestral accompaniment) with a customer, Chevalier breaks into the song's verse, which is replete with references to tailoring. Mamoulian catches him pane by pane in a suite of mirrors, a stunt right out of the Lubitsch handbook. And when Chevalier speaks of marriage and procreation—"It's a duty that we owe to France!"—the trumpets burst forth in praise of la gloire.

It's a flavorsome touch, but we're just getting started. The customer leaves the shop to lyrics calibrated to the action—retrieving his cane and fixing his tie—and now the song itself takes the lead, jumping to a passerby who hails a taxi, and we note that as the melody moves from place to place it changes character as well. It's as if "Isn't It Romantic?," like J. R. R. Tolkien's Ring of Power, needs to move from owner to owner, seeking the one who will use it most effectively—the cab passenger; soldiers who serenade him on a troop train and then take it up as a marching song on a country road; a gypsy violinist who hears them and transforms the theme once more on his fiddle, *rubato, vibrato, appassionato*; and last to the château, where, alone on her balcony, MacDonald adopts it, so longingly that, in a way, Boy has Met Girl.

Here is this book's first instance of Broadway songwriters "discovering" their own art through cinema's ability to mash time and space together. Mamoulian gets into the act, too, setting the title song into a split-screen of Chevalier and MacDonald in their separate sleeping quarters and letting them sing in voiceover. Further, Mamoulian filmed Chevalier's party piece at the château, "The Poor Apache," before a looming shadow on the wall, as if haunted by his evil twin. It's *Love Me Tonight's* only performance number, an arresting one, structurally anticipating a form Rodgers would develop with his later partner, Oscar Hammerstein: the soliloquy made of distinct musical periods instead of in AABA song form, as in *The King and I*'s "A Puzzlement" and "Shall I Tell You What I Think Of You?," and, of course, Billy's great solo in *Carousel*.

However, the lyrics of "The Poor Apache" don't really suit Chevalier. He has to that point been sunny and unselfish; suddenly he's dangerous. His sweetheart, he says, is "a treasure," making him "a gentleman of leisure," which presents him as, at worst, a pimp and, at best, an exploiter. Robert Kimball's edition of Lorenz Hart's lyrics unearthed an earlier version of the number, "Cleaning Up the Floor With Lulu," a goof on the "apache dance" in which the male brutally throws his partner around. Even as raillery, it strikes a wrong note for Maurice the tailor. True, this is a character song for an imaginary character, not the one Chevalier is portraying. Still, it seems off in some odd way, as if the authors hadn't settled on just who their hero is.

MacDonald, however, was a cinch: romantic, wistful, easily flustered, quick to quarrel, forever perplexed by the deviousness of men. In thirties operetta—of which MacDonald was shortly to become the designated queen—she offered a rich mix, especially compared with her successor at MGM, Kathryn Grayson, so cool she might have just exited an igloo. MacDonald is not only warm but pre-Code hot, notorious for her scenes in lingerie. Yet she is an outdoors type as well; Rodgers says she was an expert horsewoman. Just before she meets Chevalier, she is seen driving a one-horse carriage and singing one of the great Rodgers waltzes, a genre of its own because he of all the Harms group made three-quarter time sound American modern, not leftover Viennese.

"Lover" is the song's title, but it's zesty rather than sweet, constantly interrupted by MacDonald's instructions to her horse, from "Whoa!" to "Not too fast!" Amusingly, these exclamations cut into the sentimentality we expect from a waltz called "Lover"—so, for publication, Hart had to create a non-contextual version complete with a verse (the movie has none) and horseless lyrics.

But now for some adventure: startled by Chevalier's stalled auto on the road, the horse goes astray and MacDonald takes a tumble. Helping her to her feet, Chevalier tells her to hold onto him:

MACDONALD: (mildly outraged) Do you think I put my arms around people I don't know?
CHEVALIER: My name is Maurice.

Good, that's settled. Actually, she more or less stumbles into his arms, and they end up sitting on his running board, where this marvelous script gently reminds us that she is, after all, the sleeping princess:

CHEVALIER: Do you live down here?
MACDONALD: (sadly, resigned) I often wonder.

And now it's his turn to get a "lover" number. "Let me sing for you," he says, presently breaking into "Mimi," his nickname for her, plucked out of the air. The music is lively, not romantic, and the lyrics are daffy, because it is the special quality of these early Paramount musicals in the Lubitsch manner to blend the nutty with the amorous. Not alternate them: mix them up. So Mamoulian, and Rodgers and Hart, establish the bond of "Maurice" and "Jeanette" (for the characters bear the actors' names) by pairing the wistful "Lover" and the scatterbrained "Mimi." On Broadway, the typical romance would start with, say, the so very tender "The Best Things in Life Are Free" or "Make Believe [I love you]." But *Love Me Tonight* textures its tale. Nothing is what it seems: everything is something else.

Mamoulian's use of the Lubitschian atmosphere is so palpable that it's surprising to find neither Ernest Vajda nor Samson Raphaelson on hand, as they regularly wrote the Lubitsch musical screenplays. We remember Raphaelson from the play *The Jazz Singer*, a work that does not remotely anticipate Lubitsch's playful eros, but Raphaelson turned out to be a versatile talent—and an influential one, for *Love Me Tonight*'s authors, Samuel Hoffenstein, Waldemar Young, and George Marion Jr., have the Lubitsch tone well in hand. Movie buffs love to quote this exchange, when MacDonald faints and Ruggles seeks help from Myrna Loy:

RUGGLES: Could you go for a doctor?
LOY: Certainly, send him right in.

So the history was made—but the next Rodgers and Hart score, for *The Phantom President* (1932), is humdrum. It was an election year, and, in the spirit of the Gershwins' recent Broadway hit *Of Thee I Sing*, *The Phantom President* treated the use of show-biz tactics in a presidential election. This was a historical event, too, for, as the very first title card phrases it, "Paramount presents the first appearance on the talking screen of that eminent stage star, playwright *and* composer Mr. George M. Cohan." This was indeed Cohan's one chance to preserve his song-and-dance style (his only other talkie was non-musical), and it's fascinating, in a number called

"Maybe Someone Ought To Wave the Flag," to watch him perform the precise steps we see James Cagney go through in *Yankee Doodle Dandy*, with the patented Cohan "kangaroo" strut and his "jumping off the stage-right proscenium" turnabout.

The plot finds a dull and unscrupulous banker (Cohan) running for the highest office using as his double a charismatic medicine-show shill (Cohan). That's right: it's a dual role, good Cohan and bad Cohan (who tries to shanghai his double to the Arctic and ends up there himself). With Jimmy Durante as good Cohan's partner, enjoying his cries of injured innocence ("The ingratitude of it all! I'm aghast!"), and Claudette Colbert as the girl friend who switches sides from bad to good, the cast was fine. And Rodgers and Hart did come up with one snazzy number, "Give Her a Kiss," sung to good Cohan and Colbert, car-parking in the woods, by two birds (a boy and girl in voiceover) and a bullfrog (a bass, naturally). Clearly, the two humans should do some sparking, but nothing happens, and the number fizzles out. Like the movie generally, it's a cute idea that doesn't work.

Rodgers and Hart's follow-up, for United Artists, brought them back to their experimental mode, as much of *Hallelujah, I'm a Bum* (1933) unfolds in rhythmic dialogue or arioso conversations. This frees most of the cast from having to sing at all, allowing for odd portrayals, such as that of silent comic Harry Langdon as Egghead, a Communist sanitation worker who looks mild but is scathing in denunciation.

The star, at least, is a singer, our old friend Al Jolson as the chief of Central Park's hobo community. Yet this strange and fascinating score holds back even the ebullient Jolson. He does get a first-rate ballad, "You Are Too Beautiful." But there is no Jolson Number per se—like *The Jazz Singer*'s "Blue Skies"—and he's so busy working his way characterologically through this virtual "opera in dialogue" that he never cuts loose. After the verse of the rousing "I've Got To Get Back To New York," Jolson starts the refrain only to have the scene fade out on him after the first A strain.

Closing out their Hollywood period at MGM, Rodgers and Hart worked on *I Married an Angel*, a Lubitschian fantasy that ended up on Broadway first (four years later, in 1938).[1] The team also contributed three numbers to *Dancing Lady* (1933), MGM's answer to Warner's *42nd Street*, when musicals were making their comeback. Only one of the three was used, reminding us of the wasteful Hollywood system of trick-or-treating its scores, filling a bag with songs to sort through them and select the tastiest.

---

1. Because the *Angel* score was begun while the authors were under contract to MGM, the studio retained publishing rights, and the Broadway sheets appeared under the imprint of MGM's outfit, Robbins Music, rather than Harms.

Further, Hart ran up a new set of lyrics for the Chevalier-MacDonald *Merry Widow* (1934); both men were credited, because by contract their billing could not be broken up. A Hart operetta sounds enticing, especially as Lubitsch was directing. (On Broadway, Rodgers and Hart touched on the "uniforms, marches, and waltzes" format but once, in *Dearest Enemy* [1925]). In fact, though the movie itself is scintillating, Hart's words were no more than serviceable.

It really does seem as if Rodgers and Hart had got all they could out of Hollywood by then. True, Hart loved the night life, and its shady gay component must have tickled him. New York was bound up in subterfuges; in Los Angeles, gay life hid in plain sight. But the aforementioned "I've Got To Get Back To New York" could have been Rodgers' motto at this point. And then MGM offered the team a big project, almost an irresistible one: *The Hollywood Revue of 1933*.

This was to be a star-filled "revue with a storyline," and the studio planned to get a coalition of the willing among virtually every major MGM star (except for that professional stay-at-home Greta Garbo), even if some would take part in a mere walk-on basis. In the plot, Jimmy Durante will host, Charles Butterworth and Polly Moran will play an oil king and his socially ambitious wife, George Givot will add the plot-enhancer of a fake Greek duke coming on to Moran, Jack Pearl (then at the height of popularity as radio's Baron Munchausen) will be a guest of honor, Eddie Quillan will court June Clyde (as Moran's niece), and Lupe Velez will be tempestuous. Best of all, Rodgers and Hart will create a sizable score, as revues had a very greed for songs. This could be their *Pictures at an Exhibition*: stand-alone pieces set out on display.

But something went wrong, and the finished film, retitled *Hollywood Party* (1934) doesn't work. Most of the star drop-ins were otherwise engaged, a little Jack Pearl is too much Jack Pearl, and the narrative drive-line—about a rivalry between supposed jungle star Durante and Givot[2]—is endless and stupid. There are a few advantages. The ensemble numbers are very elaborate, using split-screens and wild camera angles. And Velez plays a very amusing game of "hits" with Stan Laurel and Oliver Hardy, who more or less invented the sport: you attack your opponent physically (in this case with raw eggs) while he just stands there, then he responds while *you* just stand there, and so on. Charles Butterworth is always fun in his

2. Have any aficionados noticed a coincidence in the casting? Two of the leads were also in a late Gershwin musical comedy (that is, before *Porgy and Bess*) on Broadway, *Pardon My English*—Pearl and Givot, who replaced Jack Buchanan during the show's sinking-ship tryout.

patented dry tenorino line readings, as when his wife thinks the fake duke is supposed to be called "[His] grace":

BUTTERWORTH: Grace? A big, strapping fellow like that?

But there's a major disadvantage, because almost everything by Rodgers and Hart was dropped. They wrote some twenty-one numbers, which have survived in some form or other (many in bootlegs of MGM music-department piano-and-vocal sheets), and one sees, once again, the sheer waste of talent. Back on Broadway, you wrote numbers for producers who wanted the numbers you and your partner would write. When Vinton Freedley and Alex Aarons commissioned a score, it was because they appreciated your ingenuity. There was no hurdle to be overcome in appeasing the narrow taste of that third audience in the small towns.

MGM did use *Hollywood Party*'s title song, solid Rodgers and Hart, with Rodgers' restlessly syncopated melody and Hart urging all in town to share the excitement—"Get up, get out, get in it!" But every other title I'm going to cite was cut, though in "You've Got That" Hart troubled to quote two numbers from MGM's flagship musical *The Broadway Melody*, and "Fly Away To Ioway" spoofs "Shuffle Off To Buffalo," from Warner's *42nd Street*.

Perhaps they seemed too "inside." And MGM must have got very nervous when the team auditioned "Black Diamond," as it's openly racial in style: ahead of its time, at least on the Coast. And what would the studio have thought of a number twitting Marlene Dietrich's fondness for men's clothes, "I'm One of the Boys"? Hart may have been larking over Dietrich's rumored bisexuality, more inside fun, at that in forbidden territory. "People ask me, 'Dearie,'" the woman sings, "'ain't you Wallace Beery?'"

Oddly, one of the unused *Hollywood Party* numbers became Rodgers and Hart's biggest hit ever. This was to be Jean Harlow's solo, "Prayer," a nobody's wish to become a Hollywood notable. Re-lyricked twice and actually used once (as "The Bad in Every Man" in *Manhattan Melodrama*, also in 1934), it still went nowhere. However, Jack Robbins, head of MGM's aforementioned music house, thought the tune had promise. It just needed third-audience appeal. One imagines him telling the boys to drop all the fancy images and Alley the number down to . . . well, how about one of those "moon" songs? Girl and Boy in the starlight of love? So Hart wrote a fourth lyric, the one that lasted: "Blue Moon."

After returning to New York, Rodgers and Hart continued to write for Hollywood, but the experimentation and madcap lyrics were over. *Mississippi* (1935) brought them into a series format, that of Bing Crosby's Paramounts, a set unlike any other in that its only fixed element was his very free, semi-jazz singing style in ballads, with a liberal use of the upper mordent and second-chorus alternate notes.

Otherwise, each Crosby was an adventure in format. *College Humor* (1933) is a fraternity-football saga in which undergraduates are played by actors apparently eligible for social security (though the program was created two years later). *We're Not Dressing* (1934) is *The Admirable Crichton*, Crosby shipwrecked with haughty lady Carole Lombard and Broadway's Ethel Merman and Leon Errol, with added hijinks from island residents Burns and Allen. *Here Is My Heart* (1934) is a crazy Society comedy with Kitty Carlisle as another haughty lady, this time a glum one. And so on—one unique piece after another, held together by the Crosby vocal brand.

So what is *Mississippi*? This one finds Bing in the Old South, where W. C. Fields runs a show boat and Joan Bennett loves Bing. But the dueling code menaces everyone, for Crosby—from Philadelphia, with a Quaker uncle—is a pacifist. Well, that doesn't work with bad guys, and Crosby, triumphant on the field of honor, becomes known as "the singing killer." As he explains it, "There's some things a man *has* to fight for!"

Nevertheless, Fields steals the film, not least with a running gag in which, every time he appears, a black servant instantly materializes with a mint julep. At one point, when the Singing Killer is about to perform, Fields tells his party, "C'mon over to the bar. We can hear better from there."

Where do Rodgers and Hart fit into this? Mainly in three of those patented Crosby ballads, a genre in themselves: "Soon," "Down By the River," and "It's Easy To Remember." Paramount plugged the melodies in the soundtrack very creatively, so that, for example, "It's Easy To Remember," a slow fox trot, turns into a gala waltz at a soirée. Still, it's Crosby's vocals that define the music, and even Hart is writing smooth, with a touch of the Alley, when "It's Easy To Remember" works its way to the line "But so hard to forget."

Came then one of the oddest jobs ever offered to Harms writers: the first musical completely in three-strip Technicolor, *Dancing Pirate* (1936). The new process, offering a fuller palette than previously, had been introduced to features in the last reel of MGM's *The Cat and the Fiddle*. But Rodgers and Hart now had the chance to officiate at the start of an era of extraordinarily color-coordinated films from *The Wizard of Oz* to *Gigi*.

What splendid history! However, why did Pioneer Pictures—formed specifically to produce in this new Technicolor, for distribution by RKO—try to get away with B-movie personnel? Roy Harris and Francis Faragoh wrote the script, Lloyd Corrigan directed, and the leads were Charles Collins, Steffi Duna, Frank Morgan, and Victor Varconi. Kids, the stars are out tonight. Bizarrely, Rodgers and Hart were used for only two songs. The film is a full musical, with six numbers, but they're mostly dances with cas-tanets and guitars or miscellaneous choruses. The hero (Collins) is a dancing teacher kidnaped by pirates in 1820 Boston. Escaping, he ends up in Spanish California, where he charms a town by teaching the women to dance, especially the daughter (Duna) of the Alcalde (Morgan, doing his standard Frank Morgan imitation). There are Indians in it, too; at one point, they go into a war dance notable for its lack of turbulence. One on-looker comments on this, and is jokingly told—typically for this humorless screenplay—"These are peaceful Indians."

The film's PR underlined that it was a "dancing" movie—but musicals need vocal substantiation, at least performance numbers if not character numbers. Edmund Burke, speaking of understanding society, said, "I must see the things, I must see the men." To paraphrase: We must hear the story, we must hear its songs. Two vocals is not a musical, though "Are You My Love?" is one of Rodgers and Hart's most wonderfully expansive ballads, however little known. The icing on the cake is the drab sets, which were bound to limit the exploitation of color in what was supposed to be a color showcase—and Pioneer had troubled to hire a noted Broadway designer, Robert Edmond Jones, billed by himself on the third title card with the credit "Designed in color by."

In filming Rodgers and Hart's 1930s stage shows, Hollywood once again abused the scores. *On Your Toes* (1939) lost everything but the two ballets. *Babes in Arms* (1939), the most hit-filled of their musicals, retained only "Where or When" and the title number. At least Rodgers and Hart got to write a new ballad each for *The Boys From Syracuse* (1940) and *Too Many Girls* (1940). The latter is quite faithful to the show, using some of the stage principals and even chorus boy Van Johnson, who can be spotted in the ensemble along with the show's and movie's vocal arranger, Hugh Martin.

However, the prize in these made-for-Hollywood insert numbers is "The Greeks Have No Word For It," a New Dance Sensation introduced in *The Boys From Syracuse* by Martha Raye and the girls. "When Orpheus started the Orpheum circuit," she begins—and Hart is already on the edge of what Hollywood tolerates in historical references (here to the famous ancient musician and the by then defunct vaudeville empire). The song's joke is that Raye never gives us the name of the dance, yet she defies the rules of the genre by giving us instructions on how to execute it. There's "lift your tunic" and "shake your toga," which is already more specific than "Black Bottom" or "The Varsity Drag" ever were.

Adaptations of the team's shows were still appearing long after the shows themselves did—a sanitized *Pal Joey* (1957) for Frank Sinatra, Rita Hayworth, and Kim Novak, and a *Jumbo* (1962) for Doris Day, with Martha

Raye again, love hunk Stephen Boyd, and, from the original 1935 stage cast, Jimmy Durante. Titled for contractual reasons as *Billy Rose's Jumbo*, the film was less a musical than an excuse to film a circus, from the parade through the town to the big top to the acrobats and trampoline jumping. Day even performed a daredevil horseback act, even if most of the footage was fulfilled by a very accomplished stunt rider.

Jumbo did trouble to reclaim much of the original score, though some lyrics were so out of date they had to be changed. In Boyd's (dubbed) solo on "The Most Beautiful Girl in the World," "[Marlene] Dietrich" became "Venus," spoiling one of Hart's snazziest rhymes, with "sweet trick." (The new rhyme was "[be]tween us.") Similarly, an allusion to "Garbo" was altered to "Juno." Was Greta Garbo, once the most famous woman in the world, really and utterly over by 1962? Or did *Jumbo* need to style Boyd as the fabled Strong, Silent Type (or, as gays term it, "trade"), unaware of anything as fey as a movie star?

Our last stop on the Rodgers and Hart tour is the bio, this one from MGM as *Words and Music* (1948). We don't look for authenticity of narrative, just some great guest-star cameos; Lena Horne is especially good in "The Lady Is a Tramp." Then, too, we enjoy the expertise of MGM's music department, using songs complete with their verses (and even the intervening "trio" sections) and including bits of the original scores that we never hear—"At the Round Table" for the onstage scene of *A Connecticut Yankee* and a taste of "A Little Birdie Told Me So" in the dance music of *Peggy-Ann*'s "Where's That Rainbow?"

For the storyline, MGM elected to focus on Lorenz Hart's problem—no, not that he was gay in a homophobic society. That he was short. The studio cast very tall men and kept setting them next to Mickey Rooney's Hart to turn him into a midget, but Rooney does trouble to recall Hart's idiosyncrasies—his habit of rubbing his hands together, his unreliability, and so on. The Rodgers, Tom Drake (the Boy Next Door in *Meet Me in St. Louis*) narrates, yet he leaves very little impression, especially considering that the real Rodgers was something of a character, sharp and fast yet enigmatic and dark on even his good days.

Still, the purpose of the song-cavalcade bio is not history but musicmaking. It contradicts Hollywood's emphasis on narrative as the primary element in the movie musical: here, the songs are everything. To put it another way: *The Broadway Melody* was about a love triangle capped by Bessie Love's Oscar-baiting mad scene, not about its Broadway melodies. Yet Broadway's greatest melodist found such a comfortable niche in Hollywood that he gave up on New York and moved to California. Let us see if he was better able than others to make the movie musical his own.

CHAPTER 6

⌒

Jerome Kern

Today, his name has somewhat faded away, except among aficionados. George Gershwin immortalized himself with his symphonic titles and *Porgy and Bess*. Richard Rodgers' colossal hits with Oscar Hammerstein keep his music in the playing loop. And Cole Porter is so permanently hip that Hollywood filmed his second bio relatively recently.

Jerome Kern has fallen behind them, though from about 1915 to his death, in 1945, he was the Harms Group's artistic leader (and, by the way, an actual partner in the Harms publishing outfit). This was partly because Kern was the most prolific of the masters of the New Music that broke away from the European models so much a part of the Victor Herbert generation.[1] For youngsters like Gershwin and Rodgers, revisiting Kern's shows again and again just to hear the music, Kern was the great begetter: of melody, yes, but also of extended musical scenes; of those aforementioned trio sections to texture character development during a number; of tiny orchestral bits between vocal phrases to soothe or excite a tune; and an extensive use of the major seventh interval in the vocal line, unheard of at the time in popular music.

Three of Kern's shows were filmed silent, says Edwin M. Bradley in *The First Hollywood Musicals*: *Oh, Boy!*, *Oh, Lady! Lady!!*, and *Sally*, with its original comic star, Leon Errol, in his stage role, opposite Colleen Moore. So far, so good—but then Kern's masterpiece, *Show Boat*, was also filmed silent.

---

1. This platitude of the musical's history is in fact only half true: the European style ruled in comic opera (the forerunner of operetta), but musical comedy had been cultivating a very native sound since the 1880s. Think, for instance, of the songs of George M. Cohan, in the very early 1900s—"The Yankee Doodle Boy," "Give My Regards To Broadway," or "Harrigan," echoing the character of an Independence Day marching band or a vaudevillian presenting the soft shoe.

Or, rather, the musical's source, Edna Ferber's eponymous *novel*, was filmed as a silent. But the talkie had become so habilitated so suddenly during the film's production that it had to be turned into a part-talkie. So music was added. But the music wasn't Kern's—and then, at the last minute, Kern's music *was* added, though most of it wasn't part of the actual narrative.

To understand these contradictory doings, we backtrack to a digest history of Universal, one of Hollywood's two oldest studios. (Paramount is the other.) By 1926, when Ferber's novel appeared, Universal had seniority the way Dracula has seniority among vampires: as the early model, outzipped by the hip kids of *True Blood* and the *Twilight* series. Revolutionary history was careening along in Hollywood, yet Universal was happy in its Stone Age, with sentimentalistic and cliché-ridden storylines played by ye olde stock company of the Heavy Father, the Perky Juvenile, the Wistful Heroine. Thus, the studio pitched its output to the third audience, which liked its art well broken-in: the good old stuff. Once a year, Universal splurged on something big for roadshow exhibition, but these à la carte premieres in the big cities were just so much appetizer to the films' real place settings out in the regions, where *The Hunchback of Notre Dame* (1923) and *Uncle Tom's Cabin* (1927) were table d'hôte.

So *Show Boat* was right up Universal's alley, because underneath Ferber's visionary American epic is a somewhat maudlin family saga enlivened by the novelty of the floating theatre and its primeval masques. The show boat puts on melodramas, and *Show Boat* itself is a melodrama. In fact, Universal was itself a kind of show boat, putting on melodrama long after the form had died out.

But then, Universal always did everything *after* the rest of Hollywood did it—reluctantly, at that. So once the studio got the rights to Ferber's novel, it scheduled it as its Big One for 1929: thus to film a silent for release in the first year of the *all-talking movie*. And of course this was to ignore the unprecedentedly popular score, above all its "Ol' Man River."

Finally, someone in power at Universal City, Hollywood, U.S.A., realized that a major film of *Show Boat* as a silent would be a commercial blunder risking industry humiliation. So the project went part-talkie, with new music. And *then* someone realized that at least a sampling of what Kern and Hammerstein had wrought had to be heard, especially as Universal's "Ol' Man River" substitution, "The Lonesome Road," by Nathaniel Shilkret and Gene Austin, was morose and repetitious where Kern's melody and Hammerstein's poetry soar. In the end—and at the eleventh hour—Universal paid a whopping $100,000 (along with profit participation) for the rights to include a two-reel prologue of some of the Broadway cast performing their numbers on stage.

So this first of three movie *Show Boat*s is not in any sense an adaptation of the musical. It follows the novel in a general way, changing many details, even omitting the miscegenation subplot, which would have irritated Universal's beloved third audience in the South. Further, Magnolia's very momentary reunion with Julie, years after the separation of these two very dear friends—a key sequence in the musical—was turned inside out for the usual bathetic Universal reasons.

Kern and Hammerstein treated this episode as ultra music theatre, built around Julie's delivering "Bill"—merry as written—as a kind of autobiographical death chant, then seeing Magnolia sweetly reprising "their" old song, "Can't Help Lovin' Dat Man," to her own guitar accompaniment. This leads Julie to sacrifice herself for Magnolia, presumably to go off on an alcoholic tear—in mid-winter—and wind up dead in Chicago's frozen streets.

None of this is in Ferber, where Julie reappears for just a second as, it seems, a clerk in a bordello; Magnolia spots her but is abruptly cut off. However, Universal sensed a Coincidence of Tearful Apocalypse in the event, and turned Julie (Alma Rubens) into the bordello *madam* who, confronted by Magnolia (Laura La Plante), calmly insists that the two have never met and sends Magnolia away. Then, alone, she weeps for lost happiness while gazing at Magnolia's photograph. One almost imagines Universal's chief, Carl Laemmle, with his picturesque German accent, purring, "Dat bit dey'll lofe in de small towns. Anoder Universal Super-Jewel!"

Critics lambasted the film, and it has no advocates today. But it is interesting to witness the sheer physics of the story   just for starters, the river and the boat itself. And while director Harry Pollard is no one's idea of an auteur, he films the termagant Parthy Ann (Emily Fitzroy) balefully "presiding" over the *Cotton Palace* (renamed from Ferber's *Cotton Blossom Floating Palace Theatre*) high over the stern as it docks. After her death, Magnolia—so unlike Parthy in every quality—takes over the family business and is seen lording it up at the stern herself in exactly the same way.

Meanwhile, 1929 saw also Hollywood's first sound adaptation of a Kern, in *Sally*. Warner Bros. already owned the rights through its adjunct studio, First National, which had made that silent *Sally* with Colleen Moore, and now Warners would unveil *Sally: The Musical*, starring the twenties' greatest woman headliner on stage, Marilyn Miller. With a fruity soprano, a sharp sense of humor, and a dreamy-crazy blond happiness look that filled the theatre, Miller was First Cinderella in a Cinderella age. And *Sally*—the waitress who crashes the *Follies*—was *her* role, on Broadway for a vast run in a giant house followed by an even vaster tour, altogether for three years.

Miller was above all a dancer, and the *Sally* film revolves around that, from the PR art of Miller in the ballerina's tutu to the first shot of her, showing only her feet and then rising to admire her gliding through her restaurant workplace fluffing out her skirt as if on stage. Rumor had it that Miller established intimate rapport with Jack Warner, and he did lavish upon her the best possible *Sally*, all in Technicolor and cast to tilt the action to her—the ever-wooden Alexander Gray as her Society Sweetheart; Joe E. Brown as the comic, working a fine chemistry with Miller (he even holds his own in a dance with her); and let us not omit Pert Kelton, not a great star but with immortality in her future as the tart-tongued Mrs. Paroo in the original stage cast of *The Music Man*, twenty-eight years later (and the movie as well).

Further, the new script, by Waldemar Young, improves a good deal on Guy Bolton's Broadway libretto, which was corny even for 1920. The new dialogue shows some awareness of the wisecrack attitudes that were taking over the national lingo, as when Miller, en masque as a continental adventuress, waves away concern over a duel supposedly fought over her between "a great Russian writer" and "the vice-president of Switzerland." Really, these petty worries over a life or two:

MILLER: There are so many Russians. And what good is a *vice*-president, anyway?

True, we have to put up with the wordy gabble of the second comic, T. Roy Barnes, one of those vaudeville hustlers who keep ad libbing and taking up space, a trial especially in the earliest talkies, when stage jesters of every rank were flooding Hollywood.

Note that this was Miller's event, not Jerome Kern's. Guy Bolton and Kern got credit on the first title card, respectively, as "Author" and "Composer" (the show counted too many lyricists to mention), but in very small lettering—and the stage score was cut back to only two numbers, "Look For the Silver Lining" and "Wild Rose." The enchanting "Whip-Poor-Will," one of Miller's best songs, was dropped, and the *Follies* ballet music, by Victor Herbert, was composed anew by unknown hands. Instead, the musical program was filled out by Joseph Burke and Al Dubin, with "All I Want To Do-Do-Do Is Dance," "If I'm Dreaming [don't wake me too soon]," "After Business Hours (That Certain Bizness Begins)," which was itself cut back to a non-vocal dance, and a new title song.[2]

A huge hit, *Sally* nevertheless did nothing for Jerome Kern's place in the Hollywood musical. He continued to work for Warner Bros., but their second filming of a Kern-Miller hit, *Sunny* (1930), trapped in the ban on

2. Every source credits this new "Sally" to Kern, but it doesn't sound remotely like him, and 78s of the number give Burke and Dubin as the authors.

musicals, sang only two songs, "Who?," from Broadway, and a new Kern tune, "I Was Alone." Written (like the rest of *Sunny*) with Otto Harbach and Oscar Hammerstein, "I Was Alone" is a strange little taste of Kern caviar. Ostensibly in AABA form, it is in fact eight variations on a four-note cell, all but one different in pitch and harmony, abutting one another in the A strains. Even odder is its tone, for the lyrics sound sad but Kern gave his partners a driving march that suggests the little tin soldier embarking on a blind date, full of hope.

The low point of Kern's Warner period was *Men of the Sky* (1931), which Kern and Harbach devised as a newfangled World War I spy drama with an operetta score and which lost nearly all its vocals. The film no longer survives, but Kern commentators who have studied the screenplay and music find it treasurable. In books entitled *Jerome Kern*, Gerald Bordman called *Men of the Sky* "One of [Kern's] sweetest, most ingratiating scores" and Stephen Banfield thought it "one of Kern's major works." Indeed, *Men of the Sky* came along when Kern was in his most ambitious period, so its loss is a tragedy: it marked the only time Kern and one of his regular Broadway collaborators sought to apply the Kern revolution in music theatre to the screen.

In fact, Kern's next movie credits consisted of adaptations of his stage shows: Fox's *Music in the Air* (1934), MGM's *The Cat and the Fiddle* (1934), Warner Bros.' *Sweet Adeline* (1935), and RKO's *Roberta* (1935). The last two are less interesting, though *Roberta* is an Astaire-Rogers title, in their third teaming. They were only featured, as the Second Couple, for Irene Dunne and Randolph Scott played the leads. Like *Sweet Adeline*, *Roberta* is faithful to the original narrative and atmosphere—American men mixed up in Parisian couture in *Roberta* and little old German-ethnic New York in *Adeline*. Coincidentally, each of the two films introduced one new Kern melody, respectively, "Lovely To Look At" (with a lyric by Dorothy Fields) and "We Were So Young" (by Oscar Hammerstein). Now things get a bit complicated, for each of the two films *also* brought over from Kern's 1934 London collaboration with Oscar Hammerstein, *Three Sisters*, one of Adèle Dixon's numbers, again, respectively, "I Won't Dance" and "Lonely Feet." Fields had to rewrite the "I Won't Dance" lyric, as Kern and Hammerstein had written it as one of those "pretty maid fends off the male chorus" numbers, and Dixon's winsome pleading wouldn't intersect with that ballroom racketeer Fred Astaire when the song was inserted into the *Roberta* movie. And of course the very notion of Astaire refusing to dance was amusing in itself. Fields fell in with the general merriment in referencing "The Continental" in the song's release.

"Lovely To Look At" became so popular that revivals of the stage show have had to absorb it. Both postwar recordings included it, and MGM used it as the title of the *Roberta* remake (1952). Yet it's a strange piece, at six-teen bars only half the length of the standard AABA pop tune—and it sounds it. True, the verse bears an exquisite ambiance in a simple melodic cell of four notes alternately descending and ascending. But that miniature chorus moves from a flowing passage to talky dotted-eighth-note pattern-ing in something like ABBCADC, and it ends very abruptly. A story goes with it, told in various versions, though Gerald Bordman seems to have reported it first: RKO was "aghast" when the music was first presented to them. Could it be that a section was missing? No: when asked for an expla-nation, Kern responded with "That's all I had to say!" And this was Pandro Berman's RKO, where the Broadway songwriter held sway. We can imagine the end of the tale: Berman shrugs and tells his minions, "Use it."

What makes *Music in the Air* and *The Cat and the Fiddle* more attractive than *Roberta* and *Sweet Adeline* is a devotion to their stage scores, though each film reflects this differently. In fact, Fox rather scanted *Music in the Air*'s musical setting, less a brace of songs than extensive musical scenes; Kern actually gave each sequence a title such as Leit Motif, Sonata, and Rondo because these were compositions in a particular structure. Further, Fox left out three of the show's most popular numbers, "In Egern on the Tegern See," "And Love Was Born," and even a standard, "The Song Is You."[3] Nevertheless, a healthy amount of the Kern-Hammerstein score is heard, including, to the aficionado's delighted surprise, the extended choral intro-duction to "I've Told Every Little Star" (adapted from the Adagio of Beethoven's Third Piano Sonata) and the lengthy through-sung episode in which the sophisticated city people demonstrate a number from their next operetta to amazed villagers, "I'm Coming Home."

And that encapsulates *Music in the Air*'s plot: two kids (Douglass Montgomery, June Lang) and her father (Al Shean) visit Munich to get a song published, bonding with a theatrical troupe led by two egocentric Characters (actor-playwright John Boles, prima donna Gloria Swanson), whereupon the Girl is given Swanson's role and undoes all the good work Ruby Keeler performed in *42nd Street* by being so terrible she's fired.

It's Plot C in reverse—and Swanson, reveling in spoofy eyes-and-teeth close-ups and end-of-days tantrums, makes *Music in the Air* a musical *Sunset Boulevard*. She also fields a rich soprano and plays wonderfully with Boles, also hamming way over the top, to contrast with the simple village kids. Or are they that simple? Montgomery is almost embarrassingly

---

3. Many sources state that "The Song Is You" is in the film, but while both it and "Egern" are heard on the accompanying soundtrack, "The Song Is You" is never sung even in part.

appetizing in the Lederhosen he wears throughout most of the picture, and Lang is not just a pretty soubrette but an adroit comic. She makes a wonderful recovery when, after fighting with Montgomery to the breaking point, she suddenly remembers that Boy gets Girl in the last reel and runs down to him, to be swept up in his arms.

And here's some interesting casting: *Music in the Air* brought in two performers from the Broadway staging, both in minor roles. One of the two, the aforementioned father, Al Shean, is very touching when defending his daughter from intensely skeptical pros, not least Joseph Cawthorn as the theatre's music director, adamant that the unseasoned Lang is not just unacceptable but *has no right* to be a performer. Are we to throw seventy people out of work, he rages, "just because a couple of amateurs want a little adventure in the theatre?"

It's another red-light-flashing New York moment in Hollywood history, because we know who is really uttering this line—Oscar Hammerstein, who had no patience with those who would substitute vanity for talent. Seeking a genuinely Bavarian flavor for its film, Fox hired three German emigrants in the top positions—producer Erich Pommer, director Joe May, and co-scenarist Billy (then spelled Billie) Wilder. Nevertheless, at the core of both show and movie is a Broadway credo that stardom is attained by charisma tempered by hard work, not by tourists with a yen.

But let us not forget the other stage veteran of *Music in the Air*, though she's in the movie for little more than five seconds. It's Marjorie Main, later famous as Humphrey Bogart's rejecting mother in *Dead End*, the amiable owner of *The Women*'s divorcées' dude ranch, and Ma Kettle in Universal's rustic B series with Pa Percy Kilbride. In *Music in the Air*, as Swanson's spectacularly affectless maid, Main gets her moment when Montgomery, fearful of strangling in the coils of these slinky city folk, sneaks out of Swanson's apartment, Lederhosen and all. Asked where the boy is, Main simply points at the exit, but in so ghostly a manner that it belongs in the supernatural wing of the Smithsonian.

The Cat and the Fiddle, written just before *Music in the Air*, and with Otto Harbach instead of Oscar Hammerstein, brings us more backstage life. But the *Cat* film is the opposite of *Music in the Air*. On the latter, Fox adhered to the story but dropped a lot of music; MGM's *Cat* changed the story while retaining virtually every melody of the original score in some form or other, sometimes with new lyrics.

Cat has a starrier cast, too. Ramon Novarro and Jeanette MacDonald are, respectively, classical and popular composers, and Frank Morgan (without his stuttering-bumbler shtick, a somewhat menacing figure) is the theatre impresario who comes between them. This much was in the stage show. But the film uses them so differently that the score as heard on Broadway no longer connected with the action—and, mind you, *Cat* is one of the most integrated musicals of its time. It's like a jigsaw puzzle: once you have completed it, you can't start moving pieces around. They fit together in only one way.

Yet this is exactly what MGM's music department did, merrily repurposing the score so that almost every major number appears in a new place in the continuity, and including the minor tunes that movie adaptations would omit almost as a rule. It's wonderful to hear all that Kern—and, better yet, MGM's clown car of screenwriters, credited and uncredited, contrived a better script than Harbach's original, severely lacking in humor. Thus, the movie's Charles Butterworth, as always delivering comedy lines with meticulous vapidity, comments on the ancient puffbag who is to go on in Novarro's operetta in place of Vivienne Segal:

BUTTERWORTH: I know she's old, but she's got good references.

This substitute is too drunk to play—and suddenly MacDonald takes over the part! So it's another Plot C tale, with a superb moment—caught from the stage-right wings looking left—as a scene ends and the traveler closes while dancing boys and girls in commedia dell'arte costumes troop on in front of the curtain for a scene-change interlude. This is one of the very few times in the 1930s in which a Hollywood backstager gives us *exactly* how stage musicals behaved at the time (and the commedia attire is a link with the original's onstage sequence built around one of Kern's best creations, "Poor Pierrot"). It's a stunning bit from director William K. Howard (or his unbilled collaborator, Sam Wood), though if you blink you'll miss it.

Indeed, MGM's *Cat* is extremely well directed, which is why its rather silly action never irritates. It's silly in an adorable way, as when, in McDonald's rooms (where "The Night Was Made For Love," on Broadway a highlight of the opening musical scene, is given a completely new role in the score), she wears a black bow tie. But I mean a gigantic black bow tie, to the point that we can speak of the Alhambra, Mt. McKinley, and Jeanette's bow tie. Still, our two directors know how to point up their storytelling, and in the last reel (using, as I've said, the new three-strip Technicolor for the first time in a feature), as Novarro and MacDonald, on stage in the finale of his operetta, give up bickering and sing their way into a love match, the camera peers into the stage-left wings. There we see Frank Morgan, witnessing the evaporation of his would-be affair with MacDonald, freezing in fury.

It's all over but "The End," so Charles Butterworth, in a characteristic masterpiece of underplaying, silently hands Morgan his hat. So long, villain.

Morgan storms off as Novarro and MacDonald seal it with a kiss. Their little operetta curtain falls, and the audience goes wild. The End.

This series of filmed Kern stage shows is capped by Universal's sound remake of its part-silent *Show Boat* (1936). Its authenticity is an article of faith among aficionados: put together by the authors themselves with some of the stage show's musical staff and a cast drawn from the Broadway run, the tour, the 1932 revival, and various regional mountings. True, some of the score is missing—even one of the six hits, "Why Do I Love You?" But it's fascinating to hear so much of the original underscoring—Parthy Ann's angry leitmotif, the convent-school theme—without alteration.[4]

Let's get our bearings on Kern's career, because his style evolved far more extravagantly than that of any of his colleagues (with the possible exception of Richard Rodgers, the silken sass with Hart suddenly replaced by a hymnal intensity for Hammerstein). Basically, there are four Kerns:

1903–1919: The deft but mainly light Kern of basic musical comedy. Sample melody: "Look For the Silver Lining" (from *Sally*), Schubertian in its purity—"naive" in Friedrich Schiller's breakdown of art as stemming from the heart (thus naive: instinctive, emotional) or from the intellect ("sentimental" in his wording, but really meaning "developed according to a plan").

1920–1927: The ever-grander Kern, working up to the stage *Show Boat*. Sample melody: "Who?" (from *Sunny*, as previously noted). This is a "sentimental" concoction, in AABBAAAC form, absurdly brilliant in that every A and B starts on the sixth of the scale, creating a pleasurable suspense that runs through the refrain till its very last measures: "No one but you!"

1928–1936: The senior Kern, masterly in the long-lined ballad, such as *Roberta*'s "Smoke Gets in Your Eyes." Now Kern dips into swing, also in *Roberta* (as in "I'll Be Hard To Handle," for Broadway's favorite Polish blonde, Lyda Roberti, sexy and adorable at once: so her music had to *sound* sexy and adorable). Swing continues to attract Kern, though he supposedly didn't like it. In Hollywood, he writes "I Got Love" for Met soprano Lily Pons to get hot with, in *I Dream Too Much* (1935), and, for Allan Jones in *One Night in the Tropics* (1940), the bluesy "Back in My Shell," subtitled "A song of renunciation in the Negro manner." From the latter film, "Your Dream (Is the Same as My Dream)" reaches its last A with the marking "Imperioso" (Imperiously), but in fact the imperious Kern of, say, "Ol' Man River" is all but over.

4. Fun fact: The dainty piano tunelet that Magnolia plays offstage just before her entrance was cut before release, though Ravenal's subsequent reference to it, and her reply, were left in.

1937–1945: The less adventurous Kern. He remains unique and wonderful—for his last new Broadway score, *Very Warm For May* (1939), he produces "All the Things You Are," which some call his greatest song ever. More: that same year, for the straight play *Mamba's Daughters*, Kern composes (to DuBose Heyward's lyrics) "Lonesome Walls," something like a woman's version of "Ol' Man River," introduced by Anne Brown, George Gershwin's original Bess. Nevertheless, the amazing Kern who inspired the next half-generation, from Rodgers to Youmans, has all but retired.

Luckily, Kern was still in his third stage when he and Hammerstein—as sole authors—created this first talkie *Show Boat*, because they decided the by then classic score had a few holes in it, which they filled with three new numbers.

This is truly surprising. *Show Boat*, the pioneer in the line of Great American Musicals, is somehow incomplete?

But, indeed, there was no number treating the development of the central romance—between the meeting ("Make-Believe") and the avowal ("You Are Love"). As it was originally played in the Washington, D.C., tryout, *Show Boat* covered this in a choral song and dance, "I Would Like To Play a Lover's Part," as the authors, thinking outside the box, let the show boat's public tell us how beautifully Magnolia and Ravenal fit together. Unfortunately, when an hour had to be cut from the overlong evening, this number was dropped. The show was playing wonderfully well on its next three stops before New York, doing such great business on its three weeks in Philadelphia (after Pittsburgh and Cleveland) that a substantial portion of its production capital was recouped even before the New York premiere. So Kern and Hammerstein left well enough alone.

Nevertheless, when they were invited to create the script and score for the remake, the pair filled this hole in the plot, writing "I Have the Room Above [her]" to look in on the budding love affair. It's one of Kern's best third-period melodies, given extra lilt by Hammerstein's conversational tone as the two sweethearts carry on a bit of nineteenth-century Mississippi hanky-panky. At the end, Kern gives them a coda to hum together, as if their rapport has moved beyond words into sheer feelings.

The second new number is "I Still Suits Me," for Joe and Queenie. This is the Kern and Hammerstein version of the De Sylva, Brown, and Henderson joshing duet, possibly added because Paul Robeson and Hattie McDaniel offered unique character opportunities unavailable to the Broadway production (especially given the poor stage deportment of the Joe, Jules Bledsoe). Interestingly, "I Still Suits Me" folds itself into the 1927 *Show Boat* composition, playing with the intervals of a third alternating with a

fourth that mark the first three pitches of "Ol' Man River" (and of its in-
verted complement, "Cotton Blossom"). However, in "I Still Suits Me" this
third-fourth alternation lies not in the vocal but in figures sitting between
the sung lines, a Kern "trick" dating back to his first period. One example:
you hear this Kern fill-in cell after each of the three A strains in "Smoke
Gets In Your Eyes," but it runs through Kern's work so indelibly that John
Kander used one of these melodic bits in *Chicago*, in the five-note lead-in to
"When You're Good To Mama," an hommage to a comparable eight-note
lead-in to *Sally*'s "Look For the Silver Lining."

The third new *Show Boat* number is the most intriguing, and, also, the
most wasted. It replaces Magnolia's dainty little piano piece (the one that,
as I've said, was cut from the release print), whose notes were then developed into a gigantic production number called "It's Getting Hotter in the
North," another casualty of the D.C. cuts. This expansion of a puerile ditty
into a vast jazz anthem was designed to balance the timelessness of the
natural world (symbolized in the "jes' keeps rollin' along" of "Ol' Man
River") with the trendy nature of the cultural world, wherein everything is
protean and unstable. *Show Boat* is epic in more than its story: it *sounds*
epic, as its music keeps getting updated as the decades pass.

Thus, having lost the marvelous ontological apotheosis of Magnolia's
theme on stage in 1927, Kern and Hammerstein wrote a new piece to undergo the same transformation on screen in 1936, "Gallivantin' Around."
This first appears as Magnolia's blackface number in the show boat olio (the
variety show that follows the melodrama), and was planned—and filmed—
to turn into the film's big finale, starting with Magnolia's daughter (Sunnie
O'Dea) on an antebellum plantation and moving to twenties Harlem, where
O'Dea is rebooted as a banjo-playing glamor flapper with the black ensemble. Unfortunately, the entire number was cut; only the stills survive.

Much else was filmed and cut, leaving the story to hasten along at a
headlong pace, just touching on arresting details in the crowd scenes as it
surges onward. (We even get Eddie Anderson, later Jack Benny's famous
Rochester, delivering one line in the excitement: "There's the show boat!")
Compared with MGM's turgid *Show Boat* remake of 1951, Universal's talkie
seems like the most vivid of musicals, and very true to the show's unique
blend of musical comedy, musical play, and operetta.

Returning to writing new scores, Kern was bound to contribute (with
Dorothy Fields) to RKO's Astaire-Rogers series, because producer Pandro
Berman was still working his way through the best of Broadway, and Kern
was the best of the best. The Kern-Fields project was called *Never Gonna
Dance* so late in its production history that "NGD" was stenciled onto the
PR stills, but the film was released as *Swing Time* (1936). This title emphasizes

an odd dichotomy in Kern's aesthetic: although he more or less hated the "latest" musical styles, he used them expertly. Perhaps as an inside joke, "The Waltz in Swing Time" fondles the old three-quarter time while striding into trendy honky-tonk.

Could *Swing Time* boast the most beguiling score in the Astaire-Rogers series? After all, in this format it is not the narrative but the decorations that matter—the support kibitzers, bingeing on tiny yet somehow earthshattering confusions; the song and dance; and of course the two bickering sweethearts. *Swing Time* has as well a genuinely hostile Other Man in Georges Metaxa, as bandleader Ricardo Romero. Nowadays, we recognize the villain because he smokes; in an Astaire-Rogers RKO, the villain is the one who's full of himself. "Where Ricardo Romero goes," he brags, "the others come."

Yet even this arrogant worm is part of RKO's love of New York and its cultural leadership, its air of being the place where the artists, opinion-makers, and their supporters congregate. On a radio hook-up, Metaxa welcomes listeners to "the starlit heavens" of his penthouse café, "on the gala night of our grand reopening. Everybody's here."

Those last two words could be this series' motto: the inspired songwriters, the great comics, the sharp writers, the whole T. B. Harms–New York kaboodle of it. And of course the outstanding songs, of *Swing Time* especially. Sophisticated: "A Fine Romance," the ultimate in savvy sarcasm. Simple: "Pick Yourself Up," though the refrain starts in not the tonic but the supertonic minor, moving through a surprising chain of chords till it finally reaches the tonic...in the eighth measure.[5] Tender: "The Way You Look Tonight," which director George Stevens amusingly undercuts by having Astaire sing it to Rogers while she's shampooing her hair—and note the typical Kern "extra" melody, a duet between two notes of wordless vocal and two beats of orchestra, back and forth thus, both to launch the tune and finish it off.

And then of course there's Astaire's blackface number. *What?* But *Swing Time* has one, "Bojangles of Harlem," a salute to Bill Robinson, probably the most prominent black dancer of the day. This number, too, is adventurous,

---

5. Kern dropped another inside joke into the first four of these measures, quoting the famous Polka from Jaromír Weinberger's opera *Švanda Dudák* (Schwanda the Bagpiper) in either precise pitches and harmony or very comparable approximations. It's logical: "Pick Yourself Up" finds Ginger Rogers teaching a supposedly lead-footed Astaire how to dance, and Švanda's playing of those pipes magically makes children of Terpsichore out of anyone who listens. To complete the merging of opera and RKO, Kern marked the published sheet's refrain "Polka-tempo," one notch below calling it "Švanda-style."

its refrain moving almost chromatically up the scale from G below middle C to the B a tenth above.

Still, the score's masterpiece is its little-known former title song, "Never Gonna Dance." A rondo with one episode using flatted blue notes and another distinguished by major seventh and ninth chords, it is Astaire's vocal solo but leads to the two stars' farewell dance duet when the romance hits what appears to be a decisive snag. This number may also be the one time in the entire Astaire-Rogers series wherein the lyricist all but takes over from the composer, for Dorothy Fields seized this occasion to give Astaire lines that connect to each other by stream of consciousness, with chance references to the "St. Louis Blues," radio talent-show host Major Bowes, two of the Marx Brothers, and French. "I'll put my shoes on beautiful trees," Astaire sings, for no reason other than there is such a thing as a shoe tree. And "My dinner clothes can dine where they please." Is this Fields' playful imitation of Gertrude Stein?

"Never Gonna Dance" really marks a summation of what Pandro Berman's outfit at RKO could do for the American story musical, especially in its unapologetic tilting of the art toward Hollywood's sophisticated first audience. It remained only for *Swing Time's* action to resolve the romance and bring the two stars together atop a skyscraper overlooking a snowy Manhattan so that Kern and Fields could give Astaire a reprise of "A Fine Romance" (with new conciliatory lyrics) while Rogers sings "The Way You Look Tonight" at the same time. Thus, two clashing melodies are married in an ivory tower above RKO's beloved New York while the achievements of Broadway's most gifted songwriters elevate the form of musical comedy itself. Everybody's here.

Unfortunately, after *Swing Time* Kern retreated from the experimentation of his earlier periods. Gone are the extensive musical scenes, the unexpected harmonic structures, even the little fill-in melodies between the vocal lines that helped reveal his individualistic flair way back in his first period. Thus, when Kern is reunited with Oscar Hammerstein for Paramount's *High, Wide and Handsome* (1937), the story is more interesting than the score. At that, the subplot (about Randolph Scott's striking oil, then trying to ship his crude to the refinery despite an impedient railroad magnate) is more interesting than the romance, between Scott and Irene Dunne.

High, Wide and Handsome is something of a western (though set in Pennsylvania), featuring action scenes, rough working men fighting wealthy dandies, a period setting (in the 1870s), a traveling medicine show, a saloon girl (Dorothy Lamour) singing to a dive filled with raucous bravos, a starchy yet lovable grandma (Elizabeth Patterson, the go-to actress for such roles), and a good old-fashioned villain. Actually, there are two: Charles Bickford plays the typical troublemaker of the minor league who does bad things because bad things are what he does; but Alan Hale is the real problem, the railroad boss who epitomizes the plutocrat greedy for not only money but the power to create misery. Yet he's no psychotic monster in the Ian Fleming Doctor No sense. Rather, Hale plays the merry goblin. He doesn't take his evil seriously; he laughs about it. At one point, director Rouben Mamoulian films Hale's laughing mug in close-up, letting it linger even as the next shot comes into view, as if Hale were a kind of comic deity, amused by the very grandeur of his nasty survey.

And this is very much Mamoulian's picture, one of the most *directed* of musicals.[6] Another of Scott's nemeses is a café owner (Akim Tamiroff), pictured as a sly and silky foreigner with a fondness for cats and the wish to grant to Scott what his oil business desperately needs . . . on one condition. He must give up the hill that he and Dunne have reserved for the house they will build as an objective-corelative of their marriage. Indeed, Kern and Hammerstein got a song out of it, "The Folks Who Live on the Hill." It is Dunne's solo, but Mamoulian films it as a duet, for Scott is as much in it as she is, touching her, gazing raptly up at her, and burying his head in her lap with a helplessly loving passion that he may never have shown in any other film. It's a wild moment, a world beyond what Maurice Chevalier and Jeanette MacDonald gave us in Mamoulian's *Love Me Tonight*—and, we should note, beyond the way romances were portrayed in Broadway musicals then.

So there is something unhappily marvelous about Tamiroff's wanting that hill. How does he even know about it? It is as though the movie wants to put Dunne and Scott through a series of trials—labors, perhaps—before they win their happy ending.

One thing about *High, Wide and Handsome* is pure Hammerstein: the strong, independent woman, for Dunne isn't content to be Scott's helpmate and nothing more. Why do men have all the fun—striking oil, getting cheated by monopolistic one per centers, battling hired thugs who keep wrecking the oil pipeline? Scott, his hair waved Byronically but bearing the flint of anger in his eye, gets great opportunities in the script. Does Alan Hale own the world?

> SCOTT: He thinks he does, him and all his friends. . . . The United States of America is just a big pie for them to cut up and pass around among themselves!

---

6. Hammerstein was billed for both screenplay (with "additional dialogue" by George O'Neil) and lyrics, but in several books historian Stanley Green claimed that Mamoulian was an uncredited co-scenarist.

And when he finds his allies abandoning him:

SCOTT: We ain't men! We're *nothing*!

How can Dunne rival this except by appearing in the center ring of a spectacular circus shot—this movie has everything—to sing "Can I Forget You," a gala love song? Wait, there's more: Dunne also coaches Lamour *during* her saloon audition on "Allegheny Al," which sounds like something Kern and Hammerstein might have written for Frank and Ellie ten years earlier, for *Show Boat*. It's a comic number with a hefty rhythmic pull to it, and Dunne really takes charge, banging out the beat for a slogging pianist, jumping into the vocal to hearten the nervous Lamour, even muttering commands as she and Lamour improvise a dance. ("Back!" cries Dunne, and "Toe!") It's a charming and even funny scene, and of course Hammerstein doesn't waste such moments, arranging for Scott to blunder in right after to find Dunne, pursuing the spirit of the occasion, singing by herself. On a table in that saloon. In the puritanical 1870s. In front of a lot of drooling creeps.

And Randolph Scott is not happy.

But then, this is a tense movie generally, confounded by menace and despair rare in films containing songs like "Allegheny Al." This is a morality tale seasoned with curios (such as the dodgy gent with the cats), taking a populist worldview to show why life isn't easy *even in a musical*. All right, Scott and Dunne work out their differences and Scott's oil pipeline makes it through all hazards to commercial success. (Alan Hale ends up with, literally, a hatful of oil.) But the good guys really have to earn their rewards in this tale.

High, Wide and Handsome can be seen as the missing link between two other Hammerstein projects, *Show Boat* and *Oklahoma!*—and of course Jerome Kern composed *Show Boat*. But by 1937 he was in his fourth period and no longer writing "super" scores. Now he just wrote songs—four some what stand-alone numbers for *Joy of Living* (1938), a screwball comedy with Irene Dunne (in her fifth and final Kern role) and Douglas Fairbanks Jr. As always in this genre, one of the leads teaches the other to stop working so hard at life and start enjoying it. Dunne's the worker, a musical-comedy star who supports her worthless family. "Scavengers," Fairbanks calls them; he's the teacher in Dunne's learning moment. "Entitled" is the word we use for these freeloaders nowadays, but they do add a lot of fun to the script, as here with Dunne's mother (Alice Brady) and father (Guy Kibbee):

BRADY: *Will* you stop drinking, for *my* sake?
KIBBEE: Who said I was drinking for your sake?

For yet more fun, Dunne models a succession of crazy hats, from one that looks like art deco Mickey Mouse ears to a box with a veil at the back that must have been lifted from the last tour of *The Vagabond King*. But she does let Fairbanks guide her in the art of cutting loose, such as getting drunk, being thrown out of a restaurant, going roller-skating, and, unfortunately, visiting a café run by Billy Gilbert, now doing his German routine.

There were so many screwball comedies in the late 1930s that a musical version of the genre should be a refreshing innovation, but *Joy of Living*'s vocals are all for Dunne (with a reprise of "You Couldn't Be Cuter" for her two little nieces), making the film less a musical than a screwball comedy hung with songs like a tiny Christmas tree. They're lovely compositions, again with lyrics by Dorothy Fields, and the big ballad, "Just Let Me Look at You," does hide one of Kern's trompe l'oeil stunts. The verse—in so many lesser hands just a question of housekeeping—is utterly remarkable. It is rich in major-seventh chords, the voice often glides down a full octave, and its main strain ("You are there...") turns up again as the refrain's release—all quite unusual, classic "sentimental" (in the Friedrich Schiller sense) Kern. Further, that refrain starts on an upward leap of a ninth, something we hear in pop music very, very seldom, and only from Broadway writers.

Nevertheless, Kern has gone movie colony on us, taking it easy in the sunshine. We wonder if two films at Columbia starring Rita Hayworth will invigorate him, as *You Were Never Lovelier* (1942) pals her with Fred Astaire and *Cover Girl* (1944) with Gene Kelly. Here are men who really *sound* like what they are, Astaire so classlessly debonair and Kelly needy and entreating. These two films follow the men, too: as Astaire sweetly woos Hayworth against the wishes of her father, Adolphe Menjou (who says, of Astaire, "He's not only a pest—he's a dancer!"); as Kelly *owns* Hayworth in mean-streets New York, all but demanding she give up a wealthy Society guy for Kelly's crass little burlesque company.

And the music follows the stories. *You Were Never Lovelier*, with Johnny Mercer's lyrics, is set in South America, though Kern lets Xavier Cugat and his band supply the local spice, while the character vocals stand firmly in Kern's North American autograph. But note that "The Shorty George," a song-and-dance duet for Astaire and Hayworth (dubbed by Nan Wynn) would be too cute, even precious, for Kelly. It's effervescent swing, and Hayworth is clearly having the time of her life with Astaire, getting something to do besides look ravishing, her usual gig at Columbia. Then, too, "I'm Old Fashioned," a ballad burnished with another of Kern's finely sculpted "extra" melodies between verse and chorus, is too confidential, too vulnerable, for Kelly to sing to anyone. But it's perfect for Astaire, because Astaire is a giving performer, while Kelly is a taking one. This is very sharp character writing—and let us note that Kern got his own title card, with his name in big letters. Mercer had to share his card with others.

Yet we're still perplexed that *You Were Never Lovelier*'s score is just songs, neat, straight-on. At least *Cover Girl*, in Technicolor to *Lovelier*'s black and white, is more elaborate, and the women's hats are once again loony oddities. (The milliner got major billing in the credits as Keneth [sic] Hopkins, though that seems to be a misspelling.) Better, Eve Arden is on hand with her Sarcastic Unmarried Lady putdowns, as a major player on the staff of a fashion magazine.

And fashion is the theme, in opposition to grunge, the world of Kelly's little neighborhood show shop. *Cover Girl*'s score (with, mainly, Ira Gershwin) reflects this in a program half-rough and half-gentle. Thus, "Put Me To the Test" is a somewhat braggy piece for Kelly—and he has an alone-at-night-on-deserted-streets dance duet (with a domineering hologram of himself) that would be unthinkable for Astaire. A hologram, okay. Dancing with a double, okay. But angry? Never.

Then, for the serene Kern, we have "Long Ago (and Far Away)," for Kelly and Hayworth (voiced by Nan Wynn again), just to establish that Kelly has a tender side. It's one of Kern's most beautiful tunes, truly haunting: and it's not enough. Our boy Kern is the champ of the Harms group. He can do haunting in his sleep, but we want something better than haunting— ambitious. We want the *Show Boat* Kern, perhaps to seize the opportunity offered by cinema the way Rodgers and Hart did in *Love Me Tonight*.

And now come two Kerns treating period Americana, Universal's *Can't Help Singing* (1944) and Fox's *Centennial Summer* (1946), both presumably in response to the phenomenal success of *Oklahoma!* on Broadway. This was initially a wartime cycle, best characterized by MGM's *Meet Me in St. Louis* (1944), so rich in imagery of American domestic life that one scarcely notices that it lacks a solid storyline.

Centennial Summer is something of a *St. Louis* moved to Philadelphia in 1876, with Walter Brennan as a crank-inventor pater familias. It's also the first musical whose leads—from Linda Darnell and Cornell Wilde to Dorothy Gish and William Eythe—neither sing nor dance. The first-billed Jeanne Crain can't even act. Why is she in a musical at all? Is it because she looked like a musical-comedy heroine? Years later, when directing Crain in *Pinky*, Elia Kazan (as he explains in his memoirs, *A Life*) assumed that she was—to put it delicately—virgo intacta, because she seemed so rosy and untried, "forever fifteen." He was shocked to discover that she was not only married but the mother, then, of four children (and two more were to follow).

Crain was, if nothing else, a movie star. But she *was* nothing else. So here again is that confusion about what talents belong in movies written by folk like Jerome Kern and his lyricists (here Leo Robin, E. Y. Harburg, and Oscar Hammerstein). The movie star is different from the talent star, above all glamorous—Elizabeth Taylor, for instance, whether or not one feels that she has thespian skills. The talent star is James Cagney or Eleanor Powell—cast because of one or more things they do well. Jeanne Crain doesn't do anything well; she can't even lip sync (to Louanne Hogan's vocals) convincingly.

So Kern is somewhat cornered on *Centennial Summer*. Movie scores tended to be written around a set cast, but it's hard to compose for Louanne Hogan or Kay St. Germain Wells (who dubbed for Linda Darnell). Worse, some of *Centennial*'s players handled their own vocals, especially on "Up With the Lark," in which Brennan's family, butter-churning maid, and visiting relation Constance Bennett take turns soloing in a number rather reminiscent of the opening song of *State Fair* the year before. Bennett's smoky bass is so unhabilitated that, faced with a high note, she simply "acts" her way through the line, with a gesture that says, "I was once the highest-paid actress in Hollywood, and suddenly I'm supposed to be Ginny Simms?"

As if answering an emergency, two specialty numbers were slotted into the score so audiences could enjoy some real singing. Taking advantage of the period setting, "All Through the Day" (the Hammerstein number) is the subject of a lantern-slide show in a "boy loves girl" motif as tenorino Larry Stevens sings the vocal. For the second chorus, he brings the ensemble in for a singalong, with some lovely choral harmony on the last A, when Kern, forever imaginative even when not making history, restates the melody a third higher in new harmony, giving it a triumphalist climax rare in a mellow ballad like this one.

Later, Avon Long and some children slip in for a black piece, "Cinderella Sue" (the Harburg number), on a melody at once mischievous and caressing. Kern analysts have speculated that both these inserts predate *Centennial Summer*—or why weren't they written with Leo Robin, like the rest of the score?

At least *Can't Help Singing* was a Deanna Durbin project, so Kern had a real vocalist to build his score around. Adept in pop and classical alike—in *That Certain Age* (1938), she sings Delibes and Mozart right along with "My Own" and "Be a Good Scout"—Durbin was really a talent star who became a movie star. She was known less for musicals than for Deanna Durbin movies in which she would sing now and again. With six numbers, *Can't Help Singing* is a full-fledged musical, but its California gold-rush setting is at war with what Kern does best. This is a "Stouthearted Men" film, a "Totem Tom-Tom" film. Even an "Ol' Man River" film; but Kern is out of the "Ol' Man River" business now.

At that, the film is most effective when it's between numbers, following two comic rogues (Akim Tamiroff, our louche cat fancier of *High, Wide and Handsome*, and Leonid Kinskey) relentlessly stalking Durbin's trunk; or a little boy named Warren whose mother keeps chiding him for twisting his hair. (Warren: "It's fun for my fingers.") *High, Wide and Handsome* had the qualities of a western, but *Can't Help Singing* really is a western. Its first shots reveal the cavalry riding furiously along the trail, and it spends most of its energy simply forging west in a wagon train. Kern (and his lyricist, E. Y. Harburg) get a song out of it, "Elbow Room." And there's a campfire dance number, "Swing Your Sweetheart," twanging like a banjo. As well, we get some lovely panoramic color photography of all that outdoors stuff.

Actually, the music fits in exactly where it would have done if the work had been written for the stage. Thus, after a scene in which Durbin and her vis-à-vis, Robert Paige, start to like each other, he goes out for a sno-kone or something and she sings one of those "Could this be love?" songs, "Any Moment Now." Later, at the appropriate moment, she caps this with "More and More," a "Yes, it *is* love" song. And the real estate is fetching—"Any Moment Now" concludes with Durbin radiant in front of what appear to be several Grand Canyons. But the sad truth of it is you could delete all the songs and nothing would be missing. The movie is movie enough, yes. But the musical isn't musical enough.

Ironically, after all the years living in Beverly Hills, Kern died on the streets of New York, in 1945, suffering a cerebral hemorrhage while readying with Oscar Hammerstein a new revisal of *Show Boat* to play the very house it had originally opened in, the Ziegfeld. One year later, the inevitable Kern bio appeared, *Till the Clouds Roll By* (1946). MGM gave it its usual "big" approach, so we get a host of guest spots, from Judy Garland to Dinah Shore, and excellent musical arrangements. But this is more than a mere cavalcade of hits: the title-card fanfare is a little-known theme from *The Cat and the Fiddle*, and the action itself starts with a fifteen-minute digest of *Show Boat* that goes beyond the hits to seek out "Where's the Mate For Me?" and "Life On the Wicked Stage."[7] Then, too, the storyline

7. The former is not a separate number in the score, forming a segment of the musical scene leading up to "Make-Believe." It is cited in the table of contents thus, though most aficionados think of it as "Who Cares If My Boat Goes Upstream?." The latter, almost invariably tagged as "Life Upon the Wicked Stage" (after its first line) in fact used *On* in the title, to revive a popular nineteenth-century phrase, as *Show Boat* narrates partly through chronological references, from the treacly parlor ballad to "dicty," black slang for "fancy." Of course, the "Wicked Stage" lyrics should have used *On* but for the extra note in Kern's melody. And once Jerome Kern composed a tune, behold *it was* very good; and he rested.

produces a splendid scene in which Van Heflin shows the young Kern (Robert Walker) how to orchestrate "Ka-lu-a" at the piano. As Heflin conjures up *divisi* strings, a solo flute, and the brass, the soundtrack produces them, a score-master's in-joke dating back at least to Rodgers and Hart's *On Your Toes* on Broadway, in 1936.

"Ka-lu-a" raises an interesting question, and Kern buffs may be wondering if MGM included the song's "Fred Fisher" bass line. Though mainly a composer, Fisher was the lyricist (and publisher) of "Dardanella," from 1919, one of the many Asian-themed Tin Pan Alley numbers of the early twentieth century. "Dardanella"'s verse and refrain run on an *ostinato* of three rising notes (C-D-E in the published sheet, in C Major), and Fisher gave fair warning to "Thieves and pirates!" in an ad on *Variety*'s front page, promising to go after any attempt to "infringe on the melody or lyric" of "Dardanella." Of course Fisher was thinking more precisely of that three-note hook, because the song's melody was rudimentary and the lyrics banal (as in "Allah knows my love for you/And he tells you to be true"). Incredibly, Kern used Fisher's hook in "Ka-lu-a," just a bit later, in *Good Morning, Dearie* (1921). Fisher sued and won, though the court granted him only $250.00; and "Dardanella" faded away, while "Ka-lu-a" remained a standard. Naturally, MGM would use it—but while Heflin is constructing its very busy orchestration, that infamous hook is nowhere to be heard.

Meanwhile, it would appear, at least so far, that our Broadway masters never quite made the movie musical their own. Each of them creates at least one unique masterpiece—but Hollywood really does want to cater to its three audiences all at once, and American musical theatre at its best has often been a first-audience art form—*Strike Up the Band*, *Porgy and Bess*, *Johnny Johnson*, *Street Scene*, *The Golden Apple*, *Candide*, *Follies*. So let us turn now to the most sophisticated of all the Harms group, to learn how he fared among the caterers and appeasers of the Hollywood ateliers.

CHAPTER 7

cVɔ

Cole Porter

Porter was gay, which made him perfect for sexy, crazy musical comedy. A composer-lyricist, he wrote with the clear-eyed perspective of the outsider who learns to imitate the "normal" folk in order to survive, giving him comprehension of their ways that they themselves do not possess.

For example, a number such as *Kiss Me, Kate*'s "Too Darn Hot," running through a list of typical love couples, blithely cites "a marine for his queen." This is the naughty and above all gay Porter, dog whistling to blasé know-it-alls like himself. You only read Winchell's column: they're *in* it.

But *Kiss Me, Kate* gives us also "So in Love," treating the mixture of passion and masochism that sustains many a relationship. And it is worth noting that Porter assembled a vast catalogue of songs written not just for women characters but looking at life from a woman's point of view, whether satiric ("A Lady Needs a Rest") or romantic ("No Lover [for me]").

In fact, Porter was utterly unlike the rest of the Harms group: a WASP of wealthy midwestern family with access to the fabled elite and a post-Yale youth spent largely in Europe, while his colleagues were first-generation Americans tied to New York. Porter's outlook was cosmopolitan and worldly; he would never have written a piece like Rodgers and Hart's "Manhattan," which is clever but corny, all about sweethearts seeing the sights. Porter's Manhattan is where Ethel Merman torches for lost love, where gangsters prowl and "rum-ridden debutramps" book suites in little-known clinics where accidents of life are neutralized. Where marriages (such as his own) are arranged because unescorted women could not go out at night and gay men must beard.

And there is this: Porter had some classical training and was ambitious and artistic, but he wanted popular success above all. He could write simple, in Alley style: "Old Fashioned Garden," "There'll Always Be a Lady Fair," "Me and Marie," "Bianca," "True Love." Yet he yearned as well to elaborate, with references to mythology, history, gilded Society names; with expansive musical structures; with discussions of no-no subject matter, a "cocotte" here and a "gigolo" there; with an obsession with sex and its sidetracks. And what of his musical subterfuges? He repeats a single pitch thirty-five times in the verse, launches the refrain in the submediant major seventh (and resolves it on not the tonic but the tonic major seventh), running the melody in a shockingly chromatic descending line for ten measures, and building the B strain on a variant of the A...all in one song, "Night and Day." And this wizard's labyrinth of pop music opens up so simply, logically, when you hear it that it stands on ASCAP's list of its ten biggest sellers.

So: how was Porter to marry his popular and elitist sides in Hollywood? Vernon Duke, Kurt Weill, and Leonard Bernstein—all classically trained composers who also wrote popular—found the movies more or less hostile. When Weill, in 1937, was in California trying to get work, producer Walter Wanger (as Weill reported to his wife, Lotte Lenya, in a missive published in their collected letters) told Weill, "Your music is distinguished and I don't want distinguished music." At just about this same time, Porter himself noted that "Polished, urbane, and adult playwrighting in the musical field is strictly a creative luxury."

But Porter loved Hollywood. Porterologist Robert Kimball has found an interview with Dorothy Kilgallen in which Porter likened life in the movie colony to "living on the moon....When I first came here they told me 'You'll be so bored you'll die; nobody talks about anything but pictures.' After I was here a week, I discovered I didn't want to talk about anything else myself."

Was that because the movies were where America's many several curiosities about beauty, power, and sex came crashing triumphantly together? Because they were what Porter was curious about, too. Irving Berlin found the whole place foolishly favoring the owners over the talent. Richard Rodgers thought the studio apparatus cumbersome, a too-many-cooks broth. Jerome Kern let its easy ways distract him from his ambitions.

But Porter liked the place. It was frisky and colorful, a musical comedy come to life. And while Famous in New York meant nothing to most movie makers, Famous for Hit Music gave one status. True, that didn't stop them from mangling Porter's scores. Paramount's *Anything Goes* (1936) retained— of a layout that produced five standards—only "I Get a Kick Out Of You" (for one verse and chorus), "You're the Top" (for the verse, multiple choruses, and a reprise), "There'll Always Be a Lady Fair," and the title song (during the credits, and only the first A of the chorus). Perhaps the studio felt the very chromatic "All Through the Night" was too lustrous a ballad, though it would have sounded great on Bing Crosby, who starred with Merman (in, of course, her original role), Charlie Ruggles as Public Enemy Number 13, and Ida Lupino as Crosby's amour. And no doubt "Blow, Gabriel, Blow" struck someone as too parodistically holy-roller in tone for the conservative but not fanatically religious second audience.

That said, *Anything Goes* is an extremely enjoyable movie. It follows the New York storyline closely, albeit rewritten by a passel of studio hirelings. Better, the director was Lewis Milestone, whose salient quality was pace, not just in playing tempo but in an avidly mobile camera that chases the story along while surprising us on the way. Thus, Ruggles needs to fashion a beard for stowaway Crosby to hide behind and lures a dowager with a pekinese into a chat while the doggy gets his hair clipped to make the whiskers. But we don't see the shaving: Milestone holds the view on Ruggles' conversation with that grandest of Hollywood grande dames, Margaret Dumont, as the two consider prison reform:

DUMONT: Surely you don't believe in capital punishment.
RUGGLES: What was good enough for my father is good enough for me!

Then Dumont gets up to leave—and Milestone finally shoots the pooch, which we had forgot about. And, sure enough, he's a Mexican hairless now.

The new numbers, all by studio people, are pleasant enough, especially the film's sole production number, "The Shanghai-De-Ho," for Merman and dancing girls in Asian mock-up style. Presumably Crosby wanted new songs he could toy with in his thirties swing manner, for he inflects both "[I'm gonna get a] Moonburn [when I'm with you tonight] and "My Heart and I" in their second choruses. And, again, Milestone uses the camera as a magician uses his rabbit hat, focusing "My Heart and I" on not the singing Crosby but the listening Lupino, thereby keeping the romance central in a script that is almost entirely farcical, almost anti-romance. It is worth adding that the very successful revision of the stage *Anything Goes* invariably in use today is at pains to emphasize the love plot in a way the original 1934 show failed to.

Interestingly, Porter was asked to create some new lyrics for "You're the Top," less to tone down its innuendo than to update its cultural references. Porter biographer William McBrien found in Yale University's Porter archives a note on this, mentioning that lyricist Ted Fetter was helping him. Still, the best new line (heard in the song's reprise) has Porter's autograph, when Crosby believes his romance is fini. "I'm the floor," he sorrowfully sings, "when the ball is over."

Two years earlier, Porter presented Broadway with an *Anything Goes* that was meant to be an Absolutely Guaranteed Popular Hit. Yes, it was sophisticated, but it was also zany fun. "After six weeks," Lynn Fontanne once said, of Broadway audiences, "it's all tourists." Meaning that, when a Porter show is hot, the Porterites flock to it, getting all the double meanings and allusions to la dolce vita. After that, a less fully evolved public misses the hottest jests. Then, in 1935, Porter presented Broadway with a show he wrote for himself, the aforementioned *Jubilee*, with his most experimental score, so vast and busy that its standards, "Begin the Beguine" and "Just One Of Those Things," did not at first get a chance to endear themselves. Despite the best set of notices till *Brigadoon*, twelve years later, *Jubilee* failed.

So Porter thought he'd best concoct another Absolutely Guaranteed Popular Hit—and that's when he went to Hollywood, working for MGM on an original, *Born To Dance* (1936), Eleanor Powell's follow-up to *Broadway Melody of 1936*. The studio was building Powell—she has, really, the title part—but it was building James Stewart as well, here in his first out-and-out lead role, a singing (and, slightly, a dancing) part at that. A three-couples tale with an injection of backstager Plot C, *Born To Dance* was also a showcase for the score. "Seven Cole Porter songs you'll love!" the ads promised—and of course MGM wanted the popular Porter. Indeed, *he* wanted the popular Porter: that's why the gods made Hollywood. Yet even here he saved a bit of the score for himself.

So *Born To Dance* comprises some songs for the masses, some songs for the first and second audiences...and one song for Porter. He's at his best here in all three idioms, but part of what makes *Born To Dance* sing so wonderfully is the MGM music department and its composer-arrangers Herbert Stothart (who was at Metro from 1929 on) and Roger Edens (who had landed at the studio in 1935). Their imagination in putting a number together, with full awareness of how the music affects the optics, was elemental in the dominance of the "MGM musical."[1]

There was not much the team could do with *Born To Dance*'s opening number, "Rolling Home." It's a clever episode made of several different themes introducing the male characters, all Navy men. Still, it's basically just an "anchors aweigh" sort of choral piece with solos (though Stewart's episode, a Hawaiian reminiscence, brings in a guitar-and-jug-band accompaniment

1. Today, this term usually denotes titles of the 1940s and 1950s. But the "MGM musical" was a concept even in the 1930s, when the studio's generous budgets provisioned spectacle scenes unknown to other studios' output. Remember, too, that while Warner Bros. pioneered sound, it was MGM that produced the first all-sound musical, the first of the *Broadway Melodys*.

that is too charmingly inane to have turned up over at Pandro Berman's soigné workshop at RKO).

Porter gets even cleverer in "Rap Tap on Wood," Eleanor Powell's first dance scene. It starts in the dominant seventh on a twisty, syncopated tune that doesn't locate the tonic till the eighth measure; the bridge develops the A strain instead of refreshing the melody as in most songs; and Porter sneaks in a four-measure coda to the bridge before returning to the A: in all, a difficult number to absorb. But once Powell has cleared the vocal, she can go into her exhibition, and this song was, indeed, born to dance. The film has been fun to this point; now it's electrifying, because for all his sophistication Porter has provided something all three audiences can respond to: a flashy turn by the greatest woman dancer in Hollywood history.

MGM's music department finally gets its showpiece in the ensuing "Hey, Babe, Hey," a quodlibet in bumptious three-quarter time wherein three different tunes are heard, one after the other and then all three simultaneously. Irving Berlin, we know, popularized the form after Gilbert and Sullivan had made it a feature of their choral writing, but these worthies mashed up only two countering melodies. Three at once is special. (And, after Porter, Harold Rome would put five or six tunes together, in *Call Me Mister*, *Fanny*, and *Destry Rides Again*.) "Hey, Babe, Hey"'s singers— Powell and Stewart, Una Merkel and Sid Silvers, and Frances Langford and Buddy Ebsen—vary from good enough to dodgy, but that only enhances the number's populist attitude. There's no question about it: this is a third-audience composition. And when Porter first auditioned it for the studio brass, they liked it so much they gathered around the piano to sing it themselves. Yes, even L. B. Mayer.

The music-department whizzes saw "Hey, Babe, Hey" as the kind of thing you hear when riding a carousel, so they scored the number within the sound style of a calliope. For its part, the choreography creates a narrative in which the six leads informally bond, each within his or her coupling and each couple within the sextet as a whole, but the aim above all is goofy charm. Thus, at one point all six line up, James Stewart looking thrillingly absurd in his officer's regal trim as he jumps to click his heels. Marrying what we hear to what we see, one episode finds Ebsen sucking up six sodas through six straws, the latter attached through a metal rod that Ebsen uses as a harmonica. Backed by four sailors playing ocarinas and a piccolo, he follows his vocal with a rubberlegs dance in the style of our old friend Al Norman: an ingratiating blend of amiable and zany.

"Hey, Babe, Hey" can be seen as Exhibit A in Hollywood's ability to coax Tin Pan Alley informality and simplicity out of the ambitious gurus of the Harms group, even as an imaginative staging gives the number a unique presence. Beyond that, it's Couples Night at MGM, and with Powell and Stewart matched, the studio must now find someone to sabotage the romance—and that would be Virginia Bruce, as a tempestuous musical-comedy diva. Paramount reveled in these glamorous characters, but MGM didn't trust them. They walk out on shows—during a Depression!—because theatre is just a hobby to them. Their day job is homewrecking.

Of course, Porter is known as the Society songwriter, where behavior is comme il faut and the parties are as exclusive as Brigadoon. Surely he will disapprove of Bruce's outlaw ways. In fact, while Porter *lived* in Society he *wrote*, very fondly, about riffraff—about Ethel Merman and Jimmy Durante, or June Havoc and Bobby Clark, the broad and the hustler. It amuses him to watch Virgina Bruce play the men. Powell has Stewart sewn up in any case; let Bruce have her fun.

So, for her establishing number, Porter went all out, and this one he wrote for Porter: a dazzling musical scene in which Bruce, as one Lucy James, cruises the ocean to arrive on shipboard, charms the captain (Raymond Walburn), and breaks into her ID solo, something like the evil twin of the Heroine's Wanting Song. This latter genre, indispensable in the classic stage musical from "Kiss Me Again" in *Mlle. Modiste* (1905) to "I'm the Greatest Star" in *Funny Girl* (1964), isn't at all common in the movie musical. When it turns up, as in *The Wizard of Oz*'s "Over the Rainbow," we are reminded of how seldom American cinema needs to "read" the heroine's motivating spirit, possibly because the close-up opens up the character to the audience visually instead of musically.

So Eleanor Powell has no Wanting Song in *Born To Dance*; rather, the aforementioned "Rap Tap on Wood" is her Wanting Dance, so to say. But Virginia Bruce gets to tell us what *she's* about, in a musical sequence made of two separate numbers. First comes "Entrance of Lucy James," which segues right into "Love Me, Love My Pekinese"—the ID solo referred to above—because the willful Miss James has a willful doggy named Cheeky, and both Must Be Obeyed. The playful lyrics (LUCY: Cheeky still thinks gentlemen are all trees. SAILORS: Cheeky, please!) sit on the bouncy rhythms with aplomb, but the real gem of the scene is the "Entrance," because it gave Porter a chance to slip into his "operetta" mode of sung conversation.

This is a perilous format, because it pushes movie realism to the crash point: not only are characters singing on a battleship (with the usual "non-existent" orchestra supporting them), but they're "conversing" in music. It's like *Aida* without the opera house. Where are we? But then, as with Rodgers and Hart's rhythmic dialogue and the Romberg-Hammerstein operetta movies, Porter's sung screenplay plays tag with the notion that movies are "real." They aren't. Like the theatre, film is fantasy. And song is fantasy; it fits right in.

Besides, Porter makes up for it with strong ballads that root the action in familiar territory. Stewart got "Easy To Love," cut from the Broadway *Anything Goes* (though restored in the current performing version), and Bruce was given a new piece, "I've Got You Under My Skin," in the "Latin rhythm" format that Porter, of all the Harms group,[2] really made his own (as with "Begin the Beguine" and "My Heart Belongs To Daddy"). We first see more than hear "Skin," used by the nightclub ballroom team of Georges and Jalna. Then, as the audience applauds, the camera picks up Bruce and Stewart at a table, and, when they're alone, she makes her move with the vocal, starting very abruptly, without a verse. Stewart does not look happy, and by the time Bruce walks out of the show and Powell goes on in her stead, Powell lifts the national morale with a mad-for-dance anthem, "Swingin' the Jinx Away."

Porter played another trick in this one. He wrote the song's verse in the minor (on the notion of a land laid low with Depression), as a chromatic melody moving by half-steps from the fifth tone of the scale to the seventh and down again. And of course the refrain (as Cab Calloway reveals the cure to F.D.R.: "Give 'em swing!") moves into the major. Writers often note Porter's use of minor keys; less commented on is his habit of shifting back and forth between them. As he stated, in a number from the stage show *Seven Lively Arts* (1944), "How strange the change from major to minor."

Note, too, that "Swingin' the Jinx Away" is a New Dance Sensation without a dance: it's a New Rhythm Sensation, what happened when the twenties jazz combo went big band in the 1930s. And this is one *big* number—the finale, in fact. Powell has taken over for Virginia Bruce with so little time to spare that the marquee for the show, *Great Guns*, still star-bills Lucy James. On stage, Frances Langford and the boys, all in white, deliver the verse and chorus, along with a patter section ("Just look at those cowboys gaily swingin' on the range…"), another songwriting element

---

2. We should note that, starting in 1936, the Harms imprint was largely (but by no means entirely) subsumed by Chappell & Co., through a reorganization of the music-publishing platform owned by Warner Bros., without altering its artistic credo in the slightest. There were odd glitches—Jerome Kern came out via Harms through his last composition, "Nobody Else But Me," for the 1946 *Show Boat*, except for the previously mentioned "Lonesome Walls," a Chappell sheet. Chappell's monopoly on the best Broadway songwriters began to give way in the 1940s, when, for instance, M. Witmark & Sons and Sam Fox, respectively, published *On the Town* and *Brigadoon*. By the 1960s, such new names as Jerry Herman, Jerry Bock and Sheldon Harnick, and John Kander and Fred Ebb signed with either Edwin H. Morris and Co., Inc. or Valando Music Corp., and Harms-Chappell lost its dominion over the sound of Broadway.

Porter used more than other writers.[3] Now the heretofore theatre-true design expands for one of those spectacles that no playhouse could contain, as Powell emerges, in black, on a six-gun battleship, and the number goes patriotic while everyone breaks into "Columbia, the Gem of the Ocean," with its key line, "Three cheers for the red, white, and blue." And that brilliant MGM music department gets the music to go big, too, letting the orchestra play the "Jinx" refrain at the same time. It's colossal: who knew that these two melodies would dovetail so neatly?—unless, of course, Porter himself wrote "Jinx" to integrate it with "Columbia" in just this way.

So Powell hits her pose-for-the-finish marks, the camera backs up to take it all in, the six big guns go boom!, and MGM gets a hit out of it all. Still, after three Powell backstagers in a row—*Broadway Melody of 1936*, *Born To Dance*, and *Broadway Melody of 1938*—the studio needed to reestablish their star as more than just a "Broadway Melody girl." It happens that one of the stage musicals bought up in 1929–30 and not filmed at the time was *Rosalie*, a Ziegfeld production for Marilyn Miller in 1928, with a co-written score, half by Sigmund Romberg and P. G. Wodehouse and half by the Gershwins. *Rosalie* was what we might call a "headline musical," uniting two of the most publicized personalities of the late 1920s, Charles Lindbergh and Queen Marie of Rumania (as it was then spelled). What if Lindbergh loves the queen's daughter, already betrothed to some noble peppernoodle, and what if she runs off to pose as . . . oh, how about in drag as a West Point cadet?

Another Ziegfeld smash. It's perfect for Powell, and as MGM's aborted 1930 *Rosalie* was going to sport a new score, why not bring Cole Porter back and make a meal of it? Why not, even, outdo *Born To Dance* in every way? That film was musical comedy. *This* film will be operetta. So let's cast a real singer opposite Powell—Nelson Eddy. And why not amplify the Porter score with classy bonus cuts—that famous Caruso aria from the opera *Martha* for Eddy to run through, a cappella; the wedding anthem "Oh, Promise Me" (which is actually an old show tune, interpolated into Reginald De Koven's *Robin Hood* [1891]); "Anchors Aweigh" and other military pep-ups; and, for the choreography, the Polovyetzki Dances from *Prince*

---

3. A distinct strain of Gilbert and Sullivan—who would appear to have introduced the patter song into the musical—runs through Porter's work, not only in his choral quodlibets but in these sections of verbal trickery found between the refrains of many numbers. In G & S, the patter is usually fast-paced (e.g., *The Pirates of Penzance*'s "I am the very model of a modern major-general . . ."), but Porter preferred slow tempos to enable clarity of diction. (In rehearsal, he would blow a whistle whenever a singer wasn't articulating the words clearly.) Perhaps the best-known Porter patter section lies inside *Kiss Me, Kate*'s "Where Is the Life That Late I Led?," beginning "In dear Milano, where are you, Momo?."

Igor and a bit of Tchaikofsky (the slow movement of the Sixth Symphony, unfortunately jazzed up a bit; the Borodin is unmolested)? And where *Born To Dance*'s big number had some two hundred people, *Rosalie*'s will have two thousand.

Though musically rich, *Rosalie* was poor in comedy, depending mainly on Frank Morgan (repeating his Broadway role as Rosalie's father, the King of Romanza) and Billy Gilbert with his asinine sneezing fits. The movie does have the wonderful Edna May Oliver as Romanza's queen. Here she is not amusingly tart as she usually was but fiercely unpleasant, so much so that Morgan hides behind a dummy he calls Nappy, who says the things Morgan's afraid to. Porter got a song out of it, "Why Should I Care?," which is the establishing song of either Morgan or the dummy, depending on how one looks at it. The melody bears a slightly folkish-Slavic (and minor-key) feeling, but it's on the dreary side, and in truth *Rosalie* isn't a great Porter event. The hits were "In the Still of the Night" and the title song, both for Eddy, and we should pause to retell a famous story about the latter.

To start with, coming up with a title number for *Rosalie* was not something Porter even wanted to do—it was MGM's need, for PR purposes. True, ten of Porter's stage shows bear title songs—but they're almost all situation numbers—"Wake Up and Dream," "Anything Goes," "You Never Know," "Kiss Me, Kate," "Can-Can." That Tin Pan Alley notion of building a eulogy around a girl's name—as with "Margie" or "Nola"—was Porter's idea of a non-event. He wrote them sporadically, but mainly under duress; *Kiss Me, Kate*'s "Bianca" was created during the tryout because the show's jeune premier, Harold Lang, threatened not to play the opening without a solo.

Stuck with having to conjure up a "Rosalie," Porter came up with five different versions, but none pleased the author till a sixth seemed to work. However, L. B. Mayer told him it was "too highbrow" (as Porter wrote to Paul Whiteman, in a letter quoted in Stanley Green's *Encyclopedia of the Musical Film*). Mayer wondered if Porter was going wrong by trying to pitch his melodies to Eddy's gala baritone. "Forget you are writing for [that particular singer]," Mayer advised him. "Simply give us a good popular song."

The seventh "Rosalie" pleased Mayer and everybody else, yet for a "popular song" it's awfully clever. For one thing, the refrain's A strain starts on the dominant seventh instead of the tonic, and Porter draws the voice from the bridge back to the A on a rising glissando—yes, in the voice!—covering a tenth. (And Eddy does sing it, though he gets through it in a split-second; Porter wrote it to cover half a measure of slow fox trot.)

It's amusing to compare this "Rosalie" with the one Jimmy McHugh and Dorothy Fields wrote for MGM's aborted 1930 *Rosalie*. Their tune is at least pleasantly banal and there's a touch of De Sylva, Brown, and Henderson syncopation in the bridge. Further, Fields asserts some good old Tin Pan Alley wisdom in the lyrics: "You must not laugh at love," the singer warns Rosalie, "or some time love will laugh at you." Still, McHugh and Fields are plucking the strings of cliché, while Porter, though pressured to write in Alley mode, nevertheless found a way to make a dopey genre his own.

More comparing: we just saw Jerome Kern writing for Fred Astaire—and now Porter writes two Astaire films, *Broadway Melody of 1940* and *You'll Never Get Rich* (1941). Kern's Astaire is tender but hip, so snazzy in "Bojangles of Harlem" but also ready for the serene, long-lined Kern legato in "The Way You Look Tonight." Porter's Astaire, however, is a smooth show-biz pro with a dreamy undertone. That is, Kern hears the different parts of Astaire—comic, lover, artist. Porter says there is only Astaire the performer, because nothing is real in Astaire's art but class and talent, and the way Astaire wears them they are one and the same.

But let's remember that "Night and Day," which Porter wrote for Astaire some years before, became one of the biggest hits of the twentieth century. They were singing it in Bali. And "Night and Day" sees Astaire—sees love, really—as obsessive. Kern's love songs are love songs. But Porter's love songs are an appeal to the gods in charge of desperate acts. So we expect to get "more" Astaire in these two Porter films.

Broadway Melody of 1940, under the surveillance of MGM's honchos, devoted above all to protecting images—of the stars, of America, of show biz, and of course of love—forces Porter to rein himself in somewhat. There is no "Love Me, Love My Pekinese" in this old-fashioned Plot A backstager (with two men instead of two women: Astaire and George Murphy vie for Eleanor Powell). Rather, Porter gives his stars show-off pieces in L. B. Mayer's "popular song" style.

So we get the ultra-basic onstage number for Astaire and Murphy, "Please Don't Monkey With Broadway," setting up a challenge dance culminating in a duel of canes. Porter left the Eleanor Powell vocal, "I Am the Captain,"[4] to others; it's specialty material, beneath him. Then comes the first ballad, "Between You and Me," given to Murphy, who even gets a post-vocal dance with Powell, which confuses us: is *he* going to get the girl? And

---

4. This number was the first time Powell sang on screen; in her earlier films she was dubbed (by Marjorie Lane), though she had sung without problems on Broadway. The movie studios were at times dub-happy to a mysterious degree. For example, Rita Hayworth was constantly dubbed, though she had a viable singing voice. While we're footnoting, despite MGM's promoting Eleanor Powell as "The Broadway Melody Girl," she was never top-billed in the series, starred only after Jack Benny, then Robert Taylor, and now Fred Astaire.

the song itself has tang, using the same syncopated, repeated-note melodic cell five times, innovatively unifying all the refrain's phrases.

Astaire gets into the love business in "I've Got My Eyes On You"—but it's an up tune, not a ballad. Starting at the piano, an accomplished player, he goes into his dance *with the song as his partner*, in a swing version of the melody, using the sheet music as his foil.[5] Okay, it's romantic, sort of. But it's a solo. And the film's second ballad, "I Concentrate on You," is given to a non-character, baritone Douglas McPhail, setting up for a rare Powell ballet sequence, complete with tutu. Rare? It's downright improbable, and it leads to a grandiose pas de deux for Powell and Astaire in matching harlequin duds. Either these two are miscast in their own dance number or this film isn't deploying its talent properly. And it compromises Astaire's image: because he's the wonderful paradox of musical comedy, the Mr. Plain whose stunning song and dance turns him into Lochinvar. But Harlequin?: no.

Maybe *Broadway Melody of 1940* is simply too lush a place for Astaire. Over at Columbia, *You'll Never Get Rich* mates Astaire and Porter much more naturally, and his co-star, Rita Hayworth, makes every scene sensual. Suddenly, Astaire sings a *love* song to his *lover*, "So Near and Yet So Far," in Porter's habitual Latin rhythm style: and he's back in form.

But then, *You'll Never Get Rich* is unpretentious, while *Broadway Melody of 1940* is the grand-opera version of a movie musical, crazed and arty. Its big number uses one of Porter's longest songs, "Begin the Beguine" (a save from Porter's *Jubilee*, as I've said), and while the words and music are about romance, the staging is about technique. All in black and white amid changing vistas, it starts with contralto Lois Hodnott's operatic vocal, after which Powell leads the corps for a while—and this segues into the first Astaire-Powell partnership, in tropical-flamenco costumes on a mirrored floor.

But we're just getting started: is this still "Begin the Beguine"? Yes: for now a girls' close-harmony quartet takes over in swing style till the two stars return, attired in white MGM ace-dancer business casual to click out rather than caress the happy ending. They don't begin the beguine. They finalize it, spectacularly, with a tops-in-taps expertise that lacks the needy wonder of the way Astaire's RKOs with Rogers used to end. But this is how Astaire and Powell conjugate the verb "to love." Professionally. Coolly.

---

5. There's a booboo in this number. An unseen Powell watches Astaire dancing, and after he finishes she claps—but, behind her, a half-hidden grip is where he shouldn't be, right in shot, moving a table. The curious can catch the moment on the DVD at 1:03:18.

Apparently Porter simply didn't hear any sweetheart music in these two. He did write "I Happen To Be in Love," presumably for one or both of them. But it's jaunty rather than fond, and while it was published with the other songs from the film with the *Broadway Melody of 1940* cover art, it isn't in the release print.

In other words, Astaire and Powell never connect vocally. *Broadway Melody of 1940* is a bit like *My Fair Lady* without "I Could Have Danced All Night" or "I've Grown Accustomed To Her Face": the cues that tell us how the central pair feel about each other. It suggests that Jerome Kern wrote more for character, while Cole Porter wrote for performers.

Now there came a bunch of adaptations from Porter's Broadway, particularly notable for how much Porter went missing: *Panama Hattie* (1942), *Du Barry Was a Lady* (1943), *Let's Face It* (1943), *Something For the Boys* (1944). The last-named retained from the New York score only the title song, and Perry Como's dégagé rendition of the sleepy "I Wish We Didn't Have To Say Good Night" (by Jimmy McHugh and Harold Adamson) reminds us once again that Hollywood wanted basic art in which the author or authors will be undetectable, and Porter was a writer whose gifts were ever on display in a personable sense. He had a style. No one else sounded like him and he never sounded like anyone else—except when he wrote his biggest hit, a "popular song" to awe even MGM's Mayer yet with quirky touches all the same.

This was "Don't Fence Me In," the plea of a cowboy threatened with, first, jail and, in the second verse, marriage. The piece is rich in imagery that is far from "basic"—"cottonwood trees," "on my cayuse" (Webster: "a native range horse"), "the ridge where the West commences." Porter had written the song in the mid-1930s, and he had a collaborator, one Bob Fletcher. Robert Kimball lays out for us the complicated saga of the number's creation in *The Complete Lyrics of Cole Porter*, but, in my own digest version: Porter needed a cowboy song for a Fox film, *Adios, Argentina*, and Fletcher, who knew the movie's producer, offered a song whose lyrics Porter drew on for a piece for which he took sole credit. To prove how much Porter owed Fletcher, Kimball reproduced the original lyric, and, indeed, Porter really did little more than shape Fletcher's evocations, including, almost verbatim, the phrases quoted above.

Adios, Argentina was never made, but "Don't Fence Me In" found its way into Warner Bros.' *Hollywood Canteen* (1944), sung by a real cowboy, Roy Rogers, and the number charmed millions to whom the name Cole Porter meant absolutely nothing. Ironically, this was the very time when Porter began to suffer his famous slump in a series of stage shows that, whether hit or failure, failed to generate the excitement attendant upon the Porter scores of the 1930s, from *Gay Divorce* to *Anything Goes* to *Du Barry Was a Lady*.

Classic Elements of Hollywood's Broadway

Rose-Marie without "Indian Love Call." This (now lost) first of three films drawn from the famous stage operetta of 1924 was a silent (1928). An operetta without its vocals is like France without champagne. But *The Jazz Singer*, released four months earlier, had only just introduced singing to Hollywood. Within a year, the studios would be producing plenty of all-talking, all-singing, all-dancing musicals, the utmost in sound films, many written fresh for the screen by Broadway masters. *Above*, left to right, Mountie Sgt. House Peters, heroine Joan Crawford, and innocent murder suspect James Murray.

Above, another lost film: Guinn Williams and the real-life Funny Girl, Fanny Brice, in a part-talkie, *My Man* (1928). A silent containing song spots for the star, in the *Jazz Singer* manner, this film was a traditional weepie with a very untraditional heroine, a New York favorite but too "special" for the national taste. It is as if Broadway and Hollywood were two different countries, with divisive sets of language, currency, mores. At times, they engage in trade. More often, however, they get into disputes, especially over how special the stars and songs of a musical can be. A smash comic and singer—the Parisian Mistinguett introduced the song "My Man," but Brice made it her own—Brice never caught on in film. Ironically, after her death, Hollywood was finally ready for her . . . as played by Barbra Streisand in *Funny Girl*.

Above, "The Wedding of the Painted Doll," in the first full-scale movie musical, *The Broadway Melody*. Note that, from the start, Hollywood needed New York as an authenticity enabler in its backstagers—it's the *Broadway* melody, because, obviously, there wasn't any Hollywood melody to speak of yet. Further, in another usage of the stage, the chorus above is all-female, even Buster Brown (at far left) and the bridegroom and preacher (at center). Women in drag had been a routine feature of the stage musical since the days of early burlesque, in the 1870s. Nevertheless, MGM commissioned *The Broadway Melody*'s songs from Nacio Herb Brown and Arthur Freed, not New Yorkers but California residents.

Two adaptations from Broadway: *above*, *The Cocoanuts* (note Zeppo and Groucho Marx and, at far right, Margaret Dumont). *Below*, *Top Speed*, with Laura Lee and Joe E. Brown.

Both *The Cocoanuts* and *Top Speed* came out in 1930, when a musical-weary public began a boycott of the form. To survive, *The Cocoanuts* dropped almost all of its score and *Top Speed* used just a few songs—new ones, by California writers. Then, in 1933, it was *Everybody onstage for the garlands number!* as *42nd Street*, *above*, brought the musical back into favor—again, with a score by a neighborhood team, Harry Warren and Al Dubin. Look for Dick Powell (at far left), director Warner Baxter (at center, back to us), and star Bebe Daniels (at right). Sharp eyes will pick out Ginger Rogers (seventh from left, sitting with the man in the dark sweater) as pretentious Anytime Annie, complete with monocle.

Each studio had a first-rate home songwriting team, like Brown and Freed or Dubin and Warren. Yet Hollywood couldn't get along without the big Broadway names, and by the mid-1930s they were dominant, as here with Irving Berlin's *Follow the Fleet* (1936), starring Fred Astaire and Ginger Rogers. *Above*, the Second Couple, Harriet Hilliard and Randolph Scott. Hilliard was a band singer (and, later, the better half of television's *The Adventures of Ozzie and Harriet*). Scott, however, neither sang nor danced. He just hunked. Hollywood created this breakaway from the Broadway model, wherein the romantic leading man sang as a rule. In the movie musical, however, not only Scott but Tyrone Power, William Holden, and many others could play a sweetheart without sharing in the music.

Cole Porter's best original Hollywood score was for *Born To Dance* (1936), *above*, with Frances Langford, Buddy Ebsen, Eleanor Powell, James Stewart, Una Merkel, and Sid Silvers. Porter's second-best was for *Broadway Melody of 1940*, *right*, with a piquant-looking Powell and Fred Astaire.

Composer Harold Arlen and lyricist E. Y. Harburg had established them-selves as a Hollywood (and Broadway) team good at non-contextual num-bers, suitable for any occasion and ideal for the revue-like song spots that Hollywood producers loved. Story numbers were too "special"—that word again. Too intellectual. Yet the Arlen-Harburg songs for *The Wizard of Oz* (1939) were so joyfully full of story content that the two writers rein-vented themselves, separately and together. Now they were admired as masters of narrative music. Broadway's *Bloomer Girl* (1944; never filmed) was their best score together, but *The Wizard* gave them their turning point. *Above*, Jack Haley, Judy Garland, and Ray Bolger about to launch the "Lions and tigers and bears" chant and meet Bert Lahr's Cowardly Lion.

Besides commissioning original work from Broadway writers and adapting their shows, Hollywood created the jukebox musical, in the song-cavalcade film. *Above*, James Cagney as George M. Cohan in *Yankee Doodle Dandy* (1942), built on a foundation of Cohan numbers. *Easter Parade* (1948) reprises forty years' worth of Irving Berlin, though "A Couple of Swells," *right*, with Judy Garland and Fred Astaire, was new.

Movie versions of shows often preserved elements of the stagings, as here with Jerome Robbins' "Small House of Uncle Thomas" ballet in *The King and I* (1956). *Above left*, Yuriko as runaway slave Eliza; *right*, Gemze de Lappe is "wicked Simon of Legree."

The *Gypsy* film (1962), *above*, retained minor Broadway cast members but replaced Ethel Merman's Rose with Rosalind Russell's (here with Karl Malden). Alan Jay Lerner, Broadway's most enthusiastic Californian, created with Frederick Loewe a new-for-Hollywood masterpiece in *Gigi* (1958). *Right*, Leslie Caron and Louis Jourdan strike a PR attitude.

On Broadway, Camelot was quite a spectacle. Mononymous couturier Adrian, who had quit when Garbo did—"Glamor is over," he explained—came out of retirement to design the costumes. (Tony Duquette took over at Adrian's death.) The resplendent movie (1968) was even grander, showing much that the stage was unable to: combat (*above*), a rite-of-spring picnic (*opposite top*, Vanessa Redgrave at left), and even the politically subversive adultery of Lancelot (Franco Nero) and Guenevere (Redgrave again), which brings down a kingdom. Still, the use of movie stars instead of singing stars turned one of Broadway's most musical of musicals into a talkeretta.

Even *Hello, Dolly!*, much tidier than *Camelot*—*Dolly!* takes place in a single day without a castle in sight—had to go big on screen (1969). Some of the vocals took to dancing all over the map in a veritable pageant of choreography. *Opposite top*, "Before the Parade Passes By" was an end-of-days explosion, the biggest number in Hollywood history. But *Dolly!* at least boasted a genuine star singer in Barbra Streisand, and, unlike the ponderous *Camelot*, it has an irresistible *joie de vivre*.

Bob Fosse's take on *Cabaret* (1972) changed everything, including the relatively innocent "Money Song" into the gruesome "Money, Money," *right*, with Liza Minnelli and Joel Grey.

As if Broadway's songwriters didn't have enough trouble competing with rock, Hollywood discovered a new market uninterested in theatre music: kids. Still, the supreme "youth" musical was yet another Broadway transfer, *Grease* (1978). High school principal Eve Arden (center) led the adults, but the public was primarily thrilled with the enfants terribles, such as John Travolta and Jeff Conaway (respectively flanking the rightward group). *Everybody onstage for the hand-jive prom number*!

Perhaps the first sign that Porter was temporarily out of inspiration was *Something To Shout About* (1943), a Fox backstager with Don Ameche, Janet Blair, and Jack Oakie. It produced a hit, a love song that, because of its historical timing, expressed the longings of the lonely wartime wife, "You'd Be So Nice To Come Home To." This was Porter in one of his sentimental moods, pure feelings free of worldly perspective.

Something To Shout About has another pleasing number, "Hasta Luego" (meaning, roughly, "Be seeing you!"). The loss of the European cinema market led Hollywood to emphasize trade with Latin America, not only in distributing its films there but in attracting local talent, from tutti-frutti songstress Carmen Miranda to bandleader Xavier Cugat, encouraging them to work in their accustomed styles. This cultural exchange went over so well that Latin American rhythm numbers took pride of place in our calendar of song genres, peaking in the early 1940s but still commanding the national listening room through the 1950s.

We already know that Porter was a specialist in the form, but "Hasta Luego" is a trick number, using its "Lively Rumba Tempo" (as Porter directs in the sheet music) to revive the nineteenth-century story ballad. The classic example in this line is Charles K. Harris' "After the Ball," an interpolation in *Show Boat* to this very day: the first verse launches the story, followed by the chorus. The second verse advances the story—but the second chorus is unchanged. The third verse ends the story, and once more the chorus, still apropos, is heard without alteration.

Thus, in "Hasta Luego"'s first verse, a señorita charms "all the ding-dong dandies," and then sings a sweet goodbye in the chorus. In the second verse, she rejuvenates a plutocrat, who contacts his wife and then sings *her* a sweet goodbye in the second chorus. Finally, the señorita takes the old guy for all he's worth, and then . . . that's right: *Hasta luego!*

The rest of *Something To Shout About*'s score, however, is third-rate,[6] and Porter's following four Broadway shows led the commentariat to declare him a has-been. Worse yet, this was when Porter suffered his big expensive

---

6. We can't move on without noting a piquant moment in this film, when Don Ameche has to use the telephone: as he picks up the receiver, some wiseguy asks him, "You sure you know how to use that thing?":

AMECHE: Are you kidding? I invented it.

This is a reference to Ameche's having played the title role in *The Story of Alexander Graham Bell* (1939)—an inside joke and an arrant violation of the movies' realism. On Broadway, such out-of-story gags were routine (only in musical comedy, of course, not in the artistically earnest musical play). On the other hand, one could view Ameche's retort as smart-ass bravado, the way one might say, "I was born telephoning," or "I've dialed more numbers than Mrs. Roosevelt has launched battleships."

famous MGM failure, *The Pirate* (1948), the first gay movie musical. Judy Garland appeared as a Caribbean lass forced into marriage with a fat frump of a mayor (Walter Slezak) while dreaming of a dashing, bloodthirsty brigand, Gene Kelly. Except Kelly is really just a strolling player. *Slezak* is the pirate.

It's a good story, and it was directed by Garland's then husband, Vincente Minnelli, with a quality seldom if ever commented on: his ability to throw every scene to his actors' unique strong points. Even the support shines here; Slezak, though a former sweetheart player (he introduced "I've Told Every Little Star" on Broadway), had grown into "characters" on the fiendish side, and his Macoco the ex-pirate is a raving bundle of fury and adventure hidden behind the facade of a humble village dignitary. It's masterly, because Slezak shows just enough menace to tip us off while gulling the other characters.

On the other hand, Kelly riots in display—at one point, he appears to swallow a lit cigarette, then shows it to us once again, exhaling the smoke. And Garland emphasizes two of her salient qualities: wistfulness and a nervous resistance to being controlled. We too easily forget what a wonderful comic she was. When she faints, her head lolls backward and, suddenly, her body just *goes*, like that, as if in a Buster Keaton silent.

Further, *The Pirate* boasts a fizzy script (by Albert Hackett and Frances Goodrich, from S. N. Behrman's adaptation of a German play for Alfred Lunt and Lynn Fontanne), because even if Macoco is a homicidal psychopath, *The Pirate* has a comic worldview. Everyone in it seems to be playing a role, so when Slezak furiously orders everyone out of a room and no one moves, Kelly very quietly snarls, "Get out," and the place instantly empties:

KELLY: (to Slezak) You should try underplaying some time. Very effective.

As well, we have director Minnelli's famous fashion sense, which moves the somewhat campy doings into the realm of the fabtastic. When Garland first meets Kelly, she is wearing the biggest and most bizarre snood in history. Even the sight of her, in her first shot, wearing a cross around her neck is startling. Yes, it's contextually correct for a young girl living a sheltered life in a Christian community. But it comes off as not a spiritual comfort but a bauble, even a minor blasphemy as a sample of Minnelli's binge accessorizing. When Kelly shows up sporting biceps rings, we wonder if this is *The Pirate* or *Rough Trade of the Caribbean*.

True, that only makes the film all the more entrancing. But Porter lets us down, with perfunctory ballads and plot numbers that do the job on site but are not worth rehearing (except for the ebullient "Be a Clown"). This was the height of the Porter slump; after a hit stay at Radio City Music Hall, *The Pirate* flopped badly, too flamboyant for the second and third audiences.

Only the arrival on Broadway of the smash *Kiss Me, Kate* reinstalled Porter as a Broadway champ. The following *Out Of This World* and *Can-Can* had wonderful scores but book problems (though *Can-Can* was a huge hit), and Porter's next new Hollywood work, MGM's *High Society* (1956), was second-division Porter. It hit his characteristic points—the Latin rhythm number in "Mind If I Make Love To You," the charm song full of syncopation and "wrong" notes in "You're Sensational." Porter even turned himself inside out in two numbers for Louis Armstrong, "High Society Calypso" (the Afro-Caribbean anticipation of reggae had just begun to trend in America) and, in duet with Bing Crosby, "Now You Has Jazz." And the film's hit, "True Love," is a waltz so simple neither the vocal nor the chorus has any syncopation whatever. This is smooth Porter, the Tin Pan Alley Porter who wants everyone to like him, even the tourists.

Everything about *High Society* is smooth—to a fault. Armstrong gives it flair, but everyone else is so relaxed he or she might be bantering between acts on a telethon. These are pale replicas of the characters so memorably portrayed in MGM's first go at this material, *The Philadelphia Story*, especially by Katharine Hepburn and Cary Grant. In their first moment, the two are in mid fight; she breaks his golf clubs and he starts to take a swing at her, recalls himself to manly grace, and simply shoves her self-satisfied mug out of shot.

This is not tough love. It's real anger, and while Philip Barry, who wrote the Broadway *Philadelphia Story*, is remembered only as a boulevardier, he was in fact a deeply religious writer who interspersed romantic comedies with allegories on the human condition, much as Cole Porter moved between popular and elite composition. Underneath Barry's Society folderol, provocative relationships undergo scrutiny as if in Christian parable; his characters are likable but worrisome—and, from First Couple Bing Crosby and Grace Kelly on down, there is nothing worrisome in this *High Society*.

And Fox's *Can-Can* (1960) is worse. The stage show was stuffed with the Parisian *belle époque*, but the movie appears to take place in Las Vegas, with leading man Frank Sinatra uttering his immortal cry, "Ring-a ding-a ding ding" and running around in "Strangers in the Night" hats to Nelson Riddle's "easy-listening LP" arrangements. Sinatra was in *High Society*, too, where he was just bland; in *Can-Can*, he's downright alien. But then, the casting generally is so out of touch with the story's placetime that the four men who perform a *danse apache* with Shirley MacLaine would be right at home in a gay bar on Clone Dress-Up Night.

Wait, there's less. The stage score is mauled with jukebox interpolations from the Porter inventory, and the numbers from *Can-Can* itself are usually assigned to the wrong character, as when the all-important "Live and Let Live"—a gay anthem as relevant as *La Cage aux Folles*'s "I Am What I Am"—is sung not by the freeliving hostess of an outlaw cabaret (as it was in the show) but by a judge. That is, the song should be Shirley MacLaine's ID number and the credo of the entire work—"Your business is your business," runs one lyric, "and my business is mine." In the movie, however, Judge Maurice Chevalier sings it, confusing the original work's association between bohemian frivolity and resolute individualism. *Can-Can*, at least on Broadway, offered a revolutionary notion to the 1950s: that what fascists call "sin" is what democrats call "liberty."

Worst of all, the direction, by Walter Lang, is so amateurish that one scene begins in sheer emptiness with Louis Jourdan gazing out a window, apparently waiting for the director to call, "Action!" He hears a knock at the door and crosses the room to open it, without a cut-in shot for kinetic pacing. He waits, he hears, he crosses. The actor is so embarrassed at this feeble setup that he calls out a "Yes?" just to do something while the camera turns.

MGM had managed the filming of *Kiss Me, Kate* (1953) and *Silk Stockings* (1957) with more aplomb, and Porter even tried out another trending pop style in a new number for *Silk Stockings*, "The Ritz Roll and Rock." (It's less rock and roll than a New Dance Sensation tricked out in brisk boogie-woogie and the blues' flatted third.) MGM even commissioned a Porter song-catalogue movie like Irving Berlin's, but *Wonderland*, with a script by Betty Comden and Adolph Green in something like 1955, was never filmed. The title refers not to Lewis Carroll's Alice but to a line from "Well, Did You Evah?," first heard on Broadway in *Du Barry Was a Lady* and slipped into *High Society* when Porter needed a duet for Crosby and Sinatra. It certainly suited the latter film's anemic atmosphere, as it features a duo trading news of disasters large and small with the utmost sangfroid. *Wonderland*'s plot told how two producers try to put together a Cole Porter bio, though Porter is disguised as "Noël Walters," possibly an amalgam of the arguably Porteresque Noël Coward and Charles Walters, who had directed films written by Comden and Green (and, by chance, had introduced "Well, Did You Evah?" with Betty Grable, in his first career, as a Broadway dancer).

A generation after *Wonderland* was canceled, a Porter jukebox feature did reach the screen. This was *At Long Last Love* (1975), directed by Peter Bogdanovich, who has very odd ideas about how musical numbers should be staged—everyone looks awkward and angry during the music, and there's a lot of it, too. And while Madeline Kahn and Eileen Brennan were musical-comedy pros, Cybill Shepherd and Burt Reynolds were not (though Reynolds acquitted himself surprisingly well). Aficionados treasure the film for having shot all its numbers live, without pre-recording, but most of the public laughed it off the screen so definitively that it didn't turn up on home media till 2014, thirty-nine years later.

Uniquely of the Harms-Chappell group, Porter got *two* Hollywood bios. *Night and Day* (1946) is traditional, with a fictional narrative and stylish musical cameos, including Mary Martin's "My Heart Belongs To Daddy." Interestingly, Jane Wyman, not known for musicals, has a singing role; in "You Do Something To Me," she and the chorus men, sporting canes, dance while guiding the canes through the air via what looks like sheer levitation. Yes, it's all done with strings, no doubt—but where are they?

Small of stature with huge eyes—an imp, really—Porter should have been hard to cast. True, in these musical bios, only Robert Alda's Gershwin resembles his counterpart in any true sense. But Porter was a classy gent, so Warner Bros. turned to the classiest gent in Hollywood, Cary Grant. In fact, *Night and Day* is the most enjoyable of the musical bios after the George M. Cohan entry, *Yankee Doodle Dandy* (1942): it moves very quickly and, for all its prevarications, is good fun.

And then came *De-Lovely* (2004), an excrescence. Kevin Kline plays a Porter reviewing his life in a theatre with Death (Jonathan Pryce), and while the film openly depicts Porter's liaisons with men, it invents a passionate and even physical relationship with his wife (Ashley Judd) that, as I've already indicated, simply didn't exist.

All Hollywood bios play hide-and-seek with the facts, but *De-Lovely*'s dishonesty is a mad havoc. The film shows a singer (John Barrowman) struggling with "Night and Day," whereupon Porter buddy Monty Woolley (Allan Corduner; Woolley played himself in *Night and Day*) says, "We should have given it to Astaire." Well, they *did* give it to Astaire; it's one of the songs he is most associated with. Further, Barrowman's rendition ignores every one of the push-beats (notes written to sound before the beat rather than precisely on the beat) that give the melody its air of breathless obsession. Yet more bizarre, "I Love You," from the stage show *Mexican Hayride*, is given to Nelson Eddy to sing in MGM's *Rose Marie* in his Mountie uniform. Yes, we remember how that crafty Porter loved to interpolate his work into MacDonald-Eddy operettas.

De-Lovely makes no attempt to simulate the singing style or orchestral sound of Porter's era, and Sheryl Crow's "Begin the Beguine" is so incorrect it recalls the two rap cuts on the Porter rock anthology *Red Hot + Blue*. When Porter's pitches go up or down, Crow does likewise, but she hits different notes than the ones Porter wrote; and the little band accompanying her makes up its own chords. Porter's songs are indestructible, and they can stand restylization; most of *Red Hot + Blue* is sort of charming. But to flout Porter's melody and harmony *in a Porter bio* is outrageous. Except for Ashley Judd, every performer in *De-Lovely* is made to look ridiculous; the sight of Kline giggling and clapping as the people of his life caper about onstage in the first sequence is appalling. This is a film produced, written, and directed by people who don't know who Cole Porter was and don't know what music is. *De-Lovely* isn't the worst of the Hollywood musical bios. It's the worst of the Hollywood musicals.

CHAPTER 8

✧

Operetta

Grace Moore's early movie appearances were not successful, but her comeback, in *One Night Of Love* (1934) was a huge hit. The film showed the struggles and sacrifices in the making of an opera career, yet it was replete with joyous music-making. Thus, having just arrived in Italy to study voice, Moore opens her apartment window on a courtyard full of the locals practicing—on violin (including three children led by their tutor), flute, clarinet, harp. It's a very carnival of music, and the impulsive Moore breaks into *La Traviata*'s "Sempre Libera." Immediately, all the players join her in a wild classical jamboree, telling us that music is the very air a musician breathes. Later, in a comparable instance, Moore takes over a restaurant with the irresistible waltz "Ciribiribin," a number that reportedly had little Italian cinemas physically shaking as audiences lustily sang along.

Despite the leaden presence of Tullio Carminati as Moore's control freak of a teacher, *One Night Of Love* proved a huge success, boosting not only Moore—a marvelous vocalist in both opera and pop—but the idea of movies built around legit singers.

Met stars Lily Pons and Gladys Swarthout were among those tapped for stardom thus, but Hollywood happened to have nurtured its own legit singer in Jeanette MacDonald. She had spent the 1920s in Broadway musicals, but almost invariably the snazzy, dizzy ones, without getting a chance to let her soprano soar. It was Hollywood that really discovered her, as we've already seen with Maurice Chevalier and Ramon Novarro. But then began her partnership with Nelson Eddy, a baritone who had started as a tenor (he had sung *Wozzeck*'s Drum Major in Philadelphia under Leopold Stokowski) and could thus astonish with unexpected high notes.

Wags dubbed them "The Iron Butterfly and the Singing Capon," mainly because most people who write about film scorn thirties musicals and the operettas in particular. But there is no arguing against great singing, and MacDonald and Eddy were both superb singers. As for operetta itself, the shows had become somewhat déclassé as sheer theatre, but the scores were still popular and the classic titles had resonance. So when MGM decided to try MacDonald and Eddy in an all-out operetta film, they chose Victor Herbert's *Naughty Marietta* rather than concoct something new in the old style.

In an interview with Tina Daniell in the aforementioned *Backstory*, screenwriter Philip Dunne recalled, "At Metro, [executive producer Irving] Thalberg always worked from the star up." Thus, MacDonald and Eddy weren't just *Naughty Marietta*'s principals: this adaptation from stage to screen was tailored to their fit. At that, the role of the rebellious and independent young noblewoman masquerading as a "casket girl" looking for a husband in old New Orleans and the backwoods soldier of fortune in buckskin suited them well. MacDonald's specialty was behaving as if all the men around her are pompous bores (the old guys) or crazy and aggressive (her love match), which gives her more to play with than stage Mariettas enjoyed, and Eddy wasn't as wooden an actor as his legend insists. Further, their new public could meet them partway, because the kind of people who liked operetta in 1935 knew *Naughty Marietta*'s main songs by heart. Her "Italian Street Song" (the one with "Zing, Zing, zizzy, zizzy, zing, zing, Boom, boom, aye"), his "I'm Falling in Love With Someone," and their "Ah! Sweet Mystery Of Life" had stood among the nation's most popular numbers for some twenty-five years, and MGM so emphasized the music that the two stars were already vocalizing during the opening credits. Operetta is back!

Further, MGM's music department—meaning, at this point, Herbert Stothart—troubled to include a great deal of the stage score. Three major numbers were missing—the title song, the hero-heroine duet "It Never, Never Can Be Love," and "Live For To-day," a huge waltz quartet with chorus. But, truth to tell, these were rather antique in sound for 1935, and a great deal of *Marietta*'s minor bits found their way into the program. On stage, the entire show takes place in New Orleans, but MGM gives us Marietta's backstory first. So we start in France (on Broadway, the heroine was Italian, because so was its creator, Emma Trentini), where she flees an arranged marriage with the usual operetta sourpuss. When she is shown her trousseau—all in black—she coldly snaps out, "Has there been a death in your family?"

Two numbers were needed for this sequence, and while the lyrics (by Gus Kahn) are new, all the music is Herbert's. Stothart contrived an establishing song for MacDonald, "Chansonette," using Herbert's piano piece "Punchinello" (1910). The men's chorus launches it, in praise of MacDonald, but then she takes over, with plenty of the rubato and portamento that were essential articles in the soprano handbook into the 1950s. Later, when MacDonald is sneaking out of Europe disguised as her maid, director W. S. Van Dyke gets a spectacle out of her ship's departure. Stothart concocts a second Herbert pastiche for a big choral scene with solos, using *Marietta's* hippety-hoppity $\frac{6}{8}$ "puppet" music (here in $\frac{4}{4}$), the "convent girls" theme from the show's opening number, and, for a prayer of Godspeed with Jeanette supplying a high descant over the choir, a melody drawn from another of Herbert's piano pieces, "Yesterthoughts" (1900).

Later, Eddy got a "new" number as well, developed out of one of the show's least-known songs, "Anybody Else But Me." Sung by the hero's comic sidekick, it runs on a craggy, emphatic tune (at "I dream that I am a pirate bold"), which Stothart molded into a showpiece for Eddy's Deep Baritone Structure With Tenor Penthouse as "The Owl and the Bobcat." These animal fables were the delight of musicals in the very early 1900s, so it was clever history to revive the genre, creating a subtle link between 1935's Herbert-Stothart and the Real Victor Herbert and his era. Unfortunately, we miss a lot of the number, as Van Dyke focuses on plot dialogue during the music. He finally rejoins Eddy for a very long-held note that has MacDonald gaping in appreciation, and our hero then adds a cadenza starting (in A Major) on the E above middle C, shuttling down an octave-and-a-half to low A, then rising to the third of the scale, at middle C sharp: sheer bravura.

MGM's *Naughty Marietta* was a tremendous hit, and the studio promptly pursued a cycle using a property it already owned (from having filmed it as a silent), *Rose Marie* (1936). *Naughty Marietta* sorta kinda followed its source's storyline except when it didn't, but *Rose Marie* retained its source's setting (Canada) and its lead Mountie (who was not actually in the love plot) but otherwise made everything up. On Broadway, the heroine was half-Indian, and MGM's 1954 remake, with Howard Keel, Ann Blyth, and Fernando Lamas, would exploit the racial angle to motivate Blyth as "difficult"—that is, naturally wary of whites and their agenda. In 1936, however, MacDonald is not only not an Indian but professionally imposing: an opera singer. We actually see her on stage in *Tosca*, most fitting because MacDonald always seemed to play a form of Tosca in her early MGMs, caught between a foolhardy hero and a sadistic villain. And that's *Maytime* (1937) and *The Firefly* (1937) in particular.

These two shows, from 1917 and 1912, respectively, were not precisely operettas of the "Stouthearted Men" and "Indian Love Call" type. Friml's *Firefly*, billed as a "comedy-opera" (a genre that didn't exist), was a musical comedy containing a very lavish soprano heroine—Emma Trentini again. Romberg's *Maytime*, billed as "a play with music," *was* an operetta, but in a transitional form leading from "comic opera"—the term denoting the Big Sing shows from the late nineteenth century to 1920—to such works as *The Student Prince*, *The Vagabond King*, and *The Desert Song*. But *Maytime*'s recurring waltz theme, "Will You Remember?," and its plangent narrative— young lovers are cruelly parted but their grandchildren, played by the same actors, achieve the happy ending—are hallmarks of operetta.

In any case, MGM again completely threw out the shows' storylines for the films, because those golden titles and the best-known numbers were all that mattered. At that, *Maytime* retained only "Will You Remember?" while *The Firefly* included five of the original songs, even as its outstanding music was a new item, "The Donkey Serenade," arranged by Stothart from an old Friml tune, lyriced by Robert Wright and George Forrest. As *The Firefly*'s setting had been changed from the show's New York and Bermuda to Spain at the time of Napoléon's invasion, director Robert Z. Leonard could build "The Donkey Serenade" into a piquant vignette as MacDonald and her duenna travel along a mountain highway in a coach driven by an older man with a guitar and a young boy piping on a little reed instrument.

Surely Nelson Eddy would be riding along to—as the song puts it— "serenade" her, only here Allan Jones is her romance, spicier than Eddy. The scene bounces along with a crazy air all its own, to a clip-clopping beat and the little boy's flutey decoration (both composed by Stothart). And we have to admit that the number is better than anything in the stage show, very musical but also written specifically for the way editing can narrate film, guiding the eye among views of the women inside the coach, the two males at the reins, Jones and his song, and even the four beasts pulling the coach. Again, it's what Hollywood can do that Broadway can't, and we're left with a quaint last shot, for Jones has fallen off his mount, and the horse comes up to nuzzle him as, in the distance, the coach wheels off on its way.

MGM's tendency to rewrite old operettas hit an apex with *Sweethearts* (1938), because, in Dorothy Parker and Alan Campbell's script, the plot is no longer European la-di-da about a laundress and a prince, only the laundress turns out to be a disguised...oh, you figured it out already? Instead, Parker and Campbell (who were man and wife) devised a new narrative, set in America, about another husband-and-wife team *appearing* in European la-di-da about a laundress and a prince.

Thus anticipating Ken Russell's filming of *The Boy Friend* some thirty-five years later, *Sweethearts* allows MGM to revel in operetta's exotic costuming and swelling choruses while constantly stepping back from them in a modern-dress Technicolor comedy about big-city characters, a first for the two stars. When onstage, the movie *Sweethearts* is the stage *Sweethearts*, in grandiose sets fit for the Hippodrome. Offstage, it's a farce in which a producer (instant Frank Morgan; just add water) and his crew try to break up the MacDonald-Eddy marriage to keep them from signing a Hollywood contract.

Incredibly, the singing lovebirds have been playing *Sweethearts* for a Broadway run of, thus far, six years, and MGM is at pains to show how much their bond shows through in their work—so much so that couples of all ages revisit the show again and again to share in its wondrous message. There's an especially mawkish bit in the theatre lobby during intermission, when the camera pauses on a young couple, cute and all dressed up and elaborately infatuated:

SHE: It's the most wonderful play in the whole world.
HE: Remember the first time we saw it?

This is pure third-audience pandering. But later, when MacDonald and Eddy give a curtain speech and direct the public in a singalong of the title song and "Auld Lang Syne," our old friend director W. S. Van Dyke brings out details in the public's reaction so realistically that we get pulled back into the film's reality—into the power of music, which is what operetta is about in the first place.

And here's an interesting difference between Broadway's business model for operetta and Hollywood's: virtually all of *Sweetheart's* leads play the comedy. In Broadway's operetta, the principals sing and emote very seriously except for one or two designated jesters. (MGM adopted this plan in that aforementioned 1954 *Rose Marie*, in which the three stars do the drama and Herman [Bert Lahr] and Lady Jane [Marjorie Main], exactly as in the 1924 stage show, handle the fun stuff.)

This *Sweethearts*, on the other hand, is stuffed with comics—for instance the composer (Herman Bing) and wordsmith (Mischa Auer) of MacDonald and Eddy's musical, the former always blowing his top and the latter a silken weasel. (He's the one who devises the plot to dismay the two stars.) But more: MacDonald and Eddy support their families in their townhouse, and these oldsters, has-been theatricals, are played as spoofs of self-important nobodies constantly recalling imaginary triumphs of long ago. We hear them invoke Reginald De Koven's *Robin Hood*, Gilbert and Sullivan, even Julian Edwards' *Dolly Varden* (one of the most obscure old operetta titles, a camp reference before camp existed). Then they get MacDonald and Eddy to join them in two numbers from—you won't believe this—*The Prince Of Pilsen* (1903), complete with fatuous dance steps (and one of the ladies gets her foot caught in her dress, and good old "One-take Van Dyke" says, "Print it!). They're old fools—yet MGM cast the roles with real-life veterans who somehow or other make these characters interesting if not lovable.

Let's go out on a limb and call *Sweethearts* MacDonald and Eddy's most enjoyable film. For one thing, the Technicolor is extraordinary, so intensely read that MacDonald's cheeks are flushed with rouge. Then, too, at nearly two hours, the film is filled with music, including a vocal version of Herbert's "Badinage" and Hermann Löhr's old chestnut "The Little Grey Home in the West." Most of the actual *Sweethearts* material was re-lyricked, by Wright and Forrest, and Stothart composed some expert "Herbert" to braid the *Sweethearts* excerpts together when necessary. But it was really the name of Victor Herbert that gave the movie its cachet; he was still that prominent, fourteen years after his death and last (posthumous) premiere. *Sweethearts*' title card gives him pride of place, and then, among "gowns by" and "sound by," stands a unique credit: "Immortal melodies by." And so they were, at the time.

Above all, *Sweethearts*, more than any other MacDonald-Eddy collaboration, celebrates their sheer love of singing. Their style contrasts with that of Lawrence Tibbett and Grace Moore in *New Moon*, highly emotional yet, visually, somewhat sedate. MacDonald and Eddy, on the other hand, revel in music-making. They're not just singing: they're sharing. In their duets they clutch each other, even seem to try to climb inside of each other, as if MGM wants them inseparable, unitary.

Their series lasted only seven years, yet in their heyday these films were commercially vital, and operetta became a Hollywood staple. It was in eclipse on Broadway, but the schmaltziest of the line thrilled New York at the vast Center Theatre—the legit counterpart of Radio City Music Hall—in 1934. This was *The Great Waltz*, a new version of an international success using the character and music of Johann Strauss. MGM ran up its own version (1938), with a new plot and a fresh set of Strauss-derived songs bearing lyrics by Oscar Hammerstein.

It's a notable film and, for all its frivolous waltzing about, a great work of cinema. All three leads were Europeans—Fernand Gravet, Luise Rainer, and Milizia Korjus—and the director was the French Julien Duvivier, who captures the very intoxication of music as no one had before. Korjus, in her only American film, is especially tasty, recalling a line from Cole Porter's *Something For the Boys*: "the missing link between Lily Pons and Mae West," meaning the stratospheric soprano who also does the Come Hither with a sardonic smirk. In Duvivier's besotted camera, Korjus can even give us cascades of notes while twirling through a ballroom or dancing with Gravet around a bandstand featuring an all-woman orchestra.

If *The Great Waltz*, why not *The Great Victor Herbert* (1939)? Isn't Herbert in some ways the father of operetta in its American form? Paramount offered this one as not a bio but a backstager Plot B and C, and Herbert himself is less important than the romance between soprano newbie Mary Martin and top Broadway tenor Allan Jones. They run into *A Star Is Born* trouble when Martin becomes the toast of Broadway and Jones starts to slide. Apparently, they appear only in Herbert's shows, often under lightly altered titles: *The Princess "Pat"* becomes *Princess Peggy*, and *Algeria* (and its revisal, *The Rose of Algeria*) becomes, after its best number, *Rose of the World*.

Though it isn't a bio, *The Great Victor Herbert* nevertheless exploits the song-cavalcade feature, and, unlike the MGM Herberts, this one has no Stothartization: every note is Herbert's. Arthur Kay, one of the outstanding musicians based in California (the reader may know him as the stage *Kismet*'s orchestrator) was the film's music director, and he made sure that the niceties of Herbert's style—the rubatos, tenutos, descants, and so on—were observed. Further, we get a lot of unusual Herbert, real rarities.[1] At one point, director Andrew L. Stone takes Jones and Martin out for a bicycle ride, a beautifully photographed sequence without any process shots or back-projection as the two pedal along a lane between banks of trees and passing carts. The whole thing looks so natural that when Martin loses control of her bike and Jones steadies it, it appears genuine, accidental art. Best of all, for much of this sequence the two converse in lyrics, singing snippets of Herbert songs, so Jones makes confession in "I'm Falling In Love With Someone" and Martin gives courtship advice with "Ask Her While the Band Is Playing."

The music even allows the two to meet cute, as a marching band and well-wishers parade up to Herbert's townhouse, where Jones sings the heck out of "Ah! Sweet Mystery of Life." Martin, a country mouse in a coat and hat twenty years out of date, is so carried away by the romance of the melody that she starts to sing along, Jones pulls her up to join him, and soon everybody else is singing, too.

It's a wonderful scene, and the film is wonderful, too. But it has its strange side. It's bemusing to encounter Martin in her early Hollywood career, fresh from attaining stardom on Broadway singing "My Heart Belongs To Daddy," because she's utterly unlike the eccentric tomboy we're used to; she sings soprano and even tries a bit of ballet. And Jones, one of operetta's sunniest people, is made to seem egomaniacal and touchy, turning against even his friends. Worse, he's always smoking. Herbert

---

1. These include a chorus drawn from that piano piece "Punchinello," just like "Chansonette" in MGM's *Naughty Marietta*. Here the melody provisions a drinking song at a party.

(Walter Connolly, who looks exactly like Herbert, by the way) is the first to see the trouble coming. "Two people, one spotlight," he says, shaking his head, of this marriage of tenor and soprano. "I don't like it."

Martin doesn't, either. Music had united them, tearing her away from the nice-guy doctor (Lee Bowman) from her hometown she was all but engaged to. Just as with the two leads in *Sweethearts*, music is love and destiny, and now it is destroying them because it has lost its faith in Jones.

Yet there's a powerful link between Martin and Jones even now: their daughter, Peggy (Susanna Foster), a very accomplished soprano with *acuti* so acute that her high B sounds like a Z. The film is framed by an onstage sequence in that aforementioned *Rose of the World*, in which Peggy goes on for her mother and suffers a panic attack. The audience rustles uncomfortably—but, lo, Jones, backstage, grabs a chorister's outfit and gets on stage to hearten his child. She recovers and triumphs—and then something odd occurs. The fadeout takes a look at neither Martin nor Jones, nor even Foster. And, no, not Herbert, either. Instead, the last character we see is that nice-guy doctor who loved Martin in vain, called from his seat in the theatre on a case. As the house roars with excitement for Peggy's debut, the good doctor takes one last look at the stage in this temple of art, then leaves. Alone of the leads, he has no music in him; it's as if he was never in the story at all.

And there the movie ends, one of the oddest of all the "Broadway operetta" films, so full of unexpected music, so banal yet so unnerving in its characterizations, so rich in talents we're not used to—Mary Martin as a housewife, Allan Jones as a selfish hothead. *The Great Victor Herbert* lacks the masterly art direction of the MGMs, yet it has something they don't: surprise.

By the 1950s, operetta had turned zombie in New York. Except for the sexy *Kismet* (and, some might say, *Candide*, though the latter scoffs at operetta's essential component, romantic longing), the form was walking dead, still around after its life was over. All its major works were almost two generations old—for example *The Student Prince in Heidelberg* (to give its full title), Sigmund Romberg and Dorothy Donnelly's 1924 adaptation of a German play and the longest-running musical of the 1920s, beating out *Blossom Time* and *Show Boat*.

MGM had filmed *The Student Prince* as a silent, with Ramon Novarro and Norma Shearer, directed by Ernst Lubitsch. So the property was theirs to remake, especially with tenor Mario Lanza, a contractee who had enjoyed a huge success in *The Great Caruso* (1951). True, this tale of a royal matriculating at Heidelberg University is quaint: he falls in love with a waitress but regretfully leaves her to honor an arranged marriage with a princess. Alas, my love, we must part—and Lanza was perhaps too ebullient for the prince, who is shy, awkward, unsocialized. Legends have grown up that further impugn Lanza's suitability, especially that his weight problem got him fired.

False! Lanza was fired, yes, but his offense was fighting with director Curtis Bernhardt, who thought Lanza's rendition of one number too outgoing for the repressed prince. The temperamental Lanza never allowed anyone to criticize his singing, and he told the studio to choose between the two men. It's Lanza or Bernhardt! he cries. Unfortunately, MGM was the producers' studio, with a power structure of mogul to supervisor to director to star—in descending order—and MGM sided with Bernhardt.

With all of Lanza's tracks already taped, MGM decided to replace him only visually. This sorely tested the new prince, Edmund Purdom (in his first Hollywood lead), for lip-synching is tricky if one isn't musical in the first place. Purdom was young, trim, and handsome, at least—though, in the number that got Lanza fired, "Beloved," Purdom's peasant's-Sunday-best regalia and red felt hat make him look like Walt Disney's Pinocchio.

Student Prince buffs will have alerted to that last song title, because of course it isn't Romberg's. Nicholas Brodsky and Paul Francis Webster wrote three new numbers, and Webster revised Donnelly's lyrics, sneakily letting the first line or two pass (because the public would remember those) and then changing everything that followed. Further, the entire score was given to the prince and waitress, with some choral work; the stage original let the various principals share in the singing. Do two characters constitute an operetta?

But then, this was not a Freed Unit project. Joe Pasternak produced it, and the Pasternak MGMs—though they utilize Judy Garland, Gene Kelly, Debbie Reynolds, and Doris Day—are not as musically sublimated as Freed's line of *Meet Me in St. Louis*, *Easter Parade*, and *Gigi*. Ironically, Curtis Bernhardt didn't direct *The Student Prince* after all; he moved on to other work in the delay in finding Lanza's replacement. Richard Thorpe took over, Ann Blyth (in a blond wig) was the waitress, and the movie came and went as a bit of kitsch that neither restored nor collapsed operetta as a form. It was a dependable second- and third-audience feature, not least for that touch of religion in one of the Brodsky additions, "I'll Walk With God."

Wasn't operetta simply too *passéiste* to go on? Warner Bros. updated *The Desert Song* with wartime hugger-mugger and Dennis Morgan (1943), then again with Gordon MacRae (1953), but the singing tamed Romberg's grandiose style. And what could be done with Friml's *The Vagabond King*? There's no way to detach this one from its dowdy setting, in that medieval Paris of the jerkins and hose and women's pointy hats. This show was a Paramount property, first filmed in 1930 with its stage François Villon, Dennis King. His Villon is poet, scamp, warrior, lover, and he knows what operetta is about, leaping and gesturing, hurling his dialogue at us. Imagine a Shakespearean actor in a Marx Brothers movie, and you'll know King cold.

There's no way to modernize that sort of thing, and Paramount didn't try. The *Vagabond King* remake (1956) is Hose and Jerkin City, though the new Villon, the Maltese tenor Oreste Kirkop (billed by first name only), plays a smoothed-out hero. Back in 1930, Dennis King is a ham, but he really gives a performance, and this wholly silly show, replete with "purloined," "hence," and "'twere," needs to go big. King was so impressive as Villon that Paramount built up his singing spots with new numbers (by Sam Coslow, Newell Chase, and Leo Robin) devoted to his rebel intensity— "King Louis," declaimed as a series of scurrilous lampoons of the monarch in iambic tetrameter; the scathing "What France Needs"; and, for Villon as swain, the slow-build ballad "If I Were King."

There are five new songs in the Oreste remake, supposedly composed by Friml himself (with lyricist Johnny Burke). Were they? Though he never wrote for Broadway after 1934, he did add a few dreary new songs to a *Rose-Marie* revival on the West Coast in 1950; and Oreste's rather grand "This Same Heart" does sound like Friml. But a crowd number, "Viva la You [viva la me]," led by Rita Moreno as Villon's sidekick (his amour is Kathryn Grayson), is irritatingly clunky in the $\frac{6}{8}$ meter that has long sounded obsolete unless used very carefully—as in *Oklahoma!*'s "Kansas City," in numerous Jerry Herman cheer-up marches, even in *A Little Night Music*'s "Every Day a Little Death." In "Viva la You," the $\frac{6}{8}$ meter is not used carefully, quite aside from the nutzoid lyrics. The truth of it is that old-time operetta had aged its way out of viability.

Friml never got a bio, but Sigmund Romberg's tale was told in MGM's *Deep In My Heart* (1954), one of its outstanding all-star song cavalcades— Helen Traubel; Gene Kelly (with his brother Fred in a beachside frolic, "I Love To Go Swimmin' With Wimmin'," reminding us that Romberg did a lively trade in musical comedy before he locked himself inside operetta); Ann Miller in a twenties production number for *The Desert Song*'s "It" (which, ironically, was left out of all three films of the show); Howard Keel, Vic Damone, and Jane Powell in two numbers from *Maytime*; and James Mitchell and Cyd Charisse dancing to "One Alone," a torrid pas de deux very impressively brought off. And here's an in-joke: backstage at one of those musical comedies, Romberg is forced to go on for an indisposed performer and is thrown into the arms of Rosemary Clooney, who thrusts him away before a stage manager pushes them both onstage for "Mr. and Mrs." And of course that's what the two of them were, for Clooney had married the Romberg, José Ferrer, just the year before.

Ferrer's performance sets *Deep In My Heart* apart from all other composer bios, because MGM gave him a genuine actor's challenge, styling Romberg's Hungarian immigrant's English using Jewish sentence structure, directing him to sing and dance in a charmingly understated way unusual in musicals, and giving him a tour de force as he puts on a frenetic digest version of a show he's working on. Every other musical-bio star plays his personal shtick—James Cagney's George M. Cohan is aggressive (far more so than Cohan himself), Cary Grant's Cole Porter is debonair, Tom Drake's Richard Rodgers and Robert Walker's Jerome Kern are more sinned against than sinning, and so on. Ferrer, however, strives to invent a character. When he and Traubel go into "Leg of Mutton," a ragtimey strut, the result is a genuine novelty: the former Met Brünnhilde dancing with oddly decorous vigor and Ferrer matching her with an expression of Mona Lisa deadpan.

Unfortunately, this film is the least plotted of the bios; all that scenarist Leonard Spigelgass had to work with was Romberg's early determination to get out of musical comedy and into operetta. *Deep In My Heart* expands it into Romberg's lifelong struggle, and pictures Romberg's bosses, the Messrs. Shubert, trying to force him out of romance and back into the silly, zany zone. In fact, they did...a little bit. Mainly, however, J. J. Shubert, who was in charge of the musicals, loved operettas, especially Romberg's, and he produced some fifteen of these, from *The Blue Paradise* (1915) to *My Romance* (1948). But then, for an MGM special, *Deep In My Heart* is unusually sloppy about details. At a party decorated with banners uniting Romberg's name with those of other composers, one reads "Ludwig Von Beethoven." It's *Van*.

Hollywood's operetta phase was more or less over by then, anyway. But the phenomenal success of *The Sound of Music* in 1965 inspired Andrew L. Stone to attempt two imitations that tilt toward operetta. Stone, a Hollywood veteran of very minor note—he directed *The Great Victor Herbert* for us a few pages ago—produced, wrote, and directed *Song of Norway* (1970) and *The Great Waltz* (1972), two of the dopiest movies ever made. The buffs revel in their blunders, which in *Song of Norway* start even before the title letters come into view: Freddy (and his fiddle) runs uphill from a fjord in black-and-red peasant garb on the tympani roll before the famous opening of Grieg's piano concerto, and just as we hear that first shrill chord in a minor, Freddy leaps into the air. It's a sort of kitsch bomb, perhaps. There's a ton of dancing for weird reasons in *Song of Norway*, as when the three leads sing the emotional "Hill of Dreams" while racing and prancing through town. Worse, two of them are Florence Henderson and Frank Poretta, who are wonderful singers, while the third is Toralv

Maurstad, whose feeble little voice utterly betrays operetta's salient quality: vocal tone.

"I never miss a Horst Buchholz musical," Bette Midler might have said of *The Great Waltz*, and Buchholz's Johann Strauss does sing and dance, though this till then straight actor was no match for soprano Mary Costa as his opera-singer wife. At one point, they enliven an outdoor wedding party with Costa at the upright and Buchholz on violin. "Corrugate the keyboard," he sings, "or we will *be* bored," and indeed the lyrics—by Robert Wright and George Forrest, who had fashioned the *Song of Norway* score from Grieg's melodies as well—are strangely terrible for this underpraised but imaginative duo.

Although MGM distributed *The Great Waltz*, the film could not be called a remake of Duvivier's version. For one thing, Stone reclaimed the son-versus-father rivalry used in the stage *Great Waltz*es, then changed the plot at the one-hour mark—this is a very long film—to a brand-new wrinkle: will he or won't he? That is, will Strauss give in to his wife and write for the voice, for the stage? Yes, he will—but it takes forever for him to get to *Die Fledermaus*. Then the plot changes again, with only twenty minutes to go; now we're in the middle of a good old spouses' quarrel, capped by Strauss' mad chase in an open horse-cab through the streets of Vienna to stop Costa from leaving him. Director Stone, who has filled *The Great Waltz* with even more bizarrely unmotivated dancing than he did *Song of Norway*, now can't resist the urge to run the cab straight into a baker's kiosk, as if this were a Laurel and Hardy short.

And that, at last, was the end of Hollywood operetta. The ever more significant youth market conclusively rejected espressivo singing, teeming choruses, lavish high notes. Rock had arrived in the 1950s, but Beatles rock (that is, their influential expansion of rock and roll's artistic horizons, starting with *Revolver* (1966) and *Sgt. Pepper's Lonely Hearts Club Band* [1967]) transformed American music—so much so that Hollywood's interest in absorbing the music of Broadway was compromised by its need to keep up with the kids. In the 1930s, Jerome Kern or Cole Porter could give the movies hit tunes. Or George Gershwin could supply the prestige of classical pop. From the 1970s on, however, Broadway's songwriters will discover that they and Hollywood have incongruent agendas.

But it's not over yet. Let us now consider three figures of slightly lesser fame than Kern, Porter, and Gershwin and how they fared in film.

CHAPTER 9

⌒∧⌒

Johnny Mercer, Frank Loesser, and Harold Arlen*

Our featured writers have been mostly New Yorkers, but Johnny Mercer, of Savannah, Georgia, prided himself on being just a bit alien among the sophisticates and theatricals of Broadway. Thus, he maintained a major singing career and even co-founded a label (Capitol Records) specifically designed to promote the latest trends in pop music. Further, though primarily a lyricist, he occasionally wrote music as well (needing, like Irving Berlin, a secretary to spell out for him the harmony he heard in his head). And while Mercer concentrated his character writing on spots in films, he returned to Broadway again and again throughout his career, for a total of seven complete scores.

Even so, Mercer didn't like Broadway, because of the gnarly personal clashes inherent in the collaborative process, especially during the black hole of tryout hell. In Hollywood, most often, the various creative platforms were segregated: songwriters didn't know scriptwriters; the director scarcely crossed paths with either. In New York, everyone was on top of everyone else, at every minute, from rehearsal to opening night—and if the show wasn't working, geschrei ensued.

Thus, on the stage show *Saratoga* (1959), Mercer found himself as the lyricist of the most expensive musical in Broadway history (at some $480,000, exactly one-third more than *My Fair Lady* had cost only three years before). Out of town, *Saratoga* looked like the flop of the decade, and, suddenly, Mercer's composer, Harold Arlen, came down with that rare

---

* A few short passages about Harold Arlen within this chapter first appeared in the *Wall Street Journal* on December 5, 2015.

disease known as Getmeoutofhereitis and abandoned the production, leaving Mercer to create words and music to new numbers entirely by himself at top speed when his habit was to dawdle.

In Hollywood, all Mercer had to do was sing the latest number in the comfortable isolation of the producer's office in his amiable baritenor with a ton of southern charm. True, except for Pandro Berman and Arthur Freed, most producers were musically illiterate; the first thing one of them said after a preview of *The Wizard of Oz* was "That 'rainbow' number has to go." Still, no one was on top of Mercer, and the pace was leisurely. Best of all, Mercer's Hollywood work seldom called for the character and situation songs endemic to the Broadway musical. On stage, characters were always *doing* something, whereas in the movies you could pluck a song out of the air.

This suggests the Tin Pan Alley aesthetic of keeping everything simple. In fact, Mercer was a good ol' boy only in part, because he was unique in his ability to blend the Harms group's rangy cultural references with a kind of poetic artlessness. A master of the Theme Song for non-musical films, Mercer could make any title lyrical. The Theme Song he wrote (with composer Henry Mancini) for *Charade* (1963), a romantic thriller with Cary Grant and Audrey Hepburn, is made of theatrical images to match the movie's "nothing is what it seems" near-Hitchcockian plotting. At one point, the singer says, "We came on next to closing"—an allusion to the star turn on a vaudeville bill, the last act before the "chaser," something ghastly to empty the house. Did many moviegoers of 1963 place the allusion? Possibly not. Yet Mercer never feels like a showoff, because of his overall ingenuous tone.

Similarly, consider *Breakfast at Tiffany*'s theme song, "Moon River," with its wonderful invention of "my huckleberry friend," suggesting a link between Truman Capote's madcap runaway and Mark Twain's Huckleberry Finn: two southern nonconformists. And isn't the notion of a river named Moon arresting in itself? (There is a Moon River, south of Savannah, Georgia, amid that city's summer-vacation islands. Officially just an inlet connecting the Vernon and Skidaway rivers, it was originally called Back River. The area now sports such tourist stops as the Moon River Kayak Tours as well—all in response to Mercer's imaginative fancy.)

Further, writing both words and music for Bing Crosby in *Rhythm on the Range* (1936), Mercer caught exactly the singer's easy-go persona in "I'm an Old Cowhand (From the Rio Grande)." Or, back on Broadway, with composer Robert Emmett Dolan, on the Bert Lahr vehicle *Foxy* (1964), Mercer needed a patter number in Lahr's unique style of goofing on pretentious twaddle. "Bon Vivant" found Lahr blithely passing himself off as an English lord "who only aims to please, punting on the Hellespont or at Milady's teas." It's the pointed cultural satire we expect from E. Y. Harburg or Stephen Sondheim, but Mercer could express it, too—when he chose to.

Was Mercer "basic" in movies and more challenging in the theatre? He actually started on Broadway, in 1930, working mainly in revue, but by 1933 he was in California. In his first films, the songs danced lightly around the story to slip in a specialty number, like "Hooray For Hollywood" (with composer Richard A. Whiting, from *Hollywood Hotel* [1937]), or "Jeepers Creepers" (with Harry Warren, from *Going Places* [1938]).

Let's take a look at Paramount's *The Fleet's In* (1942), for which Mercer wrote the lyrics to the music of the film's director, Victor Schertzinger, a versatile talent we remember as the composer also of Ernst Lubitsch's *The Love Parade*. Cliché though it be, the setting is once again a performing venue, so the score will concentrate on floor numbers—and, as films of the day loved to feature name bands, *The Fleet's In* includes Jimmy Dorsey's orchestra and his house vocalists in the cast. So we shouldn't expect plot or character songs.

Or should we? We're in and around a dance club called Swingland, where Dorothy Lamour is "the Countess," a songstress too cool for woo. Her vis-à-vis will be shy sailor William Holden, and each has a sidekick, respectively, fellow vocalist Betty Hutton and fellow sailor Eddie Bracken.

Note that we have a typical Broadway structure in the romantic First Couple (whose story it is) and a zany Second Couple (who move in and out of the story with their own concerns). So Lamour is glamorous and the twenty-two-year-old Holden unforgivably pretty, while Hutton (in her movie debut) is rambunctious and Bracken a notch above idiot. In a way, there's a Third Couple, Dorsey's vocalists Bob Eberly and Helen O'Connell, he a bit bland and she on the zesty side but present only to supply smooth vocal tone.

"Tangerine" is their main contribution, relaxed and suave, the perfect pop tune in its self-contained profile of a South American femme fatale. One might call it pure music-making, but if you listen to the words you hear Mercer create another of his "characters," as Tangerine turns out to be both sociopath and phony. Mercer gives her a twisty playout when Tangerine's "heart belongs to just one." Yes, we knew she had a secret love. Is it a sailor? A caballero? No: "Her heart belongs to Tangerine."

Except for *The Fleet's In*'s title song, every one of its eight numbers is a performance spot. Thus, Betty Hutton's comic specialties have to serve as her character songs, even though "If You Build a Better Mousetrap" is harmless enough for Eberle and O'Connell to reprise it. At that, "Arthur Murray Taught Me Dancing In a Hurry" aligns with Hutton only because they're both goofy. She sings the latter dressed to kill in a black top between shoulder pads and a skirt made of white rumba ruffles (with a matching bow atop her hair), and she really works the hall, in her characteristic Blitzkrieg manner. Mercer makes the most of this opportunity to lampoon the forties craze for wilder and wilder dances, driving Hutton mad. "To me it resembles the nine-day trembles," she cries—one of Mercer's phrase inventions. As well, he gives us another taste of his ability to place a fancy cultural footnote while remaining the guy next door, a persona far removed from those wicked sophisticates Cole Porter and Lorenz Hart. "You've heard of Pavlova?" Hutton asks, snapping back with "Well, Jack, move ovah!"

Further, composer-director and lyricist pull off a sly trick when Lamour and Hutton are in their shared apartment, with Holden and Bracken close by. We're in San Francisco, where Lamour lives atop one of those hills with the five flights of stairs. "I call it 'my discourager,'" she tells Holden. But he's undaunted, and, later, Lamour just happens to look down from her balcony and spots ... the Jimmy Dorsey band, conveniently taking the air. "Jimmy, will you play my chorus?" she asks. And the Dorseys go right into "[It's somebody else's moon above,] Not Mine," which Lamour sings as a mood piece. And then the camera moves back into the apartment, where Hutton sings it *as a plot number*, lamenting Bracken's preference for eating over romance. He even joins in, for a line or two of story information.

Mercer is hard to categorize; you could call him a Tin Pan Alleyman with the creativity of the Harms group or a poet in plain ink, an individualist who never writes down even in a business fond of uniformity. And he was something of a shape-shifter, fluent in many styles of songwriting. One year after *The Fleet's In*, he and composer Harry Warren created for MGM's *The Harvey Girls* (1946) a solid-plot-and-character score, because the Freed Unit was making original-story movies with a borrowed-from-Broadway musical structure. *The Harvey Girls* even starts with a Heroine's Wanting Song, a genre that irritates Hollywood producers because it freezes the story's motor just when it's supposed to kick into second gear (which is precisely why "Over the Rainbow" was in peril for a while). Standing at the rear of a train car gliding past western real estate, Judy Garland dreams aloud of home and marriage and watching a brand-new town grow up around her in a short piece, "In the Valley (Where the Evening Sun Goes Down)." On stage, this would have been a sort of throwaway moment, but cinematically it becomes narration, as director George Sidney uses it to establish not just Garland but the movie's geography: we're going west, experiencing a trip into as yet uncivilized territory.

Sidney provides the commentary on the DVD, and he tells us that he wanted "a train song." Warren and Mercer gave him much more than that, for "On the Atchison, Topeka and the Santa Fe" is really an "entire town song." It starts in the saloon—an important location, as it will be at war with the restaurant the Harvey girls wait table in—then moves to the train's passengers, engineers, and conductor as it pulls in and the locals look everyone over, especially the newly mustered Harveys themselves. Warren's music has imitated the train's chugging locomotion, but now comes a trio section not by Warren and Mercer (at "Hey there, did you ever see such pearly femininity..."), and the girls give us some individual backstories—one claims to have been the Lillian Russell of a small town in Kansas, and principals Ray Bolger and Virginia O'Brien each get a solo, too.

The number is not only thus detailed as a composition but gets the ultimate MGM treatment on a gigantic set with intricate interaction among the many soloists, choristers, and extras. But now it's Garland's turn to enter the number, disembark, and mix in with the crowd. According to Sidney, Garland executed everything perfectly on the first try—and it was all done in virtually a single shot. Fred Astaire would have insisted on rehearsing it for a week, but Garland was a natural. Once she understood the spirit of a number, the physics of it simply fell into place for her.

In any other film of the era, the saloon would be the place where the music was made. And Angela Lansbury, queen of the plot's rowdy element, does have a floor number, dressed in malevolent black and shocking pink topped by a matching Hippodrome hat. But every other number is a *story* number—"The Train Must Be Fed" (as the Harveys learn the art of waitressing); "It's a Great Big World" for anxious Harveys Garland, O'Brien, and a dubbed Cyd Charisse; O'Brien's comic lament, "The Wild, Wild West," a forging song at Ray Bolger's blacksmith shop; "Swing Your Partner Round and Round" at a social. Marjorie Main cues it up, telling one and all that this new dance is "all the rage way back east in Kansas City!"

It's the waltz, firming up *The Harvey Girls'* view of life as a battle of good and evil which good wins because it may be corny but evil has a crummy personality. For one thing, the bad guys don't even sing: Preston Foster is the chief villain, John Hodiak is the saloon owner (redeemed, however, by love of Garland), and Lansbury is dubbed. In fact, MGM had planned the story as a non-musical for Clark Gable, and writers beyond number—eight are credited in the titles, and there were others—labored to turn it into a musical. But then, it's not the story that beguiles: it's the sheer expertise with which the Freed Unit finds the music in, of all things, a western. George Sidney, recalling how pleasant it was to film Garland's part in his little train number, sums it up as "a lovely sunny day in Culver City," and these MGMs of the 1940s have that quality: of a bunch of pros united in love of their work.

We see this even more in *Seven Brides For Seven Brothers* (1954), with Mercer again at MGM, collaborating with composer Gene De Paul. This one has a real Broadway score, every number embedded in the characters' attitudes. Ragged, bearded, buckskinned Howard Keel has come to town to take a wife, and a local belle addresses him as "Backwoodsman": it's the film's central image, of rough men who must learn to be civilized in the company of women. The entire score has that flavor—western again, rustic, primitive, lusty. "Bless Yore Beautiful Hide," treating Keel's tour of the Oregon town where he seeks his bride, sounds like something Pecos Bill wrote with Calamity Jane. When the song sheet came out, the tune was marked "Lazily"—but that isn't how Keel sings it. He's on the hunt and he wants results, and, right in the middle of the number, he spots Jane Powell chopping wood and realizes that he has found his mate.

But he hasn't, not yet. True, she goes with him, looking forward to love and marriage. But *her* number, "Wonderful, Wonderful Day," warns us that she is of a different temperament than he: romantic, vulnerable, poetic. They don't suit each other, especially when he incites his six brothers to snatch their intended mates. Not court them: kidnap them. "Sobbin' Women" (a pun on the Sabine Women of the ancient Roman legend, which the film retells, via a story by Stephen Vincent Benét) is the number outlining the plan, in more of Keel's demanding musical tone. But the six "brides" are horrified. *Their* number, in Powell's pacifying tone, is "June Bride," and the brothers in turn offer "Lament" (usually called "Lonesome Polecat"), which reveals that they, too, have feelings. That—and the promise of good behavior—shows that they at last deserve their partners, whereupon each brother duets with each bride, in "Spring, Spring, Spring." And we note that this number completes the boys' surrender, in music that gives rather than takes.

Isn't this a Broadway score? Even: isn't this a Broadway film, in the line of the "dance musical" that had been a pride of Broadway since *The Band Wagon* (1931) and *On Your Toes* (1936)? Michael Kidd, one of New York's best choreographers, had already been working in Hollywood, but on *Seven Brides* he was essential, as his extremely athletic style matched the aggressive nature of the backwoodsman avatar. And, in a unique casting scheme, the brothers and brides were primarily dancers. Keel and Powell of course were singers, and, further, MGM was building Jeff Richards as a jeune premier and insisted on making him one of the brothers. A former baseball player, Richards was anything but a ballroom whiz, and Kidd had to work around him—Richards is especially awkward in "Goin' Co'tin'," ensconced in a chair almost throughout while Powell teaches his brothers how to dance—and, at that, MGM ended up dubbing some of the boys and girls.

But *Seven Brides* is a dance piece in a way even the Astaire-Rogers RKOs aren't. They dance because Astaire dances. *Seven Brides* dances because that's how we understand the difference between what men want women to be (chattel) and what women want men to be (nice to them).

The center of all this is the famous "Barn Raising," one of Hollywood's great set pieces and, again, entirely in Broadway style: narrative and thematic, like *Oklahoma!*'s "Laurey Makes Up Her Mind" or *On the Town*'s "Miss Turnstiles." Most of the outstanding dance numbers in Hollywood's original musicals are decorative, like "The Wedding of the Painted Doll" or "Begin the Beguine" in two of the *Broadway Melody*s. The dances in *The Harvey Girls* are decorative, too. But the "Barn Raising" pursues that notion that boys are belligerent and girls are pacifiers. Set to an irresistible country-fiddle version of "Bless Yore Beautiful Hide," it's a testosterone-challenge dance, the six younger brothers vying with the town beaux for those six incipient brides. So the girls are "traded" from the townsmen to the brothers and back, till choreogrpaher Kidd moves from dancing to track and field: feats of balance on logs, feats of strength, even feats of the brothers just being more appealing than their rivals, for, at the last moment, the six girls jump into the brothers' arms.

A gigantic hit, *Seven Brides For Seven Brothers* became a kind of landmark, often mentioned in the 1960s and 1970s when it wasn't readily available in the way such famous titles are today. On the other hand, its imitation is long forgotten: Universal's *The Second Greatest Sex* (1955). Like *Seven Brides* in color and CinemaScope, this upstart had a western feeling (it's set in Kansas but recalls *Seven Brides*' Oregon), treated gender war, looked back to an ancient tale (Aristophanes' *Lysistrata*), and even offered its own sort of "Barn Raising," choreographed by Lee Scott, featuring *Seven Brides*' brother Frank, Tommy Rall. And, like *Seven Brides*, *The Second Greatest Sex* has a Broadway score, albeit by so many different contributors that they weren't billed by name.

Further, right at the start, we hear a rollicking country tune that exactly recalls the musical tinta of *Seven Brides*, and later the women have a number, "Lysistrata," whose words and music sound like "Sobbin' Women": a brothers number revamped for brides. Because here the girls are not only peacemakers but bellicose ones: they move out of town and refuse to come back till their men give up fighting.

This is one of those amusingly terrible movies without any distinction save its omnibus casting: there's someone here for every taste. What musical of the era would be complete without Jeanne Crain, especially opposite George Nader, as he can't sing, dance, or act, either? But they look great. Sexpot Mamie Van Doren's on hand, as is Keith Andes, who for some mysterious reason had a physique almost as grand as Steve Reeves'. Unfortunately, Andes plays the town preacher, so the opportunities for scenes set at the old swimming hole or the blacksmith shop are limited. And there's Bert Lahr as the town sheriff, a wastefully serious part. As his son, teenaged Jimmy Boyd (who had had a gigantic pop hit singing "I Saw Mommy Kissing Santa Claus") is amusing enough, and the country singer billed as Cousin Emmy assists in a role so incidental that her mother would miss it. Further, Paul Gilbert plays a traveling salesman complete with establishing number and ensuing crazy dance, and Kitty Kallen, another pop singer, delivers "How Lonely Can I Get" to a ghost version of Tommy Rall. There's a lesbian in it, too; the only thing missing is Paul Henried going to the underground meeting.

Call it a potpourri: and that's the problem. If you want to imitate *Seven Brides For Seven Brothers*, you must duplicate its essential quality: consistency. *The Second Greatest Sex* is vaudeville by other means—though it is a Broadway vaudeville, telling us how influential the stage musical had finally become on screen: Hollywood's original musicals would now be more like the Astaire-Rogers RKOs and their story-and-character scores and less like, say, *The Fleet's In*, with its miscellany of performance spots.

Let us now backtrack to 1938. A strange but charming Paramount, *Sing You Sinners*, offers Bing Crosby, Fred MacMurray, and a twelve-year-old Donald O'Connor as brothers keeping themselves and their mother (Elizabeth Patterson) afloat through music. What's strange about the film is the mating of a cheery score of floor numbers with a racetrack-and-gangsters plot. Is this a musical or a crime thriller? But then, as I've already said, each Bing Crosby thirties musical tends to defy genre.

The charm inheres in the music, for the three brothers don't just sing: they play as well, Crosby on guitar, MacMurray on clarinet, and O'Connor on accordion. Their first number, "I've Got a Pocketful of Dreams," by James V. Monaco and John (later Johnny) Burke, is gentle and trim but, in performance, utterly sensational, as the trio moves around the stage of a crowded little club. They're so in tune with one other they truly seem like real-life siblings who've been performing together all their lives. And O'Connor is a scene-stealer, dancing and "pecking" like a chicken even while he's working his squeezebox. This is authentic Hollywood music-making.

Later, however, the three put on a bizarre specialty bit: a family scene in front of the façade of a house, with Crosby in a white beard as Pa, MacMurray knitting in a rocker as Ma, and O'Connor as their rakehell son, in "Small Fry." This one has lyrics by Frank Loesser, to Hoagy Carmichael's music, and the number's power rests entirely in the words because this is a conversation, as Pa chides Junior for his goings-on and Junior smarts off with backtalk. Clever and ironic, it's a vaudeville act in miniature, and it likely couldn't have been the work of the better-known Hollywood lyricists like Warner Bros.' Al Dubin or Fox's Mack Gordon. It's too smart, too precisely delineated. Yet it doesn't sound like any of Broadway's lyricists, either. The number is so outstanding that Paramount gave Loesser and Carmichael billing for that one song in the title cards, and also commissioned the Fleischer Studios to build a cartoon around it.

Though Loesser grew up in a musical family and, later on Broadway, was strictly a composer-lyricist, he almost invariably wrote only the words until his very last years of regular Hollywood work, which lasted from 1936 to 1950. At Paramount, Loesser would be spotted into usually undistinguished films, especially semi-musicals or dramas with a single song, whenever the producer wanted a lyric with a trendy air, an up-to-the-minute riff with a light touch of social observation. For *Blossoms on Broadway* (1938), a comic crime film, Loesser wrote "You Can't Tell a Man By His Hat" to Manning Sherwin's intently syncopated music, all about how guys are using their headgear as a masquerade, with "Texas sombreros on Bronx Caballeros." A year later, in *Man About Town*, Dorothy Lamour introduced Loesser's "Fidgety Joe," to Matt Malneck's jiving tune. Illustrated by the eccentric dancing of Jack Benny's sidekick Rochester (Eddie Anderson), this one told of the guy you always see compulsively moving in time with the swing band in your local night spot—again, a spry little note of cultural commentary.

Let's look at Loesser's work on a full-scale musical (to Arthur Schwartz's melodies), Warner Bros.' *Thank Your Lucky Stars* (1943). Wartime saw in a new cycle of revues, though—unlike those of 1929–30—the new batch utilized storylines to hold the star acts together. The narratives could be rudimentary, but *Thank Your Lucky Stars* isn't, centering on Eddie Cantor in a duo-role as himself and an out-of-work actor and tour guide trying to help budding singer Dennis Morgan while S. Z. Sakall and Edward Everett Horton are, in timeless Hollywood fashion, putting on a show.

That's what the film is about. What it's *famous* for is Bette Davis' singing debut, on "They're Either Too Young Or Too Old," lamenting the shortage of datable men on the homefront. Adopting a very fast tempo, Davis acts more than vocalizes, and even tries a bit of jitterbug dancing before beating a retreat from a nightclub set. She clearly does not know how to put a number over, and you'd never guess that she later starred in stage musicals and, in *Two's Company* (1952) at least, acquitted herself stylishly, albeit in a narrow vocal range and an air of self-satire.

Some of *Thank Your Lucky Stars* features celebs at their ease; Ann Sheridan, glamorous in white satin with another of those lavish Hollywood snoods, is right at home singing "Love Isn't Born [it's made]." And Humphrey Bogart has a short scene doing his tough-guy routine; no one asks him to sing, dance, or play the xylophone. However, the film does put its other tough guy, John Garfield, through a musical act, singing an interpolation not by Schwartz and Loesser, "Blues in the Night" (which comes up again at this chapter's end). First, Garfield and Cantor, before a radio audience, discuss Garfield's fee:

> CANTOR: Let's not argue over money. How much do you want?
> GARFIELD: Five thousand bucks.
> CANTOR: Let's argue.

Garfield's singing is tentative rather than catastrophic, and between the musical lines, to help him along, someone wrote him "autobiographical" recollections, sharp and jagged, taking him into comfort territory. Still, it seems odd that the studio didn't ask Schwartz and Loesser to fashion something for Garfield's tender musical abilities; "Blues in the Night" is not an easy sing. But then, we note that our two songwriters didn't even get prime billing in the titles: they share a card with the musical director, orchestrator, and vocal arranger, whereas the songwriters discussed in earlier chapters often got their own card or even with-the-title billing.

At that, *Thank Your Lucky Stars*' score is of the second or third division except in one number, "Ice Cold Katy [won't you marry the soldier?]," a black-cast production number that we see in its dress rehearsal, framed by the opening and closing of the curtain. It seems that Private Jones is about to ship out. He has both the preacher and the ring—but Miss Katy Brown is resisting. All Harlem strives with her, and finally she just gives in. With virtually no story to work with, Loesser concentrates on character, each soloist communicating in his or her unique voice; it gives us a foretaste of how well Loesser would fashion character scores for Broadway. Best of all in "Katy" is Hattie McDaniel as a sort of professional kibitzer, decked out in her Easter Sunday best and egging everyone on in an amusingly irritated way. "That's over!" she mutters, when the minister finally unites the couple. The number is one of the uncelebrated glories of the Hollywood musical, and a rare early sign of Loesser operating in a large-scale form.

Even so, when Loesser emphasized writing music as well as lyrics, in his later Hollywood years,[1] he did not seize many opportunities to distinguish

---

1. Theatre historian Thomas L. Riis, in *Frank Loesser*, has isolated the first time Loesser composed to his own words, in the title song of Paramount's updated film version of Booth Tarkington's *Seventeen*, in 1940. Jackie Cooper was the lovestruck hero and Betty Field the flirtatious Lola Pratt with the insufferable lap dog Flopit.

himself. *Neptune's Daughter* (1949), one of MGM's Esther Williams vehicles, does feature a genre Loesser would make his own, the conversational duet with interlocking lines, in "Baby, It's Cold Outside." Stanley Green tells us that Loesser originally wrote it as a specialty for him and his wife to perform at those Hollywood parties where the talent—which at various times might have included George Gershwin or Judy Garland—would go the piano to sing for supper. In *Neptune's Daughter*, a wary Williams and a seductive Ricardo Montalban worked the little gizmo of a melody: as she finished her phrase, he was starting his, then she came back in on his last note, and so on. Loesser tried it again in *Let's Dance* (1950), with Betty Hutton top-billed over Fred Astaire. This one is "Oh, Them Dudes," with the star pair in cowboy duds and mustaches, complaining that city dwellers have taken up country music, square-dancing in nightclubs and don't know what all. The movie itself has an awful lot of Hutton, so avid a performer that her co-stars are virtually wait staff, but, as so often, Astaire manages the choreography to make his partner look as good as he does. In this one number, at least, the two match up nicely.

By this time, Loesser had already launched his Broadway career, with *Where's Charley?* (1948), whose Edwardian English setting inspired him to echo, very subtly, English musical-comedy style. True, the show's hit, "Once in Love With Amy," is a soft shoe in a solid American tradition. And "Make a Miracle" was an example of Loesser's "conversational duet with interlocking lines" style. But certain *Where's Charley?* numbers— "Better Get Out Of Here" and "The New Ashmolean Marching Society and Students Conservatory Band" in particular—have the flavor of coeval West End musicals with a period setting, from *Bless the Bride* to *Chrysanthemum*.

In fact, Loesser was unique among his peers for his ability to craft each stage score ethnocentrically, so that the folkish strains of *Greenwillow* (1960) were as far from the spoofy industrial anthems of *How To Succeed in Business Without Really Trying* (1961) as Jerome Kern is from Cole Porter.

Loesser did write one last original movie score, for Samuel Goldwyn's *Hans Christian Andersen* (1952), developing a lyricism of playful innocence, suitable for the saga of an author of fairy tales. "The King's New Clothes" and "Thumbelina" are amusingly infantile, and "Wonderful Copenhagen" could be a drinking song fresh from a Danish tavern. Better, "Inchworm," which Andersen sings while his favorite audience—children—is in school, is introduced by a captivating invention, Loesser's musical setting of the addition tables teachers use to drill arithmetic into young minds. And of course he composed the mnemonics to sing simultaneously with the "Inchworm" refrain itself, a wonderful effect.

Unfortunately, the film as a whole, though extremely successful when new, does not hold up well. The dance scenes, including a fifteen-minute capsule ballet of Andersen's tale "The Little Mermaid" (the source also of the 1989 Disney cartoon feature) are impressive, especially because of the captivating Jeanmaire. And, in the title role, Danny Kaye, so manic and affected in his other performances, carefully enacts a naif utterly entranced by his own imagination. But the atmosphere of the mise en scène is suffused with fakery—fake village, fake Copenhagen, fake Europe. There are a lot of harrumphing oldsters in whiskers and frock coats or women extras in aprons bearing market baskets, clichés even an operetta would blush to present. Furthermore, at a cost of four million dollars, *Hans Christian Andersen* should look spectacular. But only the ballets fill the eye.

Goldwyn produced also—again at great expense—the film version of Loesser's *Guys and Dolls* (1955), retaining the slightly fantastical feeling of the 1950 Broadway production, presumably because Damon Runyon's outlawry of gamblers and broads is from another world in the first place. Thus, Goldwyn hired many of the show's secondary principals (and one of the leads, Vivian Blaine) and the choreographer, Michael Kidd. The result, however, is more stagey than necessary. Times Square, the nightclub, the Save-a-Soul mission, and the rest of the Runyonland theme park is *scenery*. The film lacks the validating reality we expect in "the movie version."

Another surprise: Goldwyn cast two Novelty Stars in lead singing parts without dubbing them. As Sky and Sarah, Marlon Brando and Jean Simmons couldn't possibly have handled the big duet, "I've Never Been in Love Before," which may be why it was dropped in favor of a new Loesser ballad, "[Your eyes are the eyes of] A Woman in Love." But Goldwyn's bold gamble serves us well, for Simmons and Brando *sound* like their characters in a way that dubbed actors almost never do—and *Guys and Dolls* boasts an extremely characterful score. Brando's "Luck Be a Lady" is arrestingly playful, for while Sky is gambling on his future, he is nevertheless a man who never gets weighty about anything. Some Skys implore and demand; Brando keeps it Sky-light—and Simmons' "If I Were a Bell" is surprisingly well sung. Not acted: *sung*. Her last note—on "Ding!"—is so brightly triumphant it's almost disappointing to learn that it's only the C above middle C.

Frank Sinatra wanted to play Sky, because he's the sexy, confident lead. But Goldwyn saw Sinatra as the other guy, Nathan Detroit, neither sexy nor confident. This M.O. does not make Mr. Sinatra a joyful party (to phrase it in Damon Runyon's idiom). But he was still turning his career around after a slump broken only by his Oscar win for *From Here To Eternity* two years earlier—and the famous series of Capitol LPs that established Sinatra as an archon of the American Songbook started coming out only when *Guys and Dolls* did. So even second fiddle was tempting—and, in another addition to his stage score, Loesser gave Sinatra "Adelaide," matching Sinatra's easy-peasy delivery and using gambling imagery to suit the character. Oddly, its verse is more interesting than its chorus, as when Sinatra notes that his intended wants five children after they've wed. "Five's a difficult point to make," he observes.

The entire part was a perfect fit for Sinatra, but he couldn't forgive Brando for getting the alpha-male role. Further, Brando took his time when shooting, absorbing his throughlines and assimilating character focus. Sinatra preferred to cut through the actory "process" and shoot the damn take already: the movie star versus the thespian.

As we compare stage and film musicals and the opportunities they respectively offer to songwriters, we should remember that the two forms depend on entirely different infrastructures of performing talent. They can share stars, as when, say, Ethel Merman films her stage roles in *Anything Goes* and, much later, *Call Me Madam*. But the way a Jeanne Crain or Frank Sinatra (even during his comeback phase) amplify what academia would call the "text" of a big budget Hollywood production is not at all comparable to what a Barbara Cook or Alfred Drake may represent in their Broadway assignments. A movie star always tilts a role in his or her own direction—even unwillingly.

When he was still alive, the most famous thing about Harold Arlen was that he wasn't famous. Other composers—Richard Rodgers, George Gershwin—were household names, but then they had steady partners for long periods and were thus able to build a brand: Rodgers and Hart, George and Ira Gershwin, Rodgers and Hammerstein. Arlen worked most often with Johnny Mercer, E. Y. Harburg, and Ira Gershwin (after George's death), all of them first division—but that presents a confusing game of musical chairs to the average listener. Thus, Arlen's name never caught any major traction.

Then, too, Arlen composed in densely chromatic harmony and a jazz style that resisted the evolution of popular-music jazz into swing in the 1930s and 1940s. This gave Arlen a unique voice that seemed black to many ears. "He looks white!" a bewildered Marlene Dietrich cried after meeting Arlen, in a story recorded by Dietrich's daughter, Maria Riva, in her memoirs. "How can the man who wrote 'Stormy Weather' be white?" Arlen not only wrote "Stormy Weather": he sang it, as a vocalist on commercial discs, and his singing style, too, was black, in a light baritenor given to all sorts of lilting inflections and Cotton Club "shouts" in and around the music.

Further, of Arlen's seven book shows on Broadway, five have major black characters and three of those use all-black (or nearly so) casts.

Of course, this is not the sound we hear in Arlen's music for MGM's *The Wizard of Oz* (1939), written with Harburg. On the contrary, much of this score is extremely diatonic. "Ding-Dong! The Witch Is Dead," "We're Off To See the Wizard," and "The Merry Old Land Of Oz" suggest the music small children delight in when they first start playing records. But these are the tunes of fairyland. "Over the Rainbow"—the Heroine's Wanting Song, before all the magic starts—is not only very chromatic but bears a most unusual release, with seesawing eighth notes in the tonic and then the supertonic seventh over a tonic pedal, then in the tonic and the submediant minor diminished with an added fourth, a wow of a chord that brings the entire song to an emotional climax while it's still in progress.

This isn't jazz per se. This is Broadway thinking, using different sound-scapes to define location—up-to-date and popular for the heroine but simplistic for the paradise she dreams up. (In the film, that is; in L. Frank Baum's book the visit is real.) Similarly, the three "If I Only"s for her companions, to the same music with different lyrics each time, use a loopy gavotte to characterize, in effect, three Kansas farmhands transformed into humanoid phantasms.

There was one miscalculation, in "The Jitterbug," sheer swing in which white notes flirt with black notes, much too newfangled for a number sung in a forest in Oz. It would appear that Arlen and Harburg were paying homage to Judy Garland's MGM identity as a kid who sings the latest hi-de-ho, a profile already used in a few of her pictures. But here Garland was a native of the Great Plains, a kid who probably sings little more than hymns. The number was filmed but cut, and we are always told that a jitterbug number would have dated the film in the periodic re-releases that MGM must already have had in mind for it. But I think someone at the studio realized that the song channeled the wrong Judy Garland.

Garland worked with Arlen again (now to Ira Gershwin's lyrics) on Warner Bros.' *A Star Is Born* (1954), a musical version of the 1937 Janet Gaynor film, producer David O. Selznick's despondent valentine to the industry that was his life. It's really *A Star Is Killed*, for Gaynor rises while her actor husband, played by Fredric March, falls. He ends a suicide: is this a likely musical, given the era's understanding of how a musical behaves? Besides, James Mason now had the March role, and Mason didn't sing.

The cure was to give Garland all the vocals and to build the score out of performance pieces (including "Someone at Last," wherein Garland re-creates a staging for Mason alone). Just one singer among the principals? And no character or story songs? Yet it's an astonishingly good picture, partly because of Moss Hart's script and George Cukor's direction but mainly because Garland and Mason are really thrilling. These are not "movie star" performances, in which a charismatic personality indicates and shticks his or her way through a role, as with Clark Gable in *Gone With the Wind* or the entire career of Miriam Hopkins. Mason was never considered to be part of that magnificent crew of British actors headed by Olivier, Gielgud, and Richardson, probably because he worked almost exclusively in cinema; and musical-comedy people, like Garland, are not thought of as "actors" per se. Yet both are extraordinarily persuasive,

Consider their first scene together, which gives a lift to the old meaning of "meeting cute." This meeting is dangerous. Garland and two boys are to entertain at a Major Hollywood Event, and, with the orchestra onstage, they begin "Gotta Have Me Go With You." But something's amiss backstage, and Cukor's camera moves into the wings to reveal a drunken James Mason staggering around and shoving guys out of his way as he heads for the stage. The conductor and pianist worriedly take this in, and then Garland notices. She decides to "nice" Mason, who has suddenly gained the stage, back out of sight. He resists, so she impulsively works him into the routine and, highly amused, he actually goes along with it, faking a show-biz smile and hand gestures. He even brings Garland out with him for a bow, as if the whole thing had been planned.

What fascinates is the utter naturalism that everybody brings to the number, starting with Arlen and Gershwin, who concocted one of those snappy uptunes in the composer's white style—so harmless and undramatic, the last thing you'd expect to see sabotaged by an ugly scene. And both Garland and Mason work in a reality very difficult to "stage," like a fistfight or a nervous crackup: it either "*is*" real or it looks fake. Then, too, the incident uses music to reveal character, in a way: she is the ultimate giving performer, not only to the audience but to him, and he is the ultimate self-hater, whose generosity is overwhelmed by his anger. Me can't go with you, after all. She can save him from humiliating himself, but only on stage. Not in life.

It's a drama with songs, perhaps, and the heart of it, the famous dressing-room scene in which Garland pours out her feelings to her producer boss, Charles Bickford, is an exhibition piece in two ways: one, for Garland's very moving confession, mixed of love for Mason, of protection of his pride, and of hatred for him. Yes, she says so, straight out. But the second way points up an anomaly in the very notion of a movie musical, for this one doesn't want to convey this richly emotional scene in music, even with one of the era's best singers in the role.

On Broadway, without question, this scene could have been the equivalent of *Carousel*'s "Soliloquy" or *Gypsy*'s "Rose's Turn." But Hollywood—as we have seen many times already in these pages—has always preferred to run its business hours in dialogue. Music is the coffee break.

This obtains even when one of those dramas with songs contains perhaps the greatest of all Arlen's titles (to Johnny Mercer's lyrics), "Blues in the Night." I've saved this film anachronistically for last because it is actually about music—more specifically, about a swing band struggling to survive. It, too, is called *Blues in the Night* (1941), and it has the oddest cast in the movie musical's history. For one thing, all the men are character actors—Richard Whorf, Lloyd Nolan, Jack Carson, Howard da Silva, Elia Kazan. They hitch rides on boxcars, scrounge and hustle to live. There's no singing guy, no goofy boy friend, no Ray Bolger or Dick Haymes. The two women principals are blond, helpful Priscilla Lane, the band vocalist, and Betty Field, whom we recently footnoted as a teenaged vamp in *Seventeen*. Here she is, to put it gently, evolved: dark and abrasive, eventually a murderess and then driven to her death in a car wreck by a suicidal maniac. One asks, Where does the music fit into all this? Musicals are supposed to express emotions, wishes, finding a way to get on in the world: "Happiness Is a Thing Called Joe" or "Ac-cent-tchu-ate the Positive," to name two of Arlen's Hollywood numbers.

However, in this film, music expresses the sound of the instrumentalist: the riffs and chords and rhythm that create his life. We see the band constantly at work, not just to earn a living but to explain who they are to themselves and others. At one point, they're in some night spot, listening to a rival group, and trumpeter Carson suddenly gets up and seizes a solo—not to crab the other band's act, but to establish unity with it, share in a mission of redeeming a crass world with the wonder of music, of the jazz that makes every player his own maestro because jazz is the novel that no one can write. It isn't written. It's *played*.

Arlen and Mercer were ideal for this job, as both had "black" and "white" sides. The blues itself is black, and when the movie reaches the title number, early on, the band is in jail, listening to a black prisoner launch his own personal blues. From its first line—"My mama done tol' me, when I was in kneepants"—we hear something authentic. The blacks in the scene call it "the misery," but Whorf, the band's chief and pianist, spots it as "the real lowdown New Orleans blues." The song rises out of guts and trouble with a transcendent poetry cut by a passing train whistle. It's one of the most American of numbers, folk wisdom about the ways of love packed into a sucker punch, because once the loving is done, you've only one thing left: the blues in the night.

Interestingly, though everyone in the scene is a prisoner, the whites and blacks are separated, in two different cells, and this movie is made of such separations in a kind of coherence of hostile ingredients—"good" music from "bad," for instance, when Whorf leaves the band and takes up with a festive outfit of the Paul Whiteman type, with everyone in ridiculous white tail suits, the music as dressed up as they are. While Whorf is performing, his four former male partners deliberately stand nearby to stare at and music-shame him, all immobile but for Kazan's gum-chewing. This leads to Whorf's nervous breakdown, in an imaginative montage of surreal images of dueling musics till he sees himself as an organ-grinder's monkey. He's a beast, fronting for canned melody—which of course is how his ex-bandmates see his fancy new gig.

Oddly, we never hear the title song sung from start to finish, and its return appearances are of the non-vocal, jazz-embellished sort. It's as if Warner Bros. expected Hollywood's song-hit infrastructure of radio singers, recordings, and sheet-music sales to launch the number; the other songs get more conclusive exposure. "This Time the Dream's On Me" is a suave ballad with a wistful kick to it, one of thousands such written at this time. "Hang On To Your Lids, Kids" adopts a bit of bop talk. And "Says Who? Says You, Says I!" is the film's only full-scale number, offered by that snooty orchestra Whorf temporarily joins, with dizzy vocalist Joyce Compton backed by a quartet of loco band guys, one of whom dances violently atop Whorf's grand piano. This is a tricky number to write, as Arlen and Mercer have to fashion an amusing comic novelty while marking it as a waste of our time. It's music we're supposed to hate because its characters hate it, because it's the opposite of "Blues in the Night," something contrived rather than something felt.

This is a strange film, torn over whether music is a means of deeply personal communication or just a living: sacred or profane. Even stranger, it's a musical for mostly non-singing actors and a director, Anatole Litvak, who was primarily known for dark films. Some might not see *Blues in the Night* as a musical at all—and the playing is dubbed, even Whorf's very persuasive action at the keyboard.

Yet this movie reminds us that Hollywood's definition of a musical was more fluid than Broadway's at this time, and that a *Blues in the Night* could utilize an acting ensemble far more intense than those in concurrent Broadway musicals such as *Cabin in the Sky*, *Pal Joey*, or *Lady in the Dark*. This is why musical-theatre historians, more and more, are including the Hollywood forms in their chronicles: because cinema gave our Harms and Chappell men innovative dramatic platforms. The history is incomplete without them.

CHAPTER 10

⌒∿⌒

Direct from Broadway

We've seen a tremendous variation in how Hollywood films stage shows, from the first *Desert Song*, in 1929 (using a cut-down version of the entire work), to the first *New Moon*, a year later (with a wholly different story and only some of the original's core numbers). Soon enough, Hollywood routined radical adaptations, even if the 1936 *Show Boat* is famous for its fidelity.

But that's just it: *Show Boat* stands out precisely because Hollywood was buying stage properties *with the intention of altering them in all sorts of ways.* This policy resulted in some rather alienated retoolings, as with MGM's film version of Jerome Kern and Oscar Hammerstein's *Very Warm For May.* Here are the authors of *Show Boat*: the pioneers in the revolution toward intelligent music theatre. Yet the *May* movie threw out their storyline, their entire score except for "All the Things You Are," and even their title, releasing the results as *Broadway Rhythm* (1944). The film is so little known that though Nancy Walker and Lena Horne are in it, it is never seen and never mentioned.

Then, suddenly, Hollywood launched a cycle of stage shows filmed with respect—*Annie Get Your Gun* (1950), *Call Me Madam* (1953), *Kiss Me, Kate* (1953), *Guys and Dolls* (1955). One wonders if the prestige of the forties "musical play"—the *Carousel*s and *Brigadoon*s, with their solemn intensity and hit filled cast albums—contributed to this love affair with Broadway. True, the four titles cited above are musical comedies, not musical plays. Still, the quartet displays the musical-play influence in the way each narrative makes songs necessary rather than simply makes room for songs. Think of *Annie Get Your Gun*'s "The Girl That I Marry" and "You Can't Get a Man With a Gun," counteracting statements in the two leads' personality war that runs the plot. Think of *Guys and Dolls*' "Adelaide's Lament," one of the great character numbers of all time, almost the musical's equivalent of a Shakespearean soliloquy.

As Hollywood pursued this semi-purist approach, it developed a set of Commandments for adaptations from the stage, adhered to more often than not:

I: Thou shalt cast by talent rather than by fame, if practical with the original Broadway star.

II: Thou shalt retain the original narrative structure and all or most of the score, without interpolations.

III: All right, thou mayest interpolate, but thou shalt let the original creators make the new numbers.

Thus, Warner Bros.' *The Music Man* (1962) stood in perfect alignment with the new tablets, using Robert Preston in the "lovable con man" role he had made his own on the stage. A few others of the Broadway crew repeated their parts, and the casting found interesting simulacra for the more crucial support people—bumbling Paul Ford and impervious Hermione Gingold as the mayor and his wife, Buddy Hackett as Preston's confidant.

Opposite Preston was Shirley Jones, a very able performer but, more important, extremely attractive, thus to underline that this heroine is not a wallflower: she has been spurning suitors because they don't attain to her ideal of the man who "occasionally [would] ponder what made Shakespeare and Beethoven great." This makes it all the more . . . well, philosophical . . . that she ends up with someone else entirely, for it was Broadway that touted the romantic misalliance. Hollywood's prominent musicals tended to match ego-concordant stars—Astaire and Rogers, say, or Garland and Kelly, however much they bickered. On Broadway, even in musicals written in the early twentieth century, when the star system ruled, ego-discordant match-ups were preferred, as with *Girl Crazy*, *Lady in the Dark*, *The King and I*. The dude and the western cowgirl (she's actually a postmistress); the nervous woman editor and the employee forever provoking her; and the schoolmarm and her schoolboy king, respectively, gave the stage musical its content; in the movies, the stars were the content.

The Music Man's stage score—a large one, counting nineteen numbers—was almost entirely on site, with one new piece by, again at the tablets' command, the show's author, Meredith Willson, "Being in Love." This mildly swinging, easy-listen solo replaced the heroine's semi-operatic "My White Knight," although the new song borrows some of the old one as a trio section. This fidelity to what was heard on Broadway clearly was part of Warner Bros.' plan, for the original director (Morton Da Costa) and choreographer (Onna White) were both in charge of the film as well.

And Warners treated *Gypsy* (1962) with comparable respect, albeit with Rosalind Russell replacing Ethel Merman in the role that Merman thought she had earned through a towering portrayal, the first in her career. However, the new director, Mervyn LeRoy, subtly retilted the action, seeing Rose as more than a stage mother: as an out-of-work actor. We tend to think of *Gypsy* as a family saga centered on a parent problem. LeRoy viewed it as a backstager, constantly pulling the camera into the middle of an auditorium to gaze greedily upon a stage—even during the credits, the first visual of all. Later, during the Farmboys act, when other Roses (starting with Merman on Broadway) occasionally inject themselves into the scene, LeRoy had Russell doing virtually the entire act along with the kids. So Rose's true vocation is not manager. It's performer.

Further, Russell plays an essentially innocent Rose, less the bulldozer we often see and more someone who just doesn't understand what she's up against. Most interesting, the usual Rose hits the outstanding transitional beat in the railroad station scene at the end of Act One—going numb at daughter June's desertion, then catching fire with innovative plans for daughter Louise. But Russell hits that beat earlier, in the scene at the vaudeville magnate's office, when Rose learns she could lose control of June. Most Roses get angry; Russell, instead, is stricken: at the first relization that her dream might evaporate on her. Rose needs June to reach stardom under Rose's control. Because Rose is June is Rose, in that neurosis that affects a parent living through his or her child. Take June from Rose and Rose loses her career—her stardom.

But hold: isn't Rose the musical's great singing role? Russell, while very personable in songs calibrated to her limited gifts, as on Broadway in *Wonderful Town* (1953), could not have delivered an adequate—much less superb—Rose. All the same, she pre-recorded her numbers, and Warner Bros. used her track for "Mr. Goldstone," hiring Lisa Kirk to dub most of the rest of Russell's singing (a rare case in which the vocal ghost was a major performer in her own right). At times, Kirk is "blended" in with Russell, but the very start of "Everything's Coming Up Roses"—the "I had a dream" invocation—is so Lisa Kirk in timbre that it overwhelms the dramatic moment.

In passing over Merman, Warners did sort of break the First Commandment, even if Russell had always been a talent rather than a "movie star." But, lo, the entire Jule Styne-Stephen Sondheim score was filmed,[1] and while two studio musicians were credited with the orchestrations, they are

1. "Together Wherever We Go" was cut at the very last minute, as the story slows up a bit just then. The stage musical generally likes to move along to the next number, but the Hollywood musical prefers instead to move to the next plot event. "Together" is bonused on the DVD; this is the only other song in which Russell sings without Kirk's help.

clearly drawn from the famous original set, by Sid Ramin and Robert Ginzler. Excepting *Top Banana* (1954) and *Li'l Abner* (1959), stage shows filmed, respectively, right in the theatre and on sound stages in a replica mounting, *Gypsy* might be the most faithful Broadway adaptation of the age. Little tweaks here and there only emphasize this, as in the use of the lead family's name (Hovick), never mentioned in the play text; or the introduction of Herbie (Karl Malden) early on, as the talent-show impresario Uncle Jocko, bringing him closer to the saga of Rose and her daughters than he had been on Broadway. Even the use of Jack Benny in an unbilled cameo references Broadway by irony, as he's the last performer we'd expect to see working on stage.[2] We see him swaggering into the wings after his act, to a stagehand's "What a ham." And Russell replies, "He'll never get anyplace."

Cute. Billed on Broadway as "a musical fable" (presumably to finesse its free interpretation of the lives of Gypsy Rose Lee, June Havoc, and their mother), *Gypsy* tells of vaudeville and burlesque. It's not the big time. Yet there's a paradox here, for *Gypsy* itself is the big-time Broadway musical in its essence, a smash and a classic with the American equivalent of Isolde, Manon, and Violetta as its heroine: the role without which no diva's career is complete. And, frankly, after seeing Hollywood humiliate our songwriters time and again, it's refreshing to find it almost slavishly recreating what has become one of our classic stage shows.

In fact, very little about Warner Bros.' *Gypsy* is "Hollywood," unless it be the use of Natalie Wood as Louise, though she is delightfully game and even does her own singing. There is one touch of movie-star glamor, in Rosalind Russell's last outfit, a smashing black-and-white affair with plumed hat, tie, gloves, and heels all a-match—and then Russell adds a dollop of red, plucking a rose from a bouquet. It's too high fashion for Rose. But after over two hours of realistic costuming, Russell must have asked LeRoy to let her finish up in something regal.

We're dealing with the post-studio era now, when the contract players and music departments had been let go, leaving the moguls to spend all their time negotiating with agents and each project to assemble its musical staff from scratch. We were hoping that this shakeup might bring to light new performing talent, as when Ann-Margret turned up in *Bye Bye Birdie* (1963), from the Charles Strouse and Lee Adams Broadway hit loosely premised around the drafting of Elvis Presley. Indeed, Ann-Margret is the first

---

2. Benny, in *Gypsy*'s 1962, was still very famous for a career in radio, movies, and television. He actually appeared on Broadway in revues, but was not popularly associated with the theatre in any real sense.

thing we see, setting up an out-of-story prologue-and-epilogue frame in which she hots up the screen in the title song—new for the film and, as the Commandments dictate, by Strouse and Adams themselves. Alone against a bright blue background, Ann-Margret gives us a kind of visual of a teen 45 hit, complete with privileged teen communication: she pronounces the name of her idol as "Bird-hee," thus affecting a little sob at seeing him depart.

On Broadway, Ann-Margret's character was just a Second Couple soubrette. But the movie built her up, writing her and her vis-à-vis, Bobby Rydell, special-for-the-movie vocals in "Rosie" and "A Lot of Livin' To Do." Indeed, the latter became a plot number with new lyrics, enabling Ann-Margret to defy Rydell and then fight for control in a challenge dance.

Though she had come from Sweden (at the age of six), Hollywood's new ingenue had a very American quality, but indefinably so: her look was wholesome, her attitude ambiguous. *Birdie* was not her first chance at a lead, and she was already getting typecast as a foxy sprite, even one on the dangerous side. This smudged her musical profile and hid her considerable actor's resources, which became apparent only years later. *Birdie*, however, caught her at a just-right time and place, as a good-hearted maid with a will of her own.

When not letting Ann-Margret walk away with the attention, *Birdie* had fun opening up the Broadway numbers "The Telephone Hour," frozen inside boxes on stage, now toured through town as the chorus kids anticipated the mobile phone, chatting away in the soda shop, the gym, the library, the pool. But too much of the score was cut, including "Normal American Boy," one of the great comic plot numbers of its time, simultaneously developing character, satirizing show-biz PR, and introducing the show's central character (after some film footage during the overture), Birdie himself. In a wonderful irony, he never opened his mouth: Elvis, the pop singer of the era, silent in his own establishing number!

Tempted by straight acting, Ann-Margret never did become the musical's next star. Julie Andrews did, as we'll presently see—but a new talent appeared in Barbra Streisand. Hers was an offbeat rise; David Merrick, involved in both of her Broadway shows, *I Can Get It For You Wholesale* (1962) and *Funny Girl* (1964), hated her. His show-biz woman lead would be someone like Ann-Margret, not this Jewish broad who makes no attempt to soubrette herself and make nice to skeptics in the house.

However, the real-life Funny Girl, Fanny Brice, also avoided soubretting herself. On the contrary, her act emphasized the problems of a Jewish girl of narrow cultural background getting caught up in fancy-dan adventures in the world beyond the ghetto. It's a tremendous character, especially when *Funny Girl* itself is made of Brice's real-life adventure: she feels awkward till a handsome gent's love soothes her wary heart.

The Hollywood musical needed these tremendous characters, because it was now in the business of making physically tremendous films—roadshows, to be exact. To repeat: this format called for reserved-seat showings at higher-than-usual prices, with souvenir programs, overture, intermission, and exit music, and even opening and closing curtains, just as in the theatregoer's playhouse. Only after these "hard-ticket" runs ended would the film go into general release (often losing some footage, as we have seen with *Porgy and Bess*), so there was a certain cachet attached to taking in a roadshow, like subscribing to *The New Yorker* or serving fresh caviar.

This exhibition platform dated back to D. W. Griffith's *The Birth of a Nation* (1915), but the immense success of sixties roadshows such as *West Side Story* and *My Fair Lady* inspired every studio to put roadshow commissions into production. And the Roadshow of Roadshows, *The Sound of Music*, which played hard-ticket bookings for a phenomenal four-and-a-half years, seemed to propose certain rules of engagement:

A. There should be a lot of footage, a lot of characters, and a lot of songs, aiming at at least a two-and-a-half-hour running time.
B. There should be a lot of location shooting, preferably of the Alps.
C. There should be a lot of Julie Andrews.

Andrews couldn't be in every roadshow, but Streisand would work just as well, albeit in her own way: it was the 1960s, when Different was a genre. *Funny Girl*'s second-act storyline ran thin, and Brice's love match, Nick Arnstein, lacked character content, because his role had been cut back while the troubled stage show was in tryout and fixer Jerome Robbins rearranged the work as a Streisand vehicle. But the Jule Styne-Bob Merrill score was very strong; the songs and Streisand, really, are what put the piece over.

Ironically, *Funny Girl*'s producer, Ray Stark (Brice's son-in-law, as it happens), had wanted to interpolate Brice's personal material, such as "Second Hand Rose," "I'd Rather Be Blue Over You (Than Be Happy With Somebody Else)," and her torch theme song, "My Man." Styne and Merrill blocked Stark, writing their own Brice specialties, in the "Private Schwartz from Rockaway" section of "Rat-Tat-Tat-Tat" and the somewhat "My Man"-ish "The Music That Makes Me Dance."

But that was Broadway. As we have seen over and over in these pages, the attitude and power of the Hollywood producer are overwhelming, and, now that Stark was the honcho of the movie *Funny Girl*, he deposited the three Brice specialties cited above into the continuity. Further, he dropped "Rat-Tat-Tat-Tat" and "The Music That Makes Me Dance" along with six more of the Broadway numbers, a tyrannical defiance of the Commandments. And, while we're at it, Omar Sharif makes a dull part duller, with his petit-four smile and affectless line deliveries. Further, director William Wyler, though he had steered many an actor toward an Oscar through his strangely uncommunicative multi-take style, wasn't adept in the making of musicals.

Luckily, Wyler left choreographer Herbert Ross in charge of the musical scenes, so it was Ross who filmed the first-act finale—the grandest visual in the film, as roadshow etiquette increasingly demanded—around a spectacular natural setting for "Don't Rain On My Parade." Brice abandons a tour, separating herself from a pride of Ziegfeld girls at a railroad station, and hops a train to meet Nick's Europe-bound ocean liner. The vocal, which starts with Streisand addressing the girls, slips into voiceover, and when she gains New York Harbor, right at "Here I am!," there's a marvelous glitch as both plot and the music go absolutely dead all at once: Nick's ship has departed.

Well, no problem—Fanny simply commandeers a tugboat to intercept Nick at sea. And the voiceover track "moves" with the scenery to let us hear what we see as Ross' camera pulls way, way back for a kind of Destiny and Me shot to close Act One. Broadway itself couldn't have given us a more rousing intermission curtain.

How to top that for the movie's finale? It had to be "My Man," *Funny Girl's* aria d'obbligo—the number the entire storyline has been charging up to for three hours. Of course, this takes us an ocean away from Broadway songwriters, as the authors of the piece are composer Maurice Yvain and lyricists Albert Willemetz and Jacques Charles. The first two were more or less the Rodgers and Hart of French musical comedy in the 1920s and 1930s, and the English lyrics were by Channing Pollock, a New Yorker of minor note even in his day. At that, the singer who introduced (and kept on reviving) "Mon Homme," Mistinguett, claims a European but not American fame.

So it's a foreign number. Mistinguett was actually rather playful in it, but Fanny Brice, who re-introduced the song in two different Ziegfeld shows, naturalized it in a heartfelt rendering, and Streisand turned it into a slow-build powerhouse of a piece, starting so freely that she found it impossible to lip-synch it to pre-recording. In an interview on National Public Radio in 2012, Streisand said she had to fight the usual Hollywood authorities, who don't like singing live on the set. It so upsets the protocols. "But I feel like I want to," Streisand explained all this time later, because "I don't know when I'm going to cry. I can't lip-synch that."

So Streisand sang the first chorus (the movie skipped the verse) live, taking her own individual time in the phrasing and letting the tears fall where they might. "And we had just a piano [out of view, the orchestra track to be added later], as I hear they do in *Les Mis*...because every time I did it was slightly different, you know?" At the second chorus, Streisand reverted to lip-synching, going into one of the most famous Big Sings in Hollywood history. And there *Funny Girl* fades out, stupendously.

Even before *Funny Girl* opened, to extremely good business, Streisand was making her second starring-vehicle roadshow title, Fox's *Hello, Dolly!* (1969). But 1969 was the new 1930: audiences were tiring of musicals, especially these Events, colossal to a fault. So *Dolly!*'s director, Gene Kelly—or, more honestly, *Dolly!*'s choreographer, Michael Kidd—assembled a parade on Little Old New York's Fourteenth Street for the first-act finale that was planned to be the hugest thing you ever saw on screen.

And it couldn't be a location shoot: Fox had to build an antique Fourteenth Street from scratch. The sidewalks were filled with spectators—all in period dress, mind you—and on came the marchers: a wind band; cavalrymen bearing a pennant each; a float of period beauties; a "flag" made of blue umbrellas and outstretched red and white banners; the Woman's Christian Temperance Union, looking suitably grumpy; a float devoted to Wagner's *Ring* operas; highland bagpipers; girls in red, white, and blue exercising with tiny period dumbbells; a second wind band; bicylists on those crazy period wheelers; a meat-packers' float complete with squealing period pig; the Knights of the Hudson, who include Streisand's vis-à-vis, Walter Matthau, as "the well-known unmarried half-a-millionaire" she's after; Barnum & Bailey clowns; and a Budweiser truck with a dalmation. Finally, Streisand gets some plot data out of all this, running up to Matthau, who tells her, "I came here for some privacy."

From her, he means. Because most of the above groups number some forty to fifty people each. Clearly, Fox's mogul, Darryl Zanuck, wanted this scene, built around "Before the Parade Passes By," to out-big everything that had come before, from *Cavalcade*'s departure of the troop ship and *King Kong*'s island wall to *Gone With the Wind*'s plaza of the Confederate wounded and *Ben-Hur*'s chariot race, not to mention the Babylon of *Intolerance*. Big was a genre, too.

Big meant Kidd's turning many of the songs into production numbers, so that, for instance, "Put On Your Sunday Clothes" expands into an "Everybody onstage for the train number" spectacle. True, the stage *Dolly!* went lavish for this scene, too. But filling the stage creates tidier housekeeping than filling the screen. It's worth noting that *The Sound of Music* did not enlarge on the Broadway staging beyond the use of outdoor shooting and, in one case, using the Bil Baird Marionettes.

As well, big meant bringing in no less than Louis Armstrong for the title number—a correction of history, as a black orchestra in a white establishment like the Harmonia Gardens was unofficially forbidden in the story's 1890. But of course the Streisand-Armstrong duet is matchless, and at last we learn how to pronounce his first name, at her tutorial: it's Lou-iss, not Lou-ee. The rest of the cast was modest (though Michael Crawford and Tommy Tune eventually punched out into fame), leaving only Matthau to challenge Streisand for authority control. He didn't stand a chance, which may explain why he was so hostile to her during filming. True, she's self-absorbed and demanding on the set. In a famous story, one of the *Funny Girl* crew gripes to another about the way Streisand plagues William Wyler with "suggestions," and the other crew member replies, "Don't be so hard on her. After all, it's the first film she's ever directed."

Everything was big on *Hello, Dolly!*, from the feuds (because Gene Kelly was no sweetheart, either) to the amount of money lost, because big was a trap: the concentration of these roadshow specials drained the ticket-buying pool. And just when these white elephants threatened to bankrupt Hollywood—yea, even with Julie Andrews in them—one or another would bank heavy and the studios would hurl themselves into yet more overpriced projects.

Oliver! (1968) was one of those smash hits; it even won the Best Picture Oscar. Of course, here we have not a Broadway songwriter but one from the West End, Lionel Bart. Further, *Oliver!* the movie was a purely British project. *The Boy Friend* (1971), too, though an MGM property (and, by merry chance, the show that first brought Julie Andrews to America), was made entirely under British auspices, albeit with our own Tommy Tune in the cast.

But a third English musical, like the first two a Broadway hit, merits some discussion: *Half a Sixpence* (1967), from H. G. Wells' novel *Kipps*. Paramount commissioned the film, Americans Charles H. Schneer and George Sidney produced it, Sidney directed it, and, again, there was one American in the cast, Grover Dale, repeating his Broadway role. (We should probably cite as well Cyril Ritchard, who though Australian had made his career in American theatre and television from 1947 as a sort of professional Brit.)

Here was another roadshow that lost millions. Looking back, today's commentators see *Sixpence* as twee fluff, out of its depth in the roiling, political 1960s. Even at the time, film critics who hated all musicals but especially the twee-fluff ones pounced like coyotes on a lost lambkin. In the *New York Times*, Renata Adler called *Sixpence*'s songs "trite, gay, and thoroughly meaningless, [making] no concession to anything that has happened in popular music in the last ten years."

No, actually, the songs bear the meanings that the story and characters need to project at each given point in the continuity. And why is this scold lecturing us on the sounds that a period (or any) musical should be styled in? Doesn't she really mean that the musical as a form isn't hip and relevant in the required sixties manner? But, unbeknown to Renata Adler, *Half a Sixpence*'s charming exterior fronts for a scathing exposure of the destructive one per cent, because H. G. Wells was a progressive with a hatred of the authoritarian establishment and a missionary's compassion for its victims. "They were all caught," he wrote of Arthur Kipps and his fellow workers. "All life took on the hue of one perpetual dismal Monday morning."

Half a Sixpence tells of a simple working-class lad who comes into money and *for that reason alone* is taken up by haughty bigwigs who rob him of his fortune and then abandon him. Interestingly, the far-left film director Rainer Werner Fassbinder told the exact same tale in *Faustrecht der Freiheit* (roughly, Might Makes Right), seen here as *Fox and His Friends*, in 1976. The respective settings of the two movies are very different, and instead of Tommy Steele in a musical with a heterosexual love plot, the German film gives us Fassbinder himself in the lead, the sex is gay (including frontal nudity from the auteur himself), and it's no musical. Indeed, *Faustrecht der Freiheit* ends with the protagonist's death. His fancy friends have sucked him dry as if they were vampires. As if.

There was a talkie *Kipps* in 1941, with Michael Redgrave, then the West End musical (1963), when Tommy Steele inherited the character. Steele played it in New York as well (in a slight revision), then naturally headlined in the movie, and all four versions follow Wells' story punctiliously, from the hero's poor and unhappy childhood on to his work in a dry-goods shop, thence to life among the very well-off, whom he at first emulates and finally rejects.

Director Sidney doesn't mince shots, so to speak. The dry-goods employer is a fat, ugly, self-righteous exploiter of the helpless, and the aristos are steely structures carved in flesh. True, Sidney does seem to play favorites between the two young women Kipps loves, for his working-class childhood sweetheart, Ann, is photographed straight on, no frills, while the upper-class Lorelei, called Helen, is given a halo of light (no doubt to show us how the naively smitten Kipps sees her). Anyway, her grande-dame mother and brother are creeps in plumage. Fidgeting in tails at a fancy dinner, Kipps says, of his collar, "It's cuttin' me 'ead off!":

BROTHER: My.
MOTHER: Head.
DAUGHTER: Off.

Most tellingly, during the set-piece of a boat race (the film's sole excursion into Big), Sidney establishes Ann rooting for him in the crowd, then allows Helen's umbrella to block Ann from our view, rather as the rich casually "vanish" inconvenient third parties.

A goodly portion of David Heneker's London score was cut, though that was already true in the Broadway version. But, as if to finesse the Third Commandment, the two new numbers, "This Is My World" and "The Race,"[3] are of uncertain authorship. Paramount credited the pair to Heneker and the film's music director, Irwin Kostal. Did these two really collaborate— the prolific composer-lyricist Heneker and Kostal, known mainly as a Broadway orchestrator? Is this odd byline a euphemism of some kind?

If we're missing numbers, at least there's a ton of dancing, choreographed by Gillian Lynne in her first major Hollywood job. She stages each such number to fit the dimensions of its scenery, whether in the dry-goods store's basement; on the stage of a theatre; along a river bank; or in the pub where Kipps finally marries his Ann. Over at the *Hello, Dolly!* shoot, a number like "Dancing" seems to wander widely through time and space. But the *Sixpence* dances keep the geography local.

The number at the river, "If the Rain's Got To Fall," is especially charming, featuring Kipps and a squad of scruffy children, including one small boy very into keeping up with the others yet never *quite* in sync with them. Dismaying the lyric, the rain does indeed fall   throughout much of the number—and at the end, as Steele and his muddy pack start off, the little boy feels deserted till Steele turns, signals to him, and merrily carries him off on his back. Thus, Sidney and Lynne tell us, visually, that despite Kipps' flirtation with the Great World, he will only be at home with the neighborhood guys.

One problem with *Half a Sixpence* lies with its star. A former rock and roller who switched over to the stage (including a brief spell at the Old Vic), Steele is the embodiment of Kipps. He's also a more than merely ebullient performer: a skyrocket. So a little Tommy Steele goes a long way, and, to rephrase Robert Benchley's joke about garlic, there is no such thing as a little Tommy Steele.

All the same, Steele went on to play the leprechaun in *Finian's Rainbow* (1968), so hip and relevant that it treats political corruption, the oppression of the poor, and racial bigotry. The uninitiated might think of this as a Zeitgeist film, conjured up by the concerns of the era, but the show it is very faithfully based on is from 1947. Conventional in form, it was

---

3. "The Race," which naturally accompanies the regatta scene (in Tommy Steele's voiceover), is thus named on the title card, though the song is more usually called "The Race Is On" and even "Mrs. Botting's Boating," Botting being the philanthropist sponsoring the event.

avant-garde in content, especially as it was the first famous musical truly to integrate black and white choristers, to cast blacks in some supporting roles, and to base numbers—"The Begat" and "Necessity"—on black musical styles.

By 1968, *Finian* was right in the swing of things, and its tidy budget of a mere $4,000,000 allowed it to be one of the few late-sixties roadshows to turn a profit. *Finian* is noteworthy as well because of its High Maestro director, Francis Ford Coppola—one of those know-it-all film-school kids telling everyone what a musical should be, right? In fact, Coppola, pushing thirty at the time, respected the material instead of personalizing it with idiosyncratic bric-a-brac for future academics to uncover.

Following the tablets, the screenplay copied the stage script, and only one number ("Necessity" again) was cut. And the casting emphasized not sixties cultural presences (as with *My Fair Lady*'s Audrey Hepburn or *Funny Girl*'s Dr. Zhivago) but suitable talent, with ingratiating vocalists for the sweetheart roles, Petula Clark (who sings "around" the beat, just as her Broadway predecessor, Ella Logan, did) and Don Francks (who in tone and phrasing sounds exactly like Sammy Davis Jr.). In fact, there were no movie stars in view, though Finian himself was a talent star, one of the last of the Golden Age, Fred Astaire. He hadn't filmed a musical since *Silk Stockings*, in 1957, but it was a frustrating return, for Astaire felt Coppola had no feeling for the form. And Coppola didn't—not the form of musical Astaire was used to making.

For instance, some of the show's many dance sequences became choreography by other means—a festive picnic with a tug-of-war and other contests for "If This Isn't Love." Then, too, Astaire was working with his old RKO assistant, Hermes Pan, who was suddenly fired from the picture, offending Astaire's deep-rooted sense of loyalty—to his profession, to the great songwriters who had made songs on him, and to his colleagues. Still, the movie flows along nicely with a likable confidence, not easy to bring off when the plot takes in a pot of gold that grants wishes.

While *Finian's Rainbow* proved a successful roadshow, it was almost the end of the line for that particular exhibition platform, as the last such release to make a profit—a huge one, too—came just three years later. This was *Fiddler on the Roof* (1971), very much in the style of *Finian* in overall fidelity to the stage original while simply taking it outdoors, omitting only one major number ("Now I Have Everything"),[4] and avoiding the use of movie stars.

---

4. There was to have been a new one, by the show's songwriters, Jerry Bock and Sheldon Harnick. Called "Any Day Now," it was a stirring hymn to a future in which inequality will be unknown, a more fitting piece for Perchik, the revolutionary who ends in Siberian captivity, than the dropped "Now I Have Everything." However, Paul Michael Glaser, the film's Perchik, apparently had trouble justifying the music, and it, too, was dropped.

But what to do about the obvious casting problem? Tevye, the show's protagonist, was created by Zero Mostel in a performance for which "larger than life" would be piffling understatement. Every account of the film's production tells us that the studio, United Artists, and the director, Norman Jewison, wanted instead a Tevye who could have bounded right out of the setting, the Russian village of Anatevka, in a real-life way. Mostel seemed to have come from the Planet Showbiz. In the end, they signed Chaim Topol, an Israeli who worked under his last name alone and had played the premiere Tevye in London. For support, they used "natural" rather than established performers; the only Name on the poster was that of Isaac Stern, who supplied the title role's fiddling.

One would have thought Jewison, a Canadian Protestant, would lack feeling for the subject matter, a way of life that had vanished into a folklore known only to the descendants of Jewish immigrants—a Paddy Chayevsky, say: steeped in tales of shtetl life, of how parents raised their children, of how news from the outside world was disseminated, where the food came from. (We actually see Tevye, a dairy farmer, dealing with his animals and making his rounds in town as folks gather to pick up their milk and cheese, with one young man self-importantly collecting "the rabbi's order.")

However, Jewison somehow found his way into this alien culture. His *Fiddler* is not only rich in atmosphere but one of the best directed of all this era's musicals, as shot long and short strim in with unique images—the windows of the synagogue or the vast empty magnificence of the Russia that lies beyond the train siding, where one must signal the engineer to stop for a passenger, so seldom does anyone actually visit or depart from this world closed into itself.

Broadway's *Fiddler*, directed by Jerome Robbins, was another of those very special stagings, like Robbins' *West Side Story* or Gower Champion's *Hello, Dolly!*, that would be reproduced in revival. In its place, the movie physicalizes what Robbins had to suggest—the town falling out en masse to attend a wedding and, later, to move along the village main street with their belongings to disperse throughout the world, by orders of the state.

Here is both a way of life and the death of that life, which is partly why this work, on stage and screen, has proved so compelling. We actually see its infrastructure breaking down, as children choose whom they will wed instead of accepting an "arrangement" by their elders; as men dance with women at that wedding; and as a Jewish girl, one of Tevye's daughters, partners with a Christian: all violations of taboo. Thus, strict control yields to independence, always a thrilling experience in art as in life.

So *Fiddler* is above all a vital movie, something we can't say about *Man of La Mancha* (1972), based on another special staging often revived in replica but physicalized on screen in such rudimentary and earthbound ways that its catastrophic roadshow bookings killed the reserved-seat, two-a-day showing plan forever.[5] Further, *Man of La Mancha* broke the tablets in casting Peter O'Toole and Sophia Loren when their roles demanded performers who know how musicals work. It's a specialized art—a niche art, in a way, despite the gigantic popularity of the form, because not everybody "gets" musicals. In fact, one of the best-kept secrets in Western culture is:

Not everybody gets music, period.

And Hollywood has never quite understood that, which is why, just for instance, Richard Attenborough was allowed to film a clueless debauch of *A Chorus Line* (1985). True, early in the 1950s, Broadway itself began an affair with a casting type I term the Novelty Star, a charismatic performer not associated with any sort of musical endeavor. There were fumbles—Anne Bancroft was very nearly going to play Fanny Brice in *Funny Girl* until Barbra Streisand turned up—but the experiment mostly worked well, with Rosalind Russell, Rex Harrison, Robert Preston, and Tony Randall, among others. However, it doesn't work well with everyone, and it made *Man of La Mancha* laughable. Even the set design was a failure: though shot in color, the movie seemed to play entirely in shades of brown, mahogany, and burnt umber.

Bob Fosse's *Cabaret* (1972) also defied the tablets, reconstructing the show's storyline to accord with its sources, Christopher Isherwood's so-called Berlin Stories (the books are actually entitled *Mr. Norris Changes Trains* [1935] and *Farewell To Berlin* [1939]) and John Van Druten's play drawn from them, *I Am a Camera* (1951). The new narration, bringing in characters that weren't in the stage musical, might have called for new numbers, but in fact Fosse banned all character songs, limiting the musical program to "real life" performance spots—the cabaret acts, 78s heard on a gramophone, and a group singalong, in an outdoor café, of a Nazi anthem. Yes, the score was expanded, by its original authors, Kander and Ebb, but the new tunes were all cabaret spots.

Fosse did respect one of the Commandments in retaining Joel Grey's Emcee from Broadway. Speaking of new talent for the musical, Liza Minnelli, in her first leading role in a film (after a debut in a cameo at the age of three

---

5. Bernardo Bertolucci's *Last Tango in Paris* (1972), released in the United States a year after *La Mancha*, did offer premium-priced, reserved-seat showings in a few cities, catering to the first audience, and there were a few others on a lesser level. But the global or at least national release of Hollywood pictures as roadshows truly did end with *La Mancha*.

in *In the Good Old Summertime*) was a sound choice, ideal in conveying the helplessly piquant appeal that Sally Bowles uses to hide a manipulative and self-centered personality, and of course a heck of a singer. It is a cavil to complain that she's too accomplished to appear in a dive, like resenting a Juliet who isn't, in fact, thirteen.

The rest of *Cabaret*'s cast was unexpected, actors rather than singers, because now the music focused on Minnelli and Grey. Michael York, Helmut Griem, Marisa Berenson, and Fritz Wepper, the other principals, contrasted starkly with the kind of people who turn up in musicals on Broadway—Bert Convy, Lotte Lenya, and Jack Gilford in the original *Cabaret*, for example, who among them claim singing jobs in stage shows from *No, No Nanette* through *Nine* to *The Threepenny Opera*.

Fosse's *Cabaret* was almost a musical by other means. As so often in the films outlined in this volume, it was more a movie than a movie musical, relying heavily on cinematic techniques such as cross-cutting. On stage, *Cabaret* varied story scenes with the commentative cabaret numbers, first one and then the other. The Hollywood *Cabaret* interjects the scenes *into* the numbers and vice versa, letting the action flow along in a single molecule, like a pane of glass. So the opening number, "Willkommen," is interrupted to show Michael York's train pulling into Berlin; Nazis kill Berenson's dog and leave it for her to find on her doorstep even as a girls' cabaret act turns them from dancers into goose-stepping warriors, their musical-comedy canes now repurposed as rifles.

We also get more of the cabaret acts themselves, as in one called "Arabian Night," made of silhouettes of posing odalisques to the accompaniment of "Willkommen" on the musical saw.[6] Or there is "One Man's Pleasure," which turns out to be an erotic flogging scene involving two women while a creepy gentleman looks on. Fosse was a pioneer in the inclusion of the erotic in even carefree art—he opened the musical *Redhead* (1959) with the strangling of a chorus girl, played for comedy but also for real. *Cabaret* was already somewhat edgy on stage, but the film lures the material right over the edge. Thus, in a story arc that had no place in the original, the wealthy nobleman Maximilian (Helmut Griem's role) "collects" York and Minnelli as his latest comrades in sophistication, giving in to every impulse. Early on, Griem even picks out clothing for York, making the selection of a powder-blue sweater as seductive as a naughty whisper after the lights go out.

---

6. It's exactly what it sounds like: a handsaw played with a bow, making an eerie, high-pitched noise suggestive of moaning angel cake. It was quite popular in Germany before the Nazi takeover, so its appearance in *Cabaret* is authentic. Marlene Dietrich was a devotee, even after her emigration to America; when guests became tiresome, she would take it out and play until they left.

And of course Maximilian's attentions, divided between York and Minnelli, prove very divisive indeed:

YORK: (angrily) Screw Maximilian!
MINNELLI: (after a moment, with a little laugh) I do.
YORK: (after another moment) So do I.

Do songwriters ever balk at creating new numbers for the film version? After all, they most likely came up with a lot of songs that weren't used in the stage original in the first place; suddenly, the director or producer must, absolutely must, my dear, have yet another piece or two or a specific kind (so the authors can't use the show's trunk material). And the only thing worse than the studio's asking the authors to write the new titles is the studio's asking some other team instead.

However, Kander and Ebb did balk, at least once, when working on an original, *New York, New York* (1977). And there's a story behind it, rather like the "How the Fox Got His Tail" fables of yore, recorded in *Colored Lights*, Greg Lawrence's book of Kander and Ebb conversations. Martin Scorsese's tribute to the big-band era, *New York, New York* starred Liza Minnelli—by this time virtually the "voice" of Kander and Ebb after many collaborations— opposite Robert De Niro. The latter had an unlikely role as a saxophone player, albeit an irritatingly unreliable one, something De Niro could regard as a worthy acting challenge, expressing the character's vexatious nature while keeping his sexy charm in play. Naturally, Kander and Ebb had provided a "Theme From New York, New York," which they were quite proud of. Like the "theme" tunes we met up with in the very first sound films, it was designed to encapsulate a film's emotional presence while giving it talkabout in airplay, and as far as Kander and Ebb were concerned, they had done their job and the song was going in. Still, as a formality, they performed it for Scorsese and the two stars. Scorsese was impressed and loyal Liza presumably couldn't wait to sing it. But De Niro, of all people, didn't care for it. He felt the authors could do better.

Greatly offended, Ebb was thinking something like, What does this idiot know about music? We're dubbing his saxophone! But Kander, always the peacemaker when geschrei threatens the stability of the creative process, told Ebb they had nothing to lose by writing another number.

So they did write one. And *that* one was the "Theme From New York, New York" that we all know, the one with the irresistible vamp and the "If I can make it here" meme of standoffish, fabulous show-biz Emerald City Manhattan. Amazingly, De Niro had been right after all. And that's how the fox got his tail.

For *Cabaret*, Kander and Ebb supplied three new numbers, and they had to adjust the tone of their songs to accommodate Fosse's determination to bring out the sleazy aspect of the cabaret. In this new context, Sally Bowles' establishing number on Broadway, "Don't Tell Mama," would suggest a nice girl trying to seem racy. Fosse wanted something racy, period—and with a German flavor. The replacement cut, "Mein Herr," sounds like something Marlene Dietrich might have sung in just that time and place, a perfect fit. And "Money Money," superseding a comparably themed number in the stage show, writes over its silly innocence with a grubby hunger. It also ties Grey and Minnelli together (the original number used Grey and the girls) as familiars of the fascist spirit that will crush Weimar democracy, he as its exemplar and she as its irresponsible fellow traveler.

However, the third new number, "Maybe This Time," though it gave Kander and Ebb another hit, doesn't suit the material. Apparently, the plan was to locate Sally's sentimental side. But she doesn't have one. "Cabaret" is her credo and performing is her heart: she wants applause, not love. Anyway, the music of "Maybe This Time" doesn't align with the music retained from Broadway, much less "Mein Herr" and "Money Money," and the lyrics, including a vision of Sally as "Lady Peaceful," sound like Liza Minnelli on the *Tonight Show* with Johnny Carson, not Sally Bowles.

A minor complaint. Yet I say again that *Cabaret* reminds us that movie musicals are often more about telling a story than singing a story. For all its faults, the *Hello, Dolly!* film gives us characters who open themselves up to us in music: "Just Leave Everything To Me," "It Takes a Woman," the verse to "Put On Your Sunday Clothes," "Ribbons Down My Back." The *Cabaret* film's music tells us not who the characters are but what their society is like: "She doesn't look Jewish at all." It is as far from *Born To Dance* or *Good News* as Hollywood can get.

CHAPTER 11

◦∿◦

Rodgers and Hammerstein
and Lerner and Loewe

Phil Stong's novel of 1932, *State Fair*, tells of the Iowan Frake family's visit to one, in which the parents win prizes for livestock and home cuisine and their two kids taste of love, actually having their first sexual affairs. Telling his parents that he is staying with a male friend, son Wayne is in fact spending his nights with Emily, a girl he has met on the fairgrounds. In her rooms, as he drinks his first liquor, she slips into the traditional "something more comfortable," and, as Stong relates, "There was nothing under the lovely kimono but the lovelier Emily. He had somehow known that there would not be—!"

The novel made ideal movie material the following year for Fox, most associated with folksy, rural tales, and the father and daughter would present sound opportunities to Fox's biggest draws, Will Rogers and Janet Gaynor. Rogers was one of the most beloved figures in America, but Gaynor was so big that the studio had to finesse their billing: Rogers came first on the posters while Gaynor headed the names in the title cards.

Henry King directed, but *State Fair*'s aces were scenarists Sonya Levien and Paul Green, for their work lifted characters that, in the novel, are on the flat side. One of the best-known incidents in the movie (and its two remakes) concerns the kitchen work of Mrs. Frake (Louise Dresser). In the novel, she competes at the fair for her pickles. But in the film she offers also her mincemeat—and, in the spirit of the old-fashioned "dry" Christian, a figure known to and popular with the third audience, she insists on omitting one element of the family recipe: the brandy. When she's out of range, Rogers pours in a liberal amount from the household "medicinal" bottle, and when *he's* out of range, she impulsively dumps in another wave of fire-water. She wins the prize, of course—but one of the judges comes down with delerium tremens.

Naturally, Fox could not have allowed the maidenly Gaynor to get intimate with her beau (Lew Ayres). But Wayne (Norman Foster) clearly has gotten to know Emily, for while a re-release (after the Production Code got tough on erotic narrative) cut short one scene that had some dead-giveaway material, Rogers still retained a line mentioning Wayne's "sleepin' with that fella for three nights."

Indeed, this first *State Fair* film is a vast improvement on the novel, especially in the apt casting. We should mention that Stong's one interesting character, known only as The Storekeeper, is played by Frank Craven, later to create the folksiest role in theatre history, the Stage Manager in Thornton Wilder's *Our Town*. And father Frake was clearly written as a Will Rogers part, as when he gets off one of his typical lines of homespun philosophy to one of his children: "If you think next year don't roll around quick, wait till you're old enough to pay taxes." And there is an arresting moment, when, on their last evening at the fair, mother Frake asks father to squire her on a tour of the midway. Rogers would just as soon stay at the campground reading his newspaper, so Dresser goes after him with a knitting needle, causing him to jump up in consternation amid what is unmistakably a tiny cascade of ad libs and improv. "Well, that made you move, didn't it?" she cries, victoriously, and then she grins at the camera, as if saying, I'd like to see Garbo and George Arliss top that!

By the early-middle 1940s, Fox's chief, Darryl Zanuck, thought it time to reshoot *State Fair* as a musical. The studio had been doing great business with their Alice Faye and Betty Grable backstagers, and by making Emily over into a band singer (in 1933, Sally Eilers played her as a trapeze artist), the family drama could merge with the usual Fox showbiz glitter.

Further, as Broadway's *Oklahoma!* had just emerged as a phenomenon of Americana, Zanuck felt Rodgers and Hammerstein (from now on R & H) were the men to create the score—and, as Hammerstein wrote his musicals' books, he could handle the screenplay as well. The team said yes, on the condition that they work in the east, as neither had enjoyed his stay in Hollywood. Zanuck agreed—though he thought Rodgers and Hammerstein had another think coming, as we will presently see.

The R & H *State Fair* (1945) follows the 1933 script quite closely, except in the Wayne-Emily subplot; the title cards credit not only novelist Stong (now called Philip instead of Phil) but Levien and Green. And the very first title card calls the film "Rodgers and Hammerstein's" *State Fair*: once again, Hollywood is buying New York prestige, which it admires and fears and scorns.

The casting is pure Hollywood: movie stars, singing talents, and character stalwarts. It's not at all a group that could have appeared in an R & H show on Broadway, though two of them did important work there (at very different times, Charles Winninger in the 1920s and early 1930s and Vivian Blaine a generation later). In Janet Gaynor's role was Jeanne Crain, dubbed as always, though her solo number, "It Might As Well Be Spring," still won the Oscar for Best Song. Dana Andrews played the newspaperman opposite her, hamstrung without character music, even though Andrews could sing.[1] The role is important; in a break with the novel's inconclusive ending, the 1933 *State Fair* brought the reporter and the heroine together for a romantic fadeout, and of course Zanuck wanted to honor that. Fine—but we never did get to know in musical terms this big-city type who is now going to marry a farm girl. So we have no idea what chance they have of making it work.

We're on surer ground with the farm boy and his opposite, Dick Haymes and Vivian Blaine, because they're the film's Official Vocalists, and they come through nicely. The odd thing about her "That's For Me" and his "Isn't It Kinda Fun?" is that they're performance numbers written as if they were character songs. Hearing them out of context and knowing nothing about how they are used in the movie, one would take them for her "I just met a wonderful guy" piece in something like scene three of a stage show and his confirmation of their bond near the end of the first act. But then, R & H didn't write performance numbers in any real sense; there's always a subtext. Just for instance, in *Pipe Dream* (1955), one of the three R & H shows that were never filmed, the heroine offers, as party entertainment, "Will You Marry Me?," which is announced as being "from the Hit Parade!" In fact, the song was "from" *South Pacific*, written (and later dropped) for Ezio Pinza to sing as a plot number—and, listening to the music, one can "hear" Pinza's basso coursing through the phrases.

Yet only two of *State Fair*'s six numbers are situation songs—the opening, "Our State Fair [is a great state fair]" and Crain's "Spring" number. R & H saw so much there in the latter that it is reprised twice, with different lyrics, rounding out Crain's character and setting her up as truly ready for the romance that Dana Andrews will offer. But, again, their pairing is never musicalized, as it surely would have been had R & H been writing the story as a stage show.

---

1. He does offer a solo line or two in one ensemble number, but Fox dubbed him. It is said that Andrews studied voice on the operatic level, but he sings a strophe of a number in *The North Star* (1943), and he is clearly not fielding an instrument of operatic weight.

True, Fox spent more effort in dressing Crain than in letting music place her story. On the *State Fair* DVD, commentators Richard Barrios and Tom Briggs have a hoot noting how elaborate Crain's many outfits are. "Just a simple farm girl in an organza dress," says Briggs, as Crain flutes onscreen in a fluffy white blouse with purple stars over a purple skirt. Some dozen artisanal designs later, she's in another fluffy white blouse under a high-fashion black bustier with distinct white buttons and a red bow tie, like something Snow White might have ordered from Worth's of Paris. "There are a lot of puffed sleeves in this movie," Barrios observes.

It's a disappointing film, because ninety minutes and six numbers don't give R & H a chance to relate the project to the revolution they had initiated on Broadway—one based on character songs with rich content. At least "It's a Grand Night For Singing" opens the score up, as virtually the entire cast takes part in a carefree waltz that starts in a dancing pavilion where Haymes and Blaine are on the floor. After a bandstand singer and the chorus introduce the refrain, Haymes breaks into the trio section ("Maybe it's more than the moon..."), and we think the authors have challenged the old Hollywood ban on Singing in Public. That is, Haymes is vocalizing what his character is *thinking*. He's not "really" singing at all: a paradox of the modern musical.

But no. Haymes is singing because he apparently already knows the song from somewhere—the Hit Parade again? Because the other couples on the floor are smiling at him, and Blaine—who is at first genuinely startled at his bursting into song—compliments him on his voice. Once again, we find Broadway's songwriters conforming to Hollywood's rules of engagement: characters sing in theatres and night clubs (and dance pavilions). But they talk everywhere else.

Two situation numbers and four performance numbers is so slim a setting that when Fox remade *State Fair* in 1962, Rodgers (as his own lyricist after Hammerstein's death) felt it necessary to insert new character songs to give the story more body. The film is terrible all the same. After Fox had starred a Queen of the Lot in the two prior *State Fairs*, it's odd to see the utterly unimposing Pamela Tiffin in their role—and a third Fox Queen of the Lot, Alice Faye, makes a grumpy mother Frake.

As for Darryl Zanuck, one wonders how well acquainted he was with R & H; later on, in a promotional film for Fox's *Carousel*, he said "Hammersteen" instead of the correct "Hammerstine." We recall Cole Porter's being warned that, in Hollywood, everyone talks about the movies and nothing else, and that nothing else included Broadway. Yet Zanuck's two New York authors had been very much on his mind, and—according to Rodgers' memoirs—after they had finished their work on *State Fair*, shortly before shooting began, he sent for them. He gave no reason for the summons, but Broadwayites have always been vulnerable to a Call From the Coast, and the invitation was, so to say, engraved: with a week's expenses paid, wives included. Thus, R & H could think of it as a vacation.

Yet when Zanuck finally ushered them into his presence, he simply talked of this and that for a while and then politely dismissed them. His only purpose had been to make them come to California: because a Hollywood mogul will not be outpowered by the help. This is the downside of the New Yorker's movieland experience, for the theatre world had no equivalent for this—in Rodgers' words—"ego-satisfying extravagance." Further, no producer of stage musicals would have wanted to humiliate major authors. More immediately, you don't offend writers who can make you money, and more broadly, there was a sense of community in the theatre, particularly in that wartime, when so many were banding together on writing and performance projects to keep up morale. That community, every New Yorker knew, did not exist in Hollywood. "You're only as good as your last picture" was a Hollywood slogan; there was no match for that cynical worldview on Broadway.

Meanwhile, weren't the studios clamoring for the rights to film *Oklahoma!*? Of course—but, says Rodgers, he and Hammerstein didn't want to disturb the show's New York run with competition from a movie version. And they were also aware of how ruthlessly Hollywood filleted and hashed the Broadway they filmed. So, in the end, R & H waited over a decade and then arranged to go indie as executive producers on the *Oklahoma!* movie (1955), not micro-managing but still making certain that the film presented the show they had written, even using the Agnes de Mille choreography that helped define it on Broadway.

There would be no dubbing: if you can't sing the music, you can't play the part. The film did honor the show's use of doubles for the leads in the Dream Ballet, but the notion of finding worthy singing actors who could also dance—really dance, not just hoof—was unthinkable at that time. (After Jerome Robbins cast *dancing* singing actors in the original *West Side Story*, in 1957, performers who don't need Dream Ballet doubles have taken *Oklahoma!*'s leads on stage.) Two numbers were dropped—the villain's "Lonely Room" and "It's a Scandal! It's a Outrage!," for the comic and the men's chorus (and the women sneak in on the very last line). In truth, the latter doesn't work with the rest of the score; it sounds like the things you hear in college shows. And "Lonely Room" strives to humanize a debased and evil figure in music as oddly beautiful as it is aggressive.

Everything turned out well; here was a roadshow feature that really was special, screened in the new Todd-AO process (named for producer Michael Todd and the American Optical Company) that expanded upon CinemaScope in how much one could see and hear in any given shot. And Fred Zinneman directed to fill the eye without adding much visual coloratura to what was a very simple story: landowner Laurey and laborer Curly love and bicker, reflecting the vexed relationship between the farmers and the cowmen that must be pacified if their so-called Indian Territory is to become the state of Oklahoma.

What makes this movie unusually first-rate is the choice of performers, all but one of them prominent movie veterans (that is, excepting the Curly and Laurey counterparts in the Dream Ballet, Broadway's James Mitchell and Bambi Linn). More than most New York composers, Rodgers liked real voices in his singing leads,[2] and the First Couple, Gordon MacRae and Shirley Jones, are wonderful singers. The film's action begins just a little bit before the show's first moments, as MacRae's Curly rides on horseback through the "beautiful mornin'" of cornstalks and cow herds, and the idyll of a young man in his joyful prime coursing through a golden nature to meet his lady love is strongly felt. Curlys are supposed to be handsome, captivating singers, and, in his orange shirt and bandanna, that's MacRae. Jones, as Laurey, was the film's one principal singer new to Hollywood, brought in, we presume, because the industry's resident heroines weren't as right as Jones.

The Second Couple, Gene Nelson and Gloria Grahame, are a bit of a surprise, because though he was a dancer in a dancer's role, she had no standing as a musical performer. Yet her Ado Annie is terrific, with a look and sound unlike anyone else who has played this part. Annie has no specific *Fach*: she has been cast with belters and sopranos, heroines and comics, Barbara Cook and Shelley Winters, and Grahame brings a kind of prairie fizz to the task, emphasizing by irony how introspective Laurey is, because she's so choosy about everything. Ado Annie takes everything that's offered her.

Rodgers must have loved Charlotte Greenwood's Aunt Eller, because she had been first choice for the part when the stage show was casting. Further, ornery Rod Steiger as the villain and Eddie Albert as the peddler? Aren't they ideal? True, Broadway's peddler, Joseph Buloff, specialized in ethnic portraiture (often of vague origin, from Latin America to Eastern Europe), and Albert was straight-on American. But why not "normalize" the character? He's supposed to be Persian, and casting the role ethnically in 1943

2. After his musical-comedy years with Lorenz Hart, Rodgers favored solid voices in the Hammerstein musical plays, using "Broadway" baritones like Alfred Drake and William Johnson or true-blue sopranos from Helen Traubel to Patricia Neway. Except for the musical comedy *Me and Juliet*, all the R & H shows include at least one role for an opera singer, even if it's only *Allegro*'s Annamary Dickey (who spent six seasons at the Met) or the "Love, Look Away" singer in *Flower Drum Song. South Pacific*'s Bloody Mary was created by a blues singer, Juanita Hall—yet it was really written for an operatic mezzo, and is often cast with one.

could be regarded as a fond hommage to the stereotype comedy that the stage musical doted on from about 1875 and was tiring of in the 1920s. By 1955, the type would have been a distraction.

In all, the *Oklahoma!* movie's casting is so logical it might simply have fallen into place by itself. So it's unsettling to learn that director Zinneman conducted many screen tests and auditions, taking in some performers who couldn't sing. This information appeared in 2015 in an unsigned article on the website of the Academy of Motion Picture Arts and Sciences; the piece documented its findings with scans of Zinneman's correspondence. His would-be Curlys included two non-singers, Paul Newman (whom Zinneman thought too "stiff") and James Dean ("extraordinarily brilliant" but perhaps lacking "the necessary romantic quality").

Worse, Zinneman's first choice for Curly was Frank Sinatra. Who would have been more miscast—Adlai Stevenson? Oliver J. Dragon? Hammerstein was enthusiastic, but then Hammerstein was a great writer, not a great casting consultant. At best, this partner of Romberg, Kern, and Rodgers would come up with an intriguing suggestion that, on second thought, wouldn't work at all—Dinah Shore, for instance, as Julie in the 1946 *Show Boat* revival. (Given that they were transposing Julie's music down from Helen Morgan's head-voice keys in the original, Shore's singing would have been fine. But Julie is *Show Boat*'s "acting" role, and Shore was a personality, not an actress.)

Zinneman did test a viable slate for Jud—Jason Robards, Lee Marvin (who would have made a bemusingly sexy villain), Neville Brand, and Murvyn Vye (who had created two R & H parts, *Carousel*'s villain and, out of town till they cut both of his songs, "Waiting" and "Now You Leave," the Kralahome in *The King and I*). Zimmerman even went back to the original Aunt Eller, Betty Garde, though no report known to me suggests she was anything beyond adequate, while Charlotte Greenwood was an established and delightful presence in the movies.

The Oscar site article carefully fails to tell us how the final decisions were made. Reading between the lines, however, one imagines the following: Zinneman, who was at home with dire dramas such as *High Noon* and *From Here To Eternity*, had no musical values to speak of, and his progress reports during the screen-tests phase made Rodgers extremely wary. And when it was time to go to contract, Rodgers stepped in and, executive producer as he was, tossed out everyone he didn't want—the non-singers, the movie stars, the newbies and has-beens, and, most of all, the very notion of Frank Sinatra as an imaginative, playful, ardent young cowpoke.

Yet on the movie of *Carousel* (1956)—which R & H did not produce— Sinatra was signed for another romantic lead he was wrong for, Billy

Bigelow. By hap, though, he quit on the first day of shooting, supposedly because he objected to the prospect of filming every scene twice over to accommodate a new development in CinemaScope. Famous last words: "I signed to do one movie, not two," Sinatra announces, getting into his limousine. In her at times shockingly dishy memoirs, Shirley Jones tells us what really motivated Sinatra: his wife, Ava Gardner, was shooting *Mogambo* in Africa with Clark Gable, and she told Sinatra to join her there or she'd get to know Gable really well.

So Jones, cast as *Carousel*'s Julie, gave her *Oklahoma!* Curly a call, and Gordon MacRae went on a crash diet; hied himself to the *Carousel* shoot at Boothbay Harbor, Maine; and sang a wonderful Billy. But Curly isn't Billy: MacRae was too forthright and logical a performer to play the demon-driven Billy, ever baiting authority figures and fronting his insecurity with a braggart's facade. Billy's a ne'er-do-well. A hustler. His love for Julie impels him to succeed—to fit into society's protocols and be logical. But he doesn't know how that works, and, besides, her love makes him feel unworthy and therefore excites his destructive side. This character is one of the musical's great acting roles; one cannot Curly one's way through it.

It's too bad John Raitt didn't film the Billy he created on Broadway, as he did his Sid Sorokin in the *Pajama Game* movie just a year after the MacRae *Carousel*. But more: of all the R & H titles, *Carousel* is the one distinguished by an elaborate musicalization that moves past song structures into lyrical scenes, bits and pieces, and tunelets; it's the one time R & H almost flirted with opera. Indeed, *Carousel* was the first musical to be given a "crossover" recording with opera singers, in 1955, and the show has been thus operatically treated several times since, with a Roberta Peters here and a Samuel Ramey there. Yet, even in this age of sometimes intense fidelity to Broadway, Hollywood cheated on *Carousel*, cutting much of the score back to its core material.

But then, having seen *Oklahoma!* to an authentic filming, R & H had temporarily abandoned movie producing, and *The King and I* (1956) lost a lot of music, too, not to mention the necessary dubbing of the otherwise ideal Deborah Kerr. The film does preserve the original Jerome Robbins choreography, so charming in "Getting To Know You" and imaginative in the "Small House of Uncle Thomas" ballet," both in Trude Rittman's dance arrangements, as on Broadway. And of course there's Yul Brynner's Broadway King, arguably the most unchallengeable assumption in the musical's history. There have been great Peter Pans after Mary Martin, Henry Higginses after Rex Harrison, Madam Roses after Ethel Merman. But there has never been a second King. Watch Brynner in "Shall We Dance," appearing all at once to discover a sensual match in Mrs. Anna, his sparring partner and comrade. He starts, really, to stalk her, step by step, and the famous intensity with which he takes her by the waist for their polka around the room—"Was-a ... like this ..."—is matchless.

No doubt R & H realized they were wrong to sell some titles outright to Hollywood, and while *The King and I* was a big hit, *Carousel*—from Rodgers' favorite of all his shows—actually lost money. So for the *South Pacific* film (1958), the team once again turned executive producers. This time, every single number in the score—and one cut from the show, "My Girl Back Home"—was heard. And just as the *Carousel* movie could put the world of New England fisher folk on exhibition, *South Pacific* would present the very geography of conflict, from aircraft to warships to islands in the sea.

To emphasize this, the movie reversed the order of the show's two establishing sequences. On Broadway, Nellie and Emile—the central love pair—took the first scene. Then the seabees ran on (even as the set changed) to switch focus to the military. This is where we met Bloody Mary, Luther Billis, and Lt. Cable (who forms the secondary love pair with Mary's daughter, Liat). However, even with much of the world fighting fascism, *South Pacific* concentrates on those two romances—because they're about race as much as about love. Nellie and Cable are Americans who find themselves deeply involved with Asians, the former with Emile's two mixed-race children and the latter with Liat, a Tonkinese, and the show wants to test them, to see how democratic the anti-fascist side may be.

However, Joshua Logan, who directed both play and movie, now wanted to implant the military atmosphere right from the start. So the film begins *in* the war, so to say, as Cable arrives by plane to undertake a secret mission. This leads directly to the seabees and Mary and only much later introduces us to Nellie and Emile. Such a structure feels solid and logical, but it completely destroys the innovative way in which the stage show unveiled its elements: first the racial theme (in Emile's children's "Dites-moi"), then the First Couple (the stars, Mary Martin and Ezio Pinza, who abruptly walk on after four brief offstage lines of Star Entrance preparation), then the military, then the "testing" theme (in Bloody Mary's siren's song to Cable, "Bali Ha'i"). The mysterious music promises a beautiful destiny "where the sky meets the sea": where opposing notions are harmonized if one but reach the magical island.

Cable doesn't. He gets there physically, but he can't inhabit it spiritually—can't see that "paradise" is a place of open-hearted tolerance, the opposite of fascism. All of this is in the movie, but with the emphasis falling on the wrong accents. The film is about Cable's mission—but the show was about Cable's journey and his failure to complete it. In other words, the show is a metaphor. The film is a war movie.

Even small touches in Paul Osborn's screenplay, which generally follows the stage dialogue (by Hammerstein and Logan), focus our attention on a world at war. On Broadway, early in that first Nellie and Emile scene, she ramped up to her establishing song, "A Cockeyed Optimist," by taking in the view with "Just look at that yellow sun! You know, I don't think it's the end of the world like everyone else thinks."

In the film, however, Osborn slipped new lines between those two sentences, and now Nellie notices "little white clouds." Emile tells her they might in fact be the smoke from gunfire, and she replies, "Oh, how awful. On such a [beautiful] day. Boys getting killed. People getting…" and she breaks off, to return to the second of the lines quoted above. Osborn has added in just a few words, but they are telling. They help reappoint the show from its two love stories to the larger issue of democracy fighting off its eternal enemy, fascist savages.

South Pacific was a big project, at over $5,000,000 the most expensive musical ever filmed, and it was thought that marquee names would be indispensable in selling it. Incredibly, the first choice for Nellie was Elizabeth Taylor; no, the part needs a singer and actress, not a movie star. Doris Day was the second choice, but her husband wanted too much money. Many are they who believe the film would have been much better with her, but isn't Day too strong for the part? Nellie is very young, with a limited cultural perspective and, despite a positive attitude, somewhat unsure of herself (especially with Emile, a worldly older man). R & H ended up with Mitzi Gaynor, who was not famous enough for such an imposing project but charming, pretty, and sensitive, the perfect Nellie—and the only one of the four singing leads who recorded her own vocals.

They wanted Fernando Lamas for Emile, and he could just barely have gotten away with Emile's rather operatic music. But he was engaged in a vicious feud with Ethel Merman back on Broadway in *Happy Hunting*, and as Merman was the show's (unbilled) producer, she killed his chances for a career breakout and held him to his contract. Rossano Brazzi won the part: he was dubbed. Juanita Hall re-created her Bloody Mary, but Rodgers thought her voice now in decline: she was dubbed. Finally, rather than seek out a jeune premier with the voice for Cable's numbers, R & H chose a Hollywood regular, John Kerr: he was dubbed.

This is not smart planning. Again, dubbing is all right in charm songs and the like, or even when Jeanne Crain muses on her restless feelings in a single song in *State Fair*. But a score with the espressivo of *South Pacific*'s needs singers lest it look vacant and sound false. Juanita Hall, at least, *was* a singer, and she appears at one with the music. But the two men are *clearly* not singing; their "voices" don't even sound like them, as if they came from a Secret Santa.[3] Granted, the film was a huge success. Its London roadshow run, at the sizable Dominion Theatre, lasted just about four-and-a-half years. And it has its admirers. But it is also—for various reasons, including the vulgar use of color filters for "mood"—one of the most disliked of the big famous movie musicals.

And *The Sound of Music* (1965) is one of the most ridiculed, its detractors railing at its sappy worldview in which a baron marries a nobody, religion inspires people instead of serving as a front for homophobia, and a family resists Nazism by hiking. (The Von Trapps did, in real life, escape from Nazi clutches, though instead of climbing every mountain, they simply took the train.)

Most important, *The Sound of Music* became the spectacular hit that ended forever the supremacy of the musical as a dependable Hollywood genre: because the studios' attempts to replicate it put the form into disrepute. There was an entire cycle of mediocre and even terrible musicals, and far too many of them. Why was it so hard to make a second, a third *Sound of Music*? When the movie musical was in its heyday, the studios merrily emulated *Top Hat, Born To Dance, Naughty Marietta. The Sound of Music* really isn't remarkable, however wonderful it may be. *Intolerance* and *Citizen Kane* are remarkable. Even R & H's *Flower Drum Song*, filmed in 1961, is more unusual than *The Sound of Music*, if only for its Chinese-American characters, a great rarity in the musical line.

But then, for all its devoted, repeat viewing audiences (who kept its roadshows playing for two years in many markets, with a run of three years and four months at the aforementioned Dominion in London, even before the film's general release), *The Sound of Music* is easy to underestimate. For one thing, commentators continually fail to see how special the score is, because it isn't innovative. It completely lacks those rich personal diagrams R & H laid out in other works, as when *Carousel*'s "Soliloquy" articulates the longings and drives of a ruffian that he himself doesn't understand. *The Sound of Music*'s songs are basic propositions. Not Tin Pan Alley basic, and extremely melodious and characterful, but nevertheless free of the twisty surprises that Broadway songwriters so often set off.

---

3. Brazzi's voice was even familiar, at least to some: Giorgio Tozzi, a Metropolitan Opera basso who, ironically, played Emile himself nine years later in a revival at Lincoln Center that was cast by Rodgers. At that, Juanita Hall got comparably classy dubbing, by Muriel Smith, an opera mezzo who had been London's Bloody Mary. Poor John Kerr had to settle for the unrenowned Bill Lee. Even the Stewpot, Billis' assistant, was dubbed, because Joshua Logan, the most latent heterosexual in the business, cast gleaming blond hunk Ken Clark in the role. Clark didn't sing, but his solo line in "There Is Nothing Like a Dame" took him down to M below middle Z: and he was dubbed, by Thurl Ravenscroft, who also played the voice of Frosted Flakes' Tony the Tiger.

At that, if the show's score is thus basic, the film's score is even more so, because it dropped the two cynical numbers heard on Broadway ("How Can Love Survive?" and "No Way To Stop It"). They marked the only times when the show's music broke away from the themes of inspiration, love, and happiness that otherwise pervade it. And with the film's two new numbers ("I Have Confidence" and "Something Good," entirely by Rodgers) both involving the heroine, the score was left almost entirely in the hands of nuns and children. Yes, the Baron has music, too. But "Something Good" is his quiet duet with the heroine and "Edelweiss" is a pastiche "folk song." So, unlike the stage show, the *Sound of Music* movie limits its music to unsophisticated characters, which inevitably leads to, for examples, the absurdly (but deliberately) diatonic "Do-Re-Mi" and the line about "whiskers on kittens."

The narrative, too, is simple. There isn't even a Second Couple beyond the "Sixteen Going on Seventeen" number involving two teens and, much later, the boy's treachery in giving the hiding Von Trapps away to the Nazis. (In the stage show, he protected them, albeit after thinking it over for a few very suspenseful seconds.) Yet this is in all a fairy tale, with all the power to move that we respond to in *Pinocchio* or *The Wizard of Oz*. Thus: a prince under enchantment that has frozen his heart meets a young woman of an order of healers, who frees him. Monsters overrun the land, but the healer's people open up a hidden portal of escape. It's almost a parable of dueling magics, that of the spirit versus that of destruction. And music does the healing.

So perhaps *The Sound of Music* is remarkable after all. It certainly defied imitation. Even its casting seemed unique, for while Julie Andrews was an ideal choice (and already an Oscar winner for *Mary Poppins*), the other leads were folk of little fame. Christopher Plummer, the Baron, had done many a television drama, taking on roles once played by Ronald Colman, Errol Flynn, Humphrey Bogart, John Gielgud, and Richard Burton. Big roles. But Plummer had made few films, and his ungraciously icy Baron Von Trapp did not suggest an actor trying to seize a breakout moment in his career. Moreover, the Mother Abbess was a has-been of such antiquity that she had appeared in the chorus of *Naughty Marietta* (1910), and I don't mean a revival. This was Peggy Wood, hired—I guess—because she had played the key role in television's very popular *I Remember Mama*, and Mama has the same Ms. Fix-it qualities that the Mother Abbess displays. Unfortunately, Wood not only could no longer sing but couldn't even lip-synch, and thus had to be photographed turning away in shadows during "Climb Every Mountain." It's a truly odd way to handle what is in effect the work's defining anthem.

*   *   *

R & H's influence on Broadway was immense. Their format of "musical play" was the rage, and even daffy musical comedy became rationalized. Some shows seemed to be the work of R & H in all but name, and Frederick Loewe and Alan Jay Lerner's *Brigadoon* (1947) was the main one, with its powerful sense of community, its long first act and short second, its Agnes de Mille choreography, and its thematic richness, all elements of R & H. And, as with *Carousel*, *Brigadoon*'s atmosphere was spiritual: a young man of the materialist, modernist urban world finds personal fulfillment in a timeless village bound by tribal folkways. To emphasize this, Lerner paired his hero with a cynical best friend representing the apparently soulless character of twentieth-century man. In a telling irony, he saves the village from extinction yet doesn't care about it. In the original Broadway production, the last thing the audience saw was the hero abandoning his friend at stage right to allow a character who's part-village elder and part-Druid (he's technically the schoolteacher) at stage left to usher him into the invisible city of God.

For its adaptation (1954), MGM cast Gene Kelly as the hero and Van Johnson as the cynic, and while Kelly lacked the voice needed for a score that at times leans toward operetta, Johnson is excellent in projecting his character's growing impatience with the more or less studied innocence of a magical town that exists for one single day every hundred years. A "voodoo joint," Johnson calls it, almost snarling, though he does get involved in its doings long enough to dally with a local belle (Dody Heath) even as Kelly pursues his vis-à-vis, Cyd Charisse.

By now we've seen many Broadway musicals adapted by Hollywood, and almost all were scripted by new hands. Alan Jay Lerner, an insistently bicoastal talent, was exceptional: whenever possible, he wrote the new, camera-ready scripts for his stage shows himself. Let's note that his predecessor Oscar Hammerstein did a lot of work in Los Angeles in the 1930s, including scripts as well as song lyrics. Nevertheless, in all eighteen of Hammerstein's stage works that became movies, he wrote the screenplay only once, for the 1936 *Show Boat*.

Lerner didn't share the typical New York attitude that movie work "didn't count" (except as income), and he knew how to talk to producers—a minor skill, but one most New Yorkers didn't cultivate. Ian Marshall Fisher, who runs the Lost Musicals series in London, once asked Kitty Carlisle why her late husband, playwright and director Moss Hart, worked but seldom in Hollywood, and, with a smile, Kitty replied, in a light and almost entirely non-judgmental tone, "Movies…" It's nearly as brilliant a concision as

Humbert Humbert's recollection of his mother's death ("picnic; lightning") in Nabokov's *Lolita*.

So Alan Jay Lerner wrote not only *Brigadoon*'s book and lyrics but its screenplay, his third at MGM, after *Royal Wedding* and *An American in Paris*, both in 1951. Unfortunately, this was the new MGM, no longer under the dictatorship of L. B. Mayer, who did at least love musicals. His successor, Dore Schary, held them in contempt—and he was on an economy kick, to boot. So he forbade shooting *Brigadoon* in Scotland. The soundstage look of a story that takes place almost entirely outdoors is a familiar complaint about the film, though to be fair the sets are at least functional.

No, the real problem is the severe abridgment of one of Broadway's greatest scores. Three major ballads and the soubrette's comic songs were all cut, leaving—besides "Once in the Highlands" and "Brigadoon," which together last scarcely a minute—just five numbers. The three ballads had been taped, and MGM's record department was so embarrassed at having so little music to put on the soundtrack LP that it included "Come To Me, Bend To Me" and "There But For You Go I," though they had no connection to the finished film.[4] At one point, we actually hear Van Johnson give Dody Heath the cue for her zesty romantic confessions, "The Love of My Life"—"With that philosophy, you must have had a provocative career"—but then the scene moves resolutely onward, without music. This destroys an important piece of the story's thematic presentation, for this Second Couple flirtation emphasizes by contrast the intensity of the First Couple's need for each other.

After all, like the R & H shows it imitated, *Brigadoon* is about something: the emptiness of life in an industrial—that is, a post-religious—age. Mind you, Lerner isn't advocating for organized religion. *Brigadoon*'s belief system is abstract, a series of rustic practices. But we do need the silliness of the show's Second Couple numbers (they're both hers; he doesn't sing) to contrast with the First Couple numbers, which are the opposite of silly. They move from attraction ("The Heather on the Hill") through romance ("Almost Like Being in Love") to a hymn-like purity ("There But For You Go I"). *Brigadoon* is essentially the tale of an atheist who discovers God; his best line, easy to miss because it occurs very early in the continuity, when the two buddies are lost while hunting, is "There's something about this forest that gives me the feeling of being in a cathedral."

---

4. A curiosity: the original dance music to "Come To Me, Bend To Me," featuring a new theme so beautiful that Victor found a place for it on the stage show's original-cast album, can be heard in the film during the sequence when that schoolteacher, Mr. Lundie, tells the so to say Legend of Brigadoon. While we're footnoting, it's even more curious that the three notes that launch *Brigadoon*'s title song—the town's leitmotif, really—are the same pitches, in the same harmony, as the three notes that dominate *Camelot*'s title song: *that* Lerner and Loewe show's leitmotif, in its turn.

Besides all the missing music, *Brigadoon* has a singing problem, because Kelly's wispy voice scants tunes written for a sturdy baritone, and all the other principals (except Johnson, in one brief bit) are dubbed. Indeed, Kelly is so incapable of buttoning "Almost Like Being in Love" vocally that he has to toss his hat and coat into the air, to effect a visual more than a musical conclusion.

But Kelly can dance his way into character. He and Johnson enjoy a hoofing duet during "I'll Go Home With Bonnie Jean," and it has a certain charm. But it confuses the two friends' relationship, as they aren't at all on the same page in their worldviews. We should see tension between them, not comity. Kelly—who choreographed the movie—is more successful with his romantic partner, Cyd Charisse. Not in the music, no. In "From This Day On," *Brigadoon*'s most passionate number—filmed but dropped before release—both Kelly and Charisse's voice double, Carol Richards, try to sneak around the music's grandeur with sotto voce renderings. It's risible; no wonder it was cut. Still, the ensuing dance duet (included in the DVD) conveys the longing the voices can't, and their "Heather on the Hill" dance is the movie's highlight, the one sequence that equals the magical power of the stage show.

Vincente Minnelli, *Brigadoon*'s director, provided few of those flashes of imagination he is famous for, studied pictorial effects that are cinema's equivalent of what on Broadway is called "theatrical"—Gene Kelly's aforementioned cigarette trick in *The Pirate*, for example. Worse, that scene wherein the schoolteacher catches us up on Brigadoon's "miracle" is very amateurishly filmed. It's talky and stagnant, and Minnelli makes no attempt to animate it with cut-ins or varied shooting angles. It's four people sitting there and sitting there and sitting there, dead kinetics just as the abuse of the score creates dead music.

But Minnelli directed also (most of) MGM's *Gigi* (1958),[5] Lerner and Loewe's next title after *My Fair Lady* and perhaps the greatest of all Hollywood musicals. It's supposedly based on the very short novel by

5. Charles Walters, MGM's very creative but historically underrated director, took charge of "The Night They Invented Champagne," arguably the best-staged number in the film. (It is also the only number in which the principals dance, albeit informally, and while Minnelli started on Broadway as a designer, Walters started there as a dancer—his pas de deux with June Knight to *Jubilee*'s "Begin the Beguine" was the talk of the town.) Suddenly, shortly before *Gigi* was to be released, Lerner announced that Minnelli hadn't quite topped off the piece in many needed details. Retakes were required, costing some $300,000. Loewe backed up his partner, and when MGM balked, the authors demanded to buy the movie from them for ten times that amount. Inspired by such big numbers, as Hollywood always is, MGM gave in, and it was Walters who did the topping off—really a touch-up job on some of the numbers, but an important one.

Colette, but that's a contractual euphemism. Gigi's true source was a 1949 French film of the same title, which opened up the novella's narrow geography with the outlying events we now take for granted in this storyline— the skating rink, Gaston and his uncle catching Gaston's mistress cheating on him, the trip to the seaside at Trouville. Lerner's screen play is almost entirely original on a line-by-line basis, but he followed the 1949 plot devised by the scenarist Pierre Laroche, as Colette supplied very little herself. For that matter, Anita Loos' straight-play adaptation, seen on Broadway in 1951 with Audrey Hepburn as Gilberte (Gigi's given name), did not greatly enlarge on Colette.

We should note, however, that Lerner and Loewe went off on their own in creating *Gigi*'s score, for only two of their songs are clearly cued up in Laroche's script. Gaston keeps saying "It's a bore," and that gave birth to his establishing number, with those three words as its title. Later, at Trouville, Uncle Honoré, with a contented smile, tells his latest young ladylove, "On est vieux une fois" (roughly, "You're only old once") and *that* inspired "I'm Glad I'm Not Young Anymore," in a genre that Lerner made his own, the comic lyric on the ins and outs of the erotic life.

Indeed, *Gigi* builds up this character in particular, though he has almost nothing to do with the actual storyline, serving mainly as Gaston's foil and as narrator. But then, the authors were writing the part for Maurice Chevalier, a kind of ethnic archon in the production because he's the only principal who sounds really French. Leslie Caron, the Gigi (who had played the role in the Loos version in London, in 1955), was half-American and had just the slightest of accents (and only in the dialogue, for her dubbed vocals are in Stage Atlantic). Louis Jourdan, the Gaston, spoke such good English that he has more an Anglo than a Gallic intonation, and Gigi's guardians, great-aunt Isabel Jeans and grandmother Hermione Gingold, were British.

So far, so good, but where do you go after *My Fair Lady*? Is "It's a Bore" Louis Jourdan's "Why Can't the English?" and his "Gigi" a new version of "I've Grown Accustomed To Her Face," complete with the semi-spoken gripes between the melodic sections? One of Gigi's solos, "Say a Prayer For Me Tonight," was in fact written for Eliza Doolittle (and you can still hear the first bit of its A strain, as a slow march, in *My Fair Lady*'s scene-change music leading up to the Embassy Ball). And does "The Night They Invented Champagne" recall "The Rain in Spain," as Gaston, Gigi, and her grandmother enjoy a dancey intimacy we haven't seen before—just as obtains during "Spain" with Higgins, Eliza, and Pickering?

And is the "testing" of Gigi's competence as a cocotte at Maxim's equal to Eliza's challenge at the Embassy? But enough of this, because *Gigi*'s flavor—

its colors and emphases—is very different from that of *My Fair Lady*, which in any case derives from a starchy socialist tract written by an ascetic who had no use for love and joy. The musical as a form lives on love and joy, and so did Colette. Her world is decadent, appetitive, and hedonistic, everything that *My Fair Lady*'s George Bernard Shaw hated. In a way, *Gigi* could be seen as two New Yorkers indulging in Hollywood luxury, and *Gigi* is not only risqué but the most opulent of movies. Much of it was filmed in Paris, from the Bois de Boulogne to the streets and fountains of the flâneur's itinerary, as Gaston stomps furiously through the town during the title song, working through his inchoate thoughts on exactly what Gigi means to him.

As well, the film has a very atmospheric score, for Loewe loved to style a work's setting in his music—the Scots tinta of *Brigadoon*, say, or the way he juggles *My Fair Lady*'s upper crust (in the "Ascot Gavotte") with the working class (in the music-hall abandon of "With a Little Bit of Luck" and "Get Me To the Church on Time"). Loewe did not fill *Gigi* with French pastiche; rather, the music evokes continental operetta generally, in a light polka here and a grand waltz there. Above all, this is a Broadway score—exactly the numbers Lerner and Loewe would have written had they conceived *Gigi* for the stage in the first place.

In particular, there is a musical scene in the first Maxim's sequence that rivals *Love Me Tonight*'s "Isn't It Romantic?" and *The Wizard of Oz*'s "Munchkinland" (as MGM termed the lengthy musical scene in which Dorothy is welcomed to Oz) in its absorption of plot data. In one's first experience of *Gigi*, the use of Maxim's might seem simply decorative, as it really is an eyeful, the women in spectacular gowns (the men wear regulation black tails), a young fellow in a red bellboy's outfit taking your hat to balance on his cane, and a little orchestra way in the back in a raised inset in the wall. And note that this is the real Maxim's, closed to the public so Minnelli could authenticate his tale, the sacred precincts violated with electrical cables and sound consoles.

And what happens? Not, it would seem, all that much. Maurice Chevalier retrieves his role as compère, to set the scene:

> CHEVALIER: (to us) I'm giving a small party in honor of a heavenly creature I met this afternoon. She's . . . (to a woman extra in his way as he comes toward us) excuse me . . . she's the sister of the heavenly creature I gave a party for last night.

A couple enters: an older man with his own heavenly creature. Everyone freezes and the soundtrack goes absolutely silent for a moment. Then we get "Gossip," as the company avidly deconstructs this rendezvous, their quasi-chanted lines punctuated by orchestral outbursts in can-can style. Here is *le tout Paris*, devoted to tattle and scandal, especially when Louis Jourdan comes in with Eva Gabor, his current future ex-mistress.

That future is almost here, as, in voiceover, Gaston launches the "Waltz at Maxim's," generally known as "She Is Not Thinking Of Me." Indeed, Gabor, who has secretly been carrying on with her skating instructor, is putting on a show, such as choosing Gaston's cigar, carefully rejecting the first one and delightedly accepting the second—to show her high stan-dards—and lighting it for him, each phase of this exhibition executed with tiny flourishes, all fake. Lerner's lyrics are comically ironic and Loewe un-furls a sweeping melody till the number matches that honest-to-heaven Maxim's for atmosphere. At the fadeout—to the horror of Arthur Freed, a gentleman of the Old School—Jourdan pours his champagne down Gabor's bodice.

Now, what has happened? Very little plot—but Minnelli has eloquently juxtaposed the private and public worlds that lie at the story's heart. The private world is the apartment of Gigi and her grandmother (and mother, though she appears only in the Loos adaptation). It is the place where Gaston can relax and enjoy himself, because, contrary to what he says in "It's a Bore," he isn't tired of everything. He's just tired of being famous and doing famous things.

Of course, one is famous in public—and that's why Minnelli made such a spectacle of Maxim's: it's the epicenter of the public world. And Gigi, of the private world, is being educated by her great-aunt to become famous in the public world, to be just like Gabor: Gaston's next mistress.

But Gigi doesn't want to go public. She thinks Aunt Alicia's courses in how to eat fine food and rate the quality of jewelry are absurd. There is no pretense in this girl, and the public world is all pretense. This is why, just for example, Minnelli shows us Gigi and Gaston having a ball on the beach at Trouville, far from the gossips and magazine tattlers. You can't have a ball when every move you make becomes journalism, and as Gigi later remarks:

GIGI: (To Gaston) It's not your fault you're world-famous. It's just that I haven't got a world-famous sort of nature.

Ironically, it is raw, unseasoned Gigi who teaches the worldly Gaston who he is and what he wants. In a second Maxim's scene, Gigi behaves just as Eva Gabor did, right down to the cigar business, faking everything just as she has been taught. Disgusted, Gaston drags her out of the place, and back to . . . of course!: the *private* world, her grandmother's apartment. And there he asks for Gigi's hand in marriage. Because he doesn't want an expert miotrcss. IIe wauls a romance, yes: with a *friend*. And that would be the sincere and playful Gigi—lovely, yes, but above all fun to be with. As our emcee Chevalier puts it, in derogating "sophisticated women" like his various heavenly creatures:

CHEVALIER: What can they give you? Everything but surprise.

It's an extraordinary film, commercially the most successful in the twenty-year history of the Freed Unit and one of the musicals that implanted the notion that an important film is a roadshow film. And Gigi *was* important, as the follow-up to *My Fair Lady*: its Manhattan engagement even brought it to a legit house, the Royale. Still, this high status led Hollywood to the mistaken notion that the public would see every single roadshow as important.

Certainly, Warner Bros.' *My Fair Lady* (1964) was seen so, especially as it honored the stage show to the point of replication. Ah, but Jack Warner wanted movie stars—Cary Grant, Audrey Hepburn, and James Cagney (as Doolittle)—and while he finally gave the male leads to Rex Harrison and Stanley Holloway of the stage cast, he insisted on Hepburn. Yet Julie Andrews had been as much a part of the original as the men. It made the film look guilty, even stupid—was anyone going to skip the movie version of the musical of the century just because Julie Andrews wasn't a movie star?

Ironically, by the time *My Fair Lady* was released, Andrews *was* a movie star, after her celebrated stint in Walt Disney's *Mary Poppins*, premiered four months earlier. And of course, Andrews could sing. Though Hepburn's voice is heard here and there in the songs, she had to be dubbed (by Marni Nixon): so Eliza Doolittle is not heard in any real sense, because musicals are made of music. Jack Warner paid some $5,000,000 for the property, and what he got for it was a Marni Nixon *My Fair Lady*. When Andrews accepted the Golden Globe Best Actress for *Mary Poppins*, one of those she thanked was Jack Warner.

Joshua Logan also didn't want Julie Andrews, in her second Lerner and Loewe role, as Guenevere in *Camelot* (1960). Logan intended his film (1967) of the show to bring out sensuality only latent on Broadway. After all, Guenevere is the woman who (inadvertently) destroys a kingdom, the Arthurian Helen of Troy. She must tingle with eros. Thanks to the 1966 British films *Morgan!* and *Blow-Up*, Vanessa Redgrave was trending, and as Hollywood was now dubbing-mad, her thin singing voice wouldn't be a problem. In the end, Redgrave wasn't dubbed, so her voice—not much more than competent whispering—*was* a problem. Her Arthur, Richard Harris, was also not dubbed. In fact, he insisted on singing his numbers *live*, suggesting that he did at least understand that in a musical, the production of the vocals is intrinsic to the portrayal. Franco Nero, the Lancelot, also wanted to do his own singing, and let us say that, as a singer, he looked splendid, his hair embossed in wavelets that, verily, showed us what the word "locks" really means. But Nero couldn't sing, either. The only genuine vocal tone we hear from a lead is that of Gene Merlino, and he isn't in the movie: he dubbed Nero.

Camelot the movie had worse problems. Actually, these start with the show, because its source, T. H. White's *The Once and Future King*, is too epic to shrimp down into three hours. Worse, Lerner's adaptation emphasized Arthur as a kind of Neville Chamberlain, appeasing evil because—Lerner believes—that's what men of peace do.[6] Thus, *Camelot* tells of an idealistic monarch in an age of savagery, with a wondrous queen and superhuman first knight. Arthur's bastard son (in White, he's *also* Arthur's nephew, sired on Arthur's sister) arrives at court with the intention of destroying him. And Arthur just lets it happen, because, he says, "Revenge is the most worthless of crimes." No, Arthur. Appeasement of the enemy who is determined to destroy your kingdom is the most worthless of crimes.

Arthur's son, who bears the blithely baleful name of Mordred (played by David Hemmings, also trending because of *Blow-Up*), uses the adultery of Guenevere and Lancelot as his portal to wrecking Arthur's democracy—but *are* they adulterers? On Broadway, we weren't sure: they loved, but were they physically guilty? Logan's swinging-sixties *Camelot* included shots of queen and knight in unmistakable guilt, and the Logan view of things was so persuasive that Redgrave and Nero brought forth a little Mordred of their own, and they eventually married.

Eager to naturalize what he saw as a prim operetta, Logan completely changed Lancelot's role in the jousting tournament, on Broadway an off-stage event that the onstage chorus described to the audience in a dramatic plot number, "The Jousts." Logan cut the song but of course let the Hollywood camera set the competition before us in all its bloody commotion—because Lancelot slays one of the knights. On Broadway, he brought his kill back to life through prayer. Prim, I tell you. Not swinging. So, in the film, Logan had Nero frantically pawing at the corpse, his supplication to heaven made so close to the slain knight's face that Lancelot was in effect practicing a primitive form of mouth-to-mouth resuscitation. And, lo, the knight liveth. It's effective, certainly, and it made Lancelot more interesting than he had been on Broadway in Robert Goulet's version of operetta piety.

---

6. This situation is more complexly derived in White, who weaves a tapestry of incest, Christian guilt, and the sin of Herod to smother Arthur in tragedy.

Still, as with *Brigadoon*, the *Camelot* movie shortchanged a great score and sang what was left without resonance.

Anyway, the main problem was the recklessness of John Truscott, who had designed sets and costumes for the London *Camelot* (in a different staging than in New York) and did so again for the film. Matthew Kennedy's *Roadshow!* reveals how Warners' *Camelot* became Truscott's Folly, as the studio's archives at the University of Southern California preserved pro duction notes on, among other subjects, "cosmetics in the time of King Arthur, archeology and Camelot, books on tapestries, necklaces, heraldry, Punch and Judy, castles in Scotland, drawbridges, clocks, lights, horns, gargoyles, falconry," and even "fruit in England circa 1200." And Truscott didn't stop after taking notes. Kennedy says the designer found places for "a tinsmith, blacksmith, silversmith, carpenter, tailor, and sculptor, each with his own shop." That was inside the castle grounds. Step beyond them and there were "butchers, greengrocers, bakers, weavers, ceramists, cobblers, undertakers, candlestick makers, apothecaries," eventually adding up to a negative cost of $12,000,000. This was truly alarming for 1967, and the waste can be seen in shot after shot. When Arthur and Guenevere wed, they proceed down an aisle lit by countless candles, and Redgrave seems to be wearing something spectacular, but we scarcely see it. For the first-act finale, Logan unveiled the Round Table in a hall entirely its own under a stained-glass window. The knights solemnly take their places, looking like the chorus of *Parsifal*, and it's a lovely idea—Wagner's opera, too, concerns the idealism of a visionary figure. But the film would have been a lot better with less scenery and more voice.

The policy of allowing production costs to spiral anarchically—another consequence of the break-up of the studio system, which maintained built in checks on overspending—is why roadshow-event musicals performed poorly on the accounting sheets. Even a good run couldn't recoup properly now. A film whose negative *and* release cost was $5,000,000 with a gross of $10,000,000 was a good deal. But if that same film had cost $10,000,000, there was no profit.

Thus, the musical as a dependable American form took a prestige hit. It was already under fire from certain quarters as it was: it's corny. It's politically naive. It uses old music. And in the midst of this, Alan Jay Lerner turned producer for the first time to bring forth one of the biggest bombs of the era, *Paint Your Wagon* (1969).

Lerner had never been happy with the 1951 stage show, his and Loewe's entry between *Brigadoon* and *My Fair Lady*. He revised it a bit for the national tour, and now decided to give it a completely different storyline and some new numbers to match. The results might, at least, have been a bargain, as the whole thing takes place in and around a single spot, a gold-rush town in more or less everyday (if period) clothes. As opposed to the castles in Spain where *Camelot* did much of its filming, not to mention the gargoyles and falconry.

However, anticipating the disaster-film cycle, Lerner wanted *Paint Your Wagon*'s mining town ("No-Name City. Population: Male") to sink into the earth in a catastrophe finale. Worse, production built the place from scratch in the wilds of Oregon, with no nearby living quarters for cast and crew; they had to be trucked and helicoptered in and out each day in a long and pricey commute, greatly protracting the shooting schedule. Back as director again after *Camelot*, Joshua Logan fretted about all this, but Lerner didn't care how much of Paramount's money he spent. He even hired *Camelot*'s spendthrift designer, John Truscott. In the end, it would appear that no one knows exactly how much *Paint Your Wagon* cost, but there is no doubt that it lost a vast fortune.

It deserved to. Cynically, Lerner took note of changing times and filled the film with a "youth now!" attitude and sexual freedom—refreshing if they didn't feel so commercially opportunistic. But after all, *Hair* (1967) had happened. Was Broadway urging Hollywood to go hippie, too, or would Lerner have done this anyway?

For instance, there was the use of the Nitty Gritty Dirt Band, a newish jug outfit gone electrical. This was silly pandering to the rock world, because *Paint Your Wagon* wasn't a rock movie. The Lerner and Loewe songs, along with the new inserts by Lerner and André Previn (Loewe having temporarily retired) were pure traditional Broadway in sound.

More trendy chic: the film's central romance joined a threesome of two men and one woman in "marriage" (by the rude law of the mining camp), and at one point the woman openly nursed a baby, though this was shot discreetly. Further, that threesome—stars Lee Marvin, Clint Eastwood, and Jean Seberg—were, we might say, the anti-Julie Andrews. That none of them could sing didn't trouble Lerner: singing is so Sigmund Romberg. In a way, *Paint Your Wagon* was the first "musical for people who hate musicals," to quote that repellent PR blurb used by the musical *Rent* during its Broadway run.

Seberg was dubbed, though her one number, "A Million Miles Away Behind the Door," one of the Previn-Lerners, is so gentle that she could have murmured her way through it herself. It's the dramatic numbers, I repeat, that need to look as though the character is in command of the singing, and *Paint Your Wagon*'s only powerful vocal was "They Call the Wind Maria," from the original score, and assigned to the only cast member who *could* sing, Harve Presnell. The movie's hit number, however, was Lee Marvin's "Wand'rin' Star," though no one expected Marvin to field the voice for it. His Ben Rumson is a grizzled old drunk with a 'stachezilla, so his growly chanting was suitable; at that, the original Ben Rumson, James Barton, was no Lawrence Tibbett. The show's lead voices as such were the traditional Girl and Boy: Rumson's daughter and the Mexican she loved, characters who vanished when the film's scenario was conceived.

So Lerner gave the show's main ballads, "I Talk To the Trees" and "I Still See Elisa," to Clint Eastwood. (A third ballad, the haunting "Another Autumn," was dropped.) Eastwood had a tiny voice with the amateur's vibrato, hardly right for this material, but he also got a more appropriate Previn-Lerner cut, the strangely meditative "Gold Fever." This was shot during a card game: Eastwood rises from the table of chance and wanders through a time-stopped saloon as if trying to find himself in a life whose complications overwhelm him. It proved a rare moment of...well, something or other...in a movie that was otherwise very much like a comic sixties television western—*Here Come the Brides* or *Laredo*—with songs.

The film starts well, at least, as "I'm On My Way," the men's chorus over the titles, suddenly stops dead as a wagon breaks away from the train and hurtles down a mountainside. Lee Marvin, watching, quietly says—dismissively but with some compassion—"Farmers," and goes down to investigate. Two men have been riding in the now disintegrated wagon. "Are they dead?" shouts someone on the mountaintop:

MARVIN: They better be. 'Cause I'm goin' to bury 'em!

They were brothers, and one is alive. During the roughhewn funeral for the unlucky brother, onlookers notice specks of gold in the ground, but before anything can happen, Marvin turns his eulogy into a claim—a rare link between the movie and the stage show. The view then expands as we see a town having arisen around Marvin's claim, a wonderful use of cinematic ellipsis.

The surviving brother is Clint Eastwood, so he and Marvin have met cute, and now they partner up. Indeed, "Pardner" is the only name Eastwood bears in the movie, and even though Jean Seberg becomes "their" wife, this is really a buddy movie more than a triangle. Seberg is there, really, because we need a romance, but a romance needs characters and only Marvin and Eastwood are such in any real sense.

At that, they're stereotypes—Marvin as Lovable Anarchic Drunk and Eastwood as Sensitive Hero. Seberg didn't even get a type; she was Beautiful Woman. Lerner had hired Paddy Chayevsky for the script, and Chayevsky's a wonderful writer. But Lerner changed everything; the credits had no choice but to cite Chayevsky for "adaptation" and give the primary screenplay billing to Lerner.

Part of the measly fun in screening *Paint Your Wagon* lies in picking out Lerner's emendations. It's good sport, for he typically balanced musical-play romanticism with Broadway gags (except in *My Fair Lady*, closely drawn from Shaw's 1939 *Pygmalion* screenplay), while Chayevsky switched tone from work to work, as in the contrast between *Marty*'s tortured souls and *The Tenth Man*'s Borscht Belt comix and dark rhapsody. I hear Lerner in this snippet of the scene when Marvin tours Eastwood through No-Name City. One of the sights is Harve Presnell, a card sharp ironically known as Hard Luck Willie. Eastwood doesn't need a warning:

> EASTWOOD: Oh, I don't gamble, Mr. Rumson.
> MARVIN: Neither does he.

In another link with the stage show, a Mormon arrives in the women-poor town with two wives and is forced to auction one off. This is how Seberg joins up with Marvin and Eastwood; so she, too, meets cute. And there's more Lerner when someone objects to the auction:

> SOMEONE: You can't buy a woman for money.
> RAY WALSTON: You just try and get one without it!

Yes, golden-toned Ray Walston is in this, too; with so many first-class voices crowding the screen, it's a wonder opera houses were able to function at this time.

If the *Camelot* movie unmasked the show's veiled eros, this *Paint Your Wagon* emphasized an anti-authoritarian point of view, especially when Marvin takes a starchy farmer's teenage son (Tom Ligon) for his first booze, tobacco, and sex. Here's Lerner again, always quick on the draw with a sex joke:

> LIGON: (to his father) Until you've had a good cigar and a shot of whiskey, you're missing the second and third best things in life!

The farmer and his family are living under the roof and on the generosity of Marvin, Eastwood, and Seberg, yet that doesn't stop this self-righteous peasant from throwing a tantrum. And here we get, I think, the voice of Chayevsky, who was always good on the issues, as Marvin lets loose with an opinion of every intolerant jackass in Christendom:

> MARVIN: (To Seberg and Eastwood) If he hadn't brought his goddamn respectability into this house, we'd still be a happily married [He pauses: what's the right word? Not "couple," surely. Oh, yes:] *triple*!

In all, *Paint Your Wagon* exemplifies the faults of trying to oblige the Zeitgeist with a work that has no other reason to exist. And there was, again, the music problem, for the increasingly characterful scores of Broadway—Stephen Sondheim began unveiling his mature style in *Company*, about six months after *Paint Your Wagon*'s release—demanded more than these paltry voices or actors in need of dubbing.

Moreover, even Barbra Streisand couldn't help Lerner reboot *On a Clear Day You Can See Forever* (1970), so it wasn't just the music problem. *On a Clear Day* had a viable premise (occult doctor falls in love with a woman of Regency England using her reincarnation as a medium) but no storyline (and then what happens? Nothing). Lerner even reunited with a back-in-business Frederick Loewe for *The Little Prince* (1974), a terrible movie and, mirabile dictu, terrible Lerner and Loewe.

So, once more, we find a Broadway team greatly distinguishing itself only once (on *Gigi*), otherwise to suffer a spotty Hollywood experience mostly marked by indignity and sabotage. And Lerner, too, could be his own worst enemy. These were opportunities wasted—and that would appear to be the theme of this book.

CHAPTER 12

✧

The Last Hollywood Musicals

A nnie should have been an easy show to film. A smash hit on Broadway from 1977 to 1983, it was a throwback to fifties musical comedy, an extremely uncomplicated piece with just enough eccentricity—comic villains, a cartoony Depression, and a re-creation of a radio show complete with one participant who proudly called himself "radio's only masked announcer"— to give it individuality.

Further, its leads can be played by anybody with the right look and a ready voice. However, the movie version (1982) set marquee names Albert Finney and Carol Burnett atop the cast list, with notables Tim Curry and Bernadette Peters in support. There was a marquee director as well, but producer Ray Stark hired John Huston, who apparently had never seen a musical and had no intention of learning the trade.

Thus, we sense a director who would really like to cut the music and just film the story. Why are they singing? he wonders. What's all that dancing about? Though Joe Layton, a brilliant director-choreographer on Broadway, served as Huston's supervisor of the musical numbers, most of *Annie's* choreography ended up as stupid acrobatics rather than dancing. Further, some of the show's best numbers were dropped. Unnecessary new ones were added, including "We Got Annie," written for and cut from an early version of the show and, in any case, eviscerated for the movie so that only the refrain's bridge was sung, not the A strains. "N.Y.C.," a sarcastic yet all the same infatuated hymn to New York (and the closest thing in the stage show to a production number) was dumped, but the trio "Easy Street" was aggrandized into a big dance sequence in which an entire neighborhood rose up in Depression Weltschmerz. Layton was presumably trying to put the music back into the musical—but Huston cut it. It was an expensive

mistake at the cost of something like a million dollars, and one of the reasons *Annie* did good business and still lost money.

Had Hollywood simply forgotten how to make musicals? On Broadway,
the radio show, Bert Healy's *Hour of Smiles*, came off as quaintly artless fun.
To top it, six orphan girls followed it with their imitation of Healy's format,
from the dummy act to Healy's vocal tic of the upper mordent to Healy's
"Ah, the lovely Boylan Sisters!" as a trio stepped up to the microphone
(while parking their chewing gum on it) to provide backup for his "You're
Never Fully Dressed Without a Smile." (Oldsters of the first television generation may recall Lawrence Welk's comparably doting intros of his house
quartet, the Lennon Sisters.)

Huston's version of this sequence is not at first incompetent, and he
includes the show's ventriloquist (on Broadway it was a man but here a
woman, an arresting twist) with Wacky the dummy, though the masked
announcer is gone. Too whimsical? Too sweet? Because the show was sweet
but the movie is sour. Then, too, the little pride of orphans doing their
imitation of Healy and the Boylans is overwhelmed by an inundation of
orphans jumping around in chaos. Not just the sweetness but the focus is
gone. The charm is gone. Almost no one in *Camelot* or *Paint Your Wagon*
could sing, but they still were musicals. To rephrase *Rent*'s PR blurb, *Annie*
was made by people who hate musicals.

But producer Stark presented also *Funny Lady* (1975), the sequel to
Funny Girl, with Barbra Streisand now opposite James Caan as Fanny
Brice's real-life second husband, Billy Rose. This was going to be a copy of
Funny Girl in a general sort of way, with onstage numbers both dramatic
and comic, with the nonsexual male buddy (here Roddy McDowall), the
outdoor "travel" number while Streisand sings an "I shall prevail" anthem,
all as in the earlier movie.

However, Caan was very, very different from the likable rogue that Omar
Sharif had played. Actually, the real-life Rose was a hateful rogue, one of
the two or three most infamous men in show business. There was a joke at
the time concerning the Brice-Rose marriage:

QUESTION: Who has the biggest prick on Broadway?
ANSWER: Fanny Brice.

But Caan's Rose isn't hateful. He's clumsy, pushy, and arrogant, a slob
whose work clothes might be a tuxedo jacket over his pajamas. Although
Caan does indulge in actory tricks—half-baked gestures at nothing,
tiny shrugs, half-laughs—he gives the romance a presence it lacked in
Funny Girl.

But then, this romance isn't a love story. As Streisand says to Caan, "If we hate the same people and you get your suit cleaned, it's a match." Or, as she tells Roddy McDowall, referring to Rose's songwriting collaborations, "I think I'll marry him, I hate paying for material." Or even, as Streisand sings "Isn't This Better" on a train, as Caan sleeps like a child with his head in her lap: isn't a good working partnership preferable to love, with its tendency to tear your heart apart? Or, simply, as she admits to us, "I fell in like with him."

For years, wags had predicted that Barbra Streisand would return to her career-making role of Fanny Brice. *Funny Crone!* Yet there was nothing to return to. Brice had gone on to marriage with the distinctly unglamorous Billy Rose and, mostly, radio and movie work and retirement. All the "story" of her life lay in the first film, even in the first half of the first film, when she was the neighborhood kid struggling for acceptance. By the time of *Funny Lady*, Brice is a confident and worldly woman. Before, she was a know-it-all, but ignorant, untested. Now she's still a know-it-all, but she's always right.

Nevertheless, Streisand owed Stark another picture, and Fanny Brice's daughter—Ray Stark's wife—was determined to see more of Streisand's electrifying glorification of her mother. So Streisand had to make *Funny Lady* just to keep the peace in Ray Stark's family. As well, Streisand needed a hit to affirm her success in *The Way We Were*—and a musical, after all, would place her back in her element. If, from Streisand's viewpoint, *Funny Girl* had a problem, it was its director, the exasperatingly uncommunicative William Wyler. But on *Funny Lady* the director was Herbert Ross, who had handled *Funny Girl's* musical sequences. And Ross, who always walked away with the notices when choreographing on Broadway, really knew what a musical was.

More: there would be a brace of new Kander and Ebb songs, along with a ton of old numbers, most of which bore Billy Rose's byline (though it is believed that Rose had more to do with negotiating terms than writing lyrics). The Rose titles included "I Found a Million Dollar Baby (In a Five and Ten Cent Store)," "Great Day," and "It's Only a Paper Moon": onetime hits that had gone into semi-limbo. Rejuvenating classics was a Streisand specialty, so even though she didn't want to do a sequel to anything, this one really looked promising.

With these period pieces—most of *Funny Lady* is set in the 1930s—we are interested in how authentically the film observes the era. There's one arresting touch, when Streisand is about to record a song and we see an assistant lightly brushing the matrix disc to keep off the dust, a true precaution of the day. But we get as well musical-comedy producer Caan hectoring his chorus dancers even when they aren't doing anything wrong, an idiotic cliché going back to the earliest talkies. And the use of black choristers in a white show is wholly anachronistic. Color-blind casting keeps a democracy fit, but in this case we are given the impression that theatre was racially integrated in the 1930s in a casual and even long-established way. No: integration came late, and only through bold violations of unwritten law.[1]

All the same, authenticity of setting was less important than Streisand's return to the musical after five talkies. Harold Arlen and Vincent Youmans represent the Harms/Chappell group, and Kander and Ebb are in fine form. In one spot, the two newbies write *with* Arlen, running Streisand's "I Like Him" and Caan's "I Like Her" simultaneously with "It's Only a Paper Moon," thus to blend a classic emptyheaded charm song with twin character pieces in the modern Broadway style.[2]

Amusingly, while Jule Styne and Bob Merrill gave their Fanny Brice a few comic numbers, it was Kander and Ebb who actually created one in Brice's unique genre of the Jewish kid trying out the alien ways of the world beyond the ghetto: "Becky Is Back in the Ballet," "Modernistic Moe," even "I'm an Indian." (Cole Porter wrote one, too, "Hot-House Rose," a twist on the model because, in this one, Brice never gets out of her tenement room and workplace.) The Kander and Ebb version, which launches *Funny Lady* during the credits, is "Blind Date," because now our intrepid cultural tourist, here called Rosalie, abjures the prim "arranged" courtship of the Old Country for the daring American habit of young people making their own arrangements.

However, as with the mating of "Paper Moon" and "I Like Him," this scene combines new and old art. The former, a sort of prelude in song, finds Brice agonizing, in real life, over her imminent rendezvous with Nick Arnstein after a long separation. This runs right into the old art, "Blind Date" itself, a perfect way to usher us into the show biz that Brice inhab-

---

1. This subject needs its own book, but very briefly: once upon a time, show business was divided into the so-called white time and black time, each with its own infrastructure, performers, and audience. On Broadway, where American theatrical precedent is made, Ziegfeld integrated his *Follies* with Bert Williams, from 1907 on, but the experiment wasn't at first repeated. (In *Funny Lady*, Ben Vereen impersonates a Williams knock-off as Bert Robbins in a highly energetic style alien to Williams' own sly underplaying; Vereen sounds like Al Jolson.) Sam H. Harris (and silent partner Irving Berlin) restarted the Ziegfeld experiment using Ethel Waters in *As Thousands Cheer*, in 1933. By the mid-1940s, black choristers were turning up in white musicals, and Duke Ellington's *Beggar's Holiday* (1946) used both black and white principals and introduced the musical's first interracial romance.

2. Everyone thinks "Paper Moon" is a pop tune, but it was actually a lone song decorating a straight play, *The Great Magoo*. The credited lyricists are Billy Rose and E. Y. Harburg.

lted. And as Kander and Ebb knew they were writing for Streisand, this jaunty two-step matches the star's inflections. Thus, fearing (like the real-life Brice in the little prelude, but now comically) a disaster, Rosalie hides under the bed, the blind date arrives and gives up, and when Rosalie is told that he was "a Rudolph Valentino from the movies," she is crushed. "What'll I do now?" she asks, "maybe become a nun?" Then the punchline, in pure Streisandese: "*That's* . . . impossible."

If *Annie* was an old-fashioned show even when new and *Funny Lady* featured some old-fashioned music, *Mame* (1974) offered an old-fashioned star, Lucille Ball. Her notices and talkabout were so bad she fled back to and remained in television for the last twelve years of her career. Why didn't Warner Bros. go with Angela Lansbury, who had had such a stunning success as Mame on stage? But we've seen this over and over—with Ethel Merman and *Gypsy*, Julie Andrews and *My Fair Lady*.

Ball herself didn't want Madeline Kahn in *Mame* (as Agnes Gooch, one of the two comic supporting roles), and had her fired after one day's shooting. The story comes to us in versions. In one, Ball thinks the curvy Kahn is too appealing to play a wallflower (though Kahn had been wonderfully persuasive in just such a part in the Streisand comedy *What's Up, Doc?*). In another telling, Kahn's methodical, deliberating approach to performing irritates Lucy's just-do-it efficiency; a third explanation is that the uniquely impish Kahn could have stolen the picture.

Because all the standard criticisms of Ball are correct. She was too old for the role, she couldn't sing, and she wasn't personally right for the suave patrician of Beekman Place. Mame and sitcom Lucy meet halfway, in that both are scatterbrained nonconformists.[3] But Mame is cultured (however vaguely) and she knows how to move among the gentry; Lucy typified the uninformed bourgeoise, awkward in the great world.

Even so, Lucy wanted that movie. She actually hung around backstage in New York studying Lansbury's performance; Angela later said this was when she realized she wasn't going to get the film. Ball even volunteered to lay down her own vocal tracks. Or, to be blunt, she insisted on it, though her singing was dodgy and "If He Walked Into My Life" wholly inadequate. Still, wasn't Ball's voice just too familiar to dub?

And isn't there something touching about Ball's intense need to cap a major career and a secure legacy with a role that was more than a bit of a dare, and to insist on doing it without a net? It could be called gallant. Yes,

---

3. The character is written scatterbrained, but never seemed so because Rosalind Russell and Angela Lansbury, the most apparent Mames of the era, could not help but radiate intelligence, no matter what they did.

Ball was miscast. But she was determined to play Mame Dennis, not Lucy Ricardo. Veiled behind soft-focus filters—so she did use a net, after all— she still looks great. And she's game in the choreography, though dancing was not one of her fortes. In her participation in the title song (filmed in a reproduction of the Broadway staging while using a vast chorus in those color-mad fox-hunt get-ups), one sees why she thought a Lucille Ball Mame would work. As she slowly makes her way between two lines of admirers and the men fall one by one to their knees, sweeping off their black top hats, we almost feel the film is saluting not just Mame but Ball's eminence in American entertainment. True, the chorus men had hailed Lansbury in just this way on stage (albeit with far fewer people and from a different perspective rather than head-on). Nevertheless, the moment really is quite thrilling.

But if Ball is not all that Mame should be, it's really the movie as a whole that disappoints, though it was filmed by its Broadway director and choreographer, Gene Saks and Onna White. In accordance with the Commandments, the score was largely intact, with an added number by the show's songwriter, Jerry Herman, for Robert Preston, "Loving You," in Herman's once-around-the-dance-floor fox-trot style. Further, Beatrice Arthur and Kahn's replacement, Jane Connell, were preserving their stage roles. So the movie should have re-created what had seemed so fresh and crazy in New York in 1966.

But something went wrong, perhaps in the rewriting of the Jerome Lawrence-Robert E. Lee stage script. Paul Zindel, who had attracted attention for *The Effect of Gamma Rays on Man-in-the-Moon Marigolds* on off-Broadway, was a man of the hour, and, in the Hollywood fashion, all the studios wanted to try him out. But Zindel had no feeling for the material. Whenever he departed from the stage libretto, what had sailed along on daffy energy on stage now felt slow and leaden.

Meanwhile, the professional intellectuals who had been grousing about Broadway's reliance on a traditional musical vocabulary were probably not mollified by either *Grease* (1978) or *Hair* (1979), because, as I've said, professional intellectuals hate musicals in the first place. *Hair* was wonderfully directed, by Milos Forman, in effect restyling what on stage had been vaudeville-with-a-plot into a cogent narrative. But *Grease* completely overshadowed it as a kind of antidote, for *Hair*, devoted to the sixties counterculture, ran on composer Galt MacDermot's very free use of "pop with a beat" music, while *Grease* was grounded in fifties teen conformist culture and pastiched that world's rock and roll into character and situation numbers. Then, too, Paramount's *Grease* movie troubled to cast two then-current teen idols as Danny and Sandy, John Travolta and Olivia Newton-John.

Wisely, Paramount retained choreographer Patricia Birch from the original staging, for most of the film's high energy level resides in the way the songs are presented. In fact, one of them, "Summer Nights," the establishing number for both Danny and Sandy simultaneously (but separately), may be one of the best of its kind: on the first day of school, the two kids reveal their recent vacation dating to their comrades, the boys on football-field bleachers and the girls at a lunch table. Line by vocal line, their schoolmates get involved, the boys stamping, grabbing, bragging, bullying, moving in Birch's precise patterns up and down the bleacher planks, while the girls are less physical, concentrating on getting the story's details down: "Like, does he have a car?" Each of the two groups thinks this piquant love story has ended. "Wonder what she's doin' now," Danny softly tells us. But *we* know that, as they speak, they are but inches apart, for Sandy has transferred (from Australia, apparently) to his school, Rydell High.

The allusion to *Bye Bye Birdie*'s jeune premier, Bobby Rydell, tells us that *Grease* is a comedy, though less spoofy in flavor than the stage show was. Comparably, *Hair* had been rather merry in New York but got edgy in California. Thus, Forman gives "Black Boys/White Boys" to two girls' trios, whites singing about black boys and blacks singing about white boys—just as in the show. But then Forman slips in shots of Army officers singing the number as they inspect naked draftees, the whites admiring a black recruit and the blacks admiring a white recruit, their toes tapping to the beat. This was an extremely provocative mise en-scène for the day.

As for the music, *Grease* broke a Commandment by inserting numbers not by the original authors, Jim Jacobs and Warren Casey, including the very popular title song. But "Grease," by Barry Gibb (of the Bee Gees), unlike the rest of the *Grease* score, sings from a perspective that no character in the story commands. Grease, we learn, "is the time, is the place, is the motion"—but to Danny and Sandy, grease is nothing more than the stuff boys run through their hair when they comb it. These are kids, not philosophers. True, the song is heard over the opening titles, not within the action. But the vocalist is Frankie Valli (of the Four Seasons), thus addressing us as a member of the tribe.

Hair, on the other hand, added just one number, "Somebody To Love" (by the show's authors: again, Galt MacDermot, with James Rado and Gerome Ragni) while dropping rather a lot from the lengthy stage score. Even the semi-standard "[I met a boy called] Frank Mills" was omitted, though it had been recorded and was included on the soundtrack release. It was, admittedly, a pallid rendition; Broadway's Shelley Plimpton was much better, with a uniquely clumsy wistfulness in a more interesting orchestration.

The "down with musicals" crowd might have welcomed the *Little Shop of Horrors* movie (1986), because its sources were, more immediately, an off-Broadway show, and, originally, the blithely raunchy black comedy from the atelier of Roger Corman (1960). So the material had "experimental" street cred. And its characters—basically woebegone zombies and a man-eating plant—could be called "socially enlightening" for the emphasis on folk of the lower depths.

However, Alan Menken and Howard Ashman were not writing experimentally; their sound is up-to-date Broadway plot-and-character observation (with rhythm and blues for the plant, the black from another planet). Further, Frank Oz directed this so to say off-Hollywood movie musical as suavely as if it were *Funny Lady*. The film is filled with clever show-biz touches, as in the use of the stage show's three sarcastic black commères. They should be too theatrical a conceit for film, narrating (in song) as out-of-story guides. But Oz tucks them into many a sequence as extras, changing their outfits: as nurses, bridesmaids, secretaries, and, mainly, stalking through the blasted despair of Skid Row in mauve prom dresses and pearls. This is the modern musical, meta-theatre—yes, even on film—mixing its elements of realism and fantasy the way Ernst Lubitsch did when he had Maurice Chevalier complaining or bragging to the audience about how the story was going.

Unfortunately, Oz did cut away from Ellen Greene's "Somewhere That's Green" to substantiate her vision of suburban bliss, with TV dinners, *I Love Lucy*, and a Howdy Doody marionette. On stage in New York, Greene made something very special of this number, turning it almost into a little show of its own, and Oz lost the chance to preserve it thus.

Although my topic is Broadway songwriters, one foreign group has had major impact on Broadway and therefore begs inclusion: the authors of European pop opera. Often enjoying very long runs (the New York *Phantom of the Opera* is in its twenty-seventh year at this writing), the form has influenced in particular the singing of what are now termed "power ballads." Some dare call it screaming, and the style has given rise to many a spoof. Still, pop opera's strength does lie in its intensity, dealing as it does with larger-than-life figures, from Jesus Christ to Madame Butterfly.

Typically, then, Andrew Lloyd Webber and Tim Rice's *Evita*, filmed in 1996, treats the rise, rule, and death of one of the most charismatic yet reviled political figures in history, Eva Perón. However, the original London and New York staging, by Harold Prince, was a trick mounting in a concept-show mash-up of time and space with a narrator, Che, who also takes part in the action while remaining outside it.

The film's director, Alan Parker, could have cut hack the concept-show stuff and simply told the story using only the parts of the score that support it naturalistically. Instead, he decided to go wild, in a cocktail of equal parts concept show and realism. In the latter vein, the first of several gigantic crowd scenes is one of the biggest things ever filmed—Eva's state funeral, with the military, dignitaries, children, a flaming urn, the catafalque hauled on white cords by sixty men, the draped coffin raised up as if an offering to the gods. There are, we are told, four thousand extras in sight, and it's easy to believe; this was a spare-no-expense project, though it must have been a long shot. Most people don't like opera, and these shows aren't called pop operas for nothing. Except for the odd spoken line, the piece is through-sung, and the movie retains not only the self-contained numbers but the musical dialogues as well.

There is some neatening up of the music's focus, as when "Another Suitcase in Another Hall," sung on stage by a minor character who doesn't deserve a number, is reassigned to Eva, quite logically. Later, when that minor character has her brief scene, Parker allows a tiny reprise for her, Eva, and Perón that caps the sequence with a rightness that the show lacked.

On the other hand, Parker let the concept-show aesthetic assert itself as well. Yes, right there on the screen, bold art, because it is what it is. After all, *Evita* started as a two-disc LP song cycle, free of the "time and place" exigencies of cinematic narrative. This work is something like the *Tristram Shandy* or *Naked Lunch* of musicals, scorning your classical unities, your dainty little How To Make a Musical for the suburban devotee. This is a shattering work. But, once again, because it's a musical, it gets no respect. Even the intellectuals who admire musicals—and I know them both—would not give praise to anything by Andrew Lloyd Webber.

We can praise Alan Parker, because he must have understood what an unusual piece he was working with and decided to make it into an unusual film. What to do with all those clusters of choristers sharing with us what they are actually only thinking—the grousing aristos, the wary army officers? Film them as they are. How to finesse the moments when Che glides into view to sing at or with someone in the story while he sings at us as well? Is he *there* or is he *here*? Then there's that physically impossible duet, the "Waltz For Eva and Che." It's not real, because he's a theatrical invention, so we cut it, right? No: we film it. A big story needs big imagery. *It is what it is.*

As we noticed, Frank Oz did a bit of this in a little story, *Little Shop of Horrors*. But *Evita* revels in this paradox of fantasy-realism, as when Parker's Che turns up everywhere in the continuity—a waiter, an apartment-building janitor in a wife-beater, the emcee of a fancy charity show,

Perón's newsreel projectionist, a bartender supplying an obbligato in "Another Suitcase."

However, this very innovative film is vexed in part by casting. The Che, Antonio Banderas, is marvelous, taking on his countless roles so casually that he naturalizes the bizarre—which is exactly how the concept musical works. And, unlike many movie stars going musical—Johnny Depp in *Sweeney Todd*, for instance—Banderas really can sing.

The Perón, however, is weak. It's Jonathan Pryce, a resourceful performer who, on stage, dominated another pop opera, *Miss Saigon*, as a sort of back-alley Perón: a hustler, but, in this case, of sex work instead of politics. Somehow, projecting the saturnine air of the military man sapped Pryce's vitality. But then it is a difficult part to elaborate on. Al Jolson himself might have disappeared in it.

And Madonna is Evita. It must have seemed like a perfect fit, for, like Eva Perón, Madonna is a Warholian figure, known more for who she is than for what she does. There are other parallels: both are sexy, glamorous, and unpredictable; loved by millions but despised by the elite; and experts at provoking the self-elected protectors of Good Taste. And, indeed, Madonna's portrayal is well judged, even expertly so. Yet it never connects with the opportunities. Again, pop opera delights in hyper characters and needs hyper performances. In "Rainbow High," Eva sings, "Make me fantastic," and Madonna's supposed to be. But she isn't. She looks great, in something like eight zillion costume changes. And she is Evita, more or less. She just isn't Madonna.

Lloyd Webber's *The Phantom of the Opera* (2004) also benefits from a naturalistic realization of this extravagant story. The original staging, like *Evita*'s directed by Harold Prince for both London and New York (and seen in replicas throughout the world) was pure fourth-wall realism with no concept-show meta-theatre. On the contrary, Maria Björnson's stormload of scenery locked the action into precise locales, with no room for a Che and his autonomous out-of-story mischief. So the movie, directed by Joel Schumacher, concentrates on opening Björnson's theatre up with Hollywood's First Advantage Over the Stage: you get to see what everything actually looks like.

Even better, you watch Schumacher *invoke* the story into being. He opens in black and white (in the present), then slips into color (for the past) as the broken chandelier of the ruined Opéra Populaire is set back into place. Dust that had collected on it for forty-nine years flies into the air as the auditorium comes back from the dead—the footlights flaming up one by one, the rows of seats reappearing, the boxes aglow, ready for music, altogether a fabulous conjuration of a tale that is at once a spoof of opera, a magic show, and a celebration of the power of song.

Comparably, the Septet of the Letters (so to call it), staged in the show in a single set, here takes up a very geography of shots, from the opera-house lobby to the managers' office, from the fans waiting outside to the corridors backstage, where the fatuous prima donna La Carlotta (with a headdress three feet tall) is borne to the stage on a palanquin. Interestingly, someone took the trouble to mike the septet's separate voice lines distinctly enough for one to differentiate what the various parties are saying; in the stage show, all seven lines come forth in a mush.

And now the singing. *The Phantom* really is an opera, calling for the higher end of the "show biz" voice—people like Sarah Brightman, Colm Wilkinson, Davis Gaines, or Judy Kaye, who have the tone to support the work's grand manner without technically being opera singers. The movie compromises on this somewhat, with very musical sweethearts (Emmy Rossum, Patrick Wilson), the managers (Ciarán Hinds, Simon Callow) just bearable, a dubbed Carlotta (Minnie Driver, who can in fact sing, but not the soprano's coloratura the role requires), and a Phantom (Gerard Butler) on the sour side, though he does hit the notes.

To the film's credit, it makes no apology for its lavish music and grotesque storyline; a happy aspect of the current resurgence of the movie musical is its willingness to let Broadway and the West End do what they're good at doing, as if filming entirely for the first audience. Thus, this cinema *Phantom* is almost startlingly faithful to the stage show. It does omit the second-act rehearsal of the Phantom's own particular opera, an important scene revealing that the music he composes is as advanced and impenetrable as his hideaway under the opera house: the compleat magician. (The opera's ascending eight-note theme, gruesomely avant-garde for its era, is heard a few times on the movie's soundtrack accompaniment.) On the other hand, we get a new sequence, a flashback telling of how Mme. Giry, the ballet mistress (Miranda Richardson), came to be the Phantom's familiar, which does explain—as the show never did—why she is strangely sympathetic to him.

Les Misérables (2012), the last of these three classic pop-opera titles, shares with the other two an elaborate realization of the sheer physics of the story, stylized on stage but in the cinema thrillingly spacious. Still, *Les Mis* is unique for its solution to a problem almost as old as the talkie itself: how to project above all dramatic music when the actors aren't being musically dramatic during the actual shooting. When they are, in fact, simply mouthing along with a pre-recorded track, thinking more about matching their lip movements to the guide vocal than about what the music is supposed to express.

This wasn't a problem for a long time, because not till late in the musical's history did the more impetuously delineated character song—"A Puzzlement," say, or "And I Am Telling You I'm Not Going"—turn up. This is heavy personal communication, and I say again that it needs to be sung, not synched. The closer we get to opera, the less effective pre-recording becomes. This is why almost no studio-made opera films work. Yes, there are exceptions, such as Michael Powell and Emeric Pressburger's *Tales of Hoffmann*, as much danced as sung and specifically meant as a primarily visual delight. Far more typical is, for example, Francesco Rosi's *Carmen*, very imaginatively directed but so phony in its voice-to-sync relationship that Rosi keeps shooting from a distance, as if embarrassed to show us that his singers aren't singing at all.

Perhaps Hollywood's canned vocals are valid except when they aren't. So director Tom Hooper filmed *Les Misérables* with the principals all doing their singing live on the set, to the point of closing in on Anne Hathaway's "I Dreamed a Dream" in one long take, thus virtually to torture the music out of her. *Les Mis* tells of people living momentously, intensely, calamitously—the bandit (Hugh Jackman) redeemed by Christian charity; the law officer (Russell Crowe) stalking him on the belief that the outlaw cannot (or, given his perverted worldview) must not be redeemed; the revolutionaries (Eddie Redmayne, Aaron Tveit); the criminal tavern keepers (Sacha Baron Cohen, Helena Bonham Carter); the young girl (Amanda Seyfried) living in despair till the bandit pays his redemption forward and saves her in turn; the tavern keepers' daughter (Samantha Barks), wretched in love and therefore happy in death.

It's a pop opera because the story is too big for a musical; only the musical-comedyesque taverners get "fun" music. And the Claude-Michel Schönberg-Alain Boublil-Jean-Marc Natel score (in the familiar English translation by Herbert Kretzmer) needs very strong singers. As with the *Phantom* film, some of Hooper's cast can and some sort of can't, but only Russell Crowe truly fails to justify his music. Worse, his role may be the most impossible in the classic pop-opera calendar, lumbered with the obsessive monosyllabic end-rhymes that have haunted the genre after the ambitious Tim Rice broke up with Lloyd Webber. Javert is already crashingly nasty; doggerel lyrics serve only to cartoon him.

So it is less the music than the visuals that compel us to screen this by now venerable work, first staged, in Paris, in 1980. The movie's opening sequence, of convicts dragging a great ship into drydock, is spectacular, as is Jackman's disposing of his hated convict's papers, tearing them apart to flutter in the air high above a mountain village, in a perspective suggestive of the heavens looking down. We even get a view of Napoléon's ruined elephant statue in Paris—not used on stage but important in Victor Hugo's novel as a symbol of the one per cent rotting away as uprisings seek to empower the *misérables*—a clumsy word denoting the unhappy but also the worthless and, especially, the harmful.

Interestingly, pop opera on stage revives the profile that old-time operetta used to claim, with lots of spectacle and voice, while pop opera on film emphasizes spectacle over voice. None of these three movies counts even one gala singing star in the Tibbett-Moore or MacDonald-Eddy manner. But then, there is a fourth audience now: the uncultured, intolerant of anything they're not used to and particularly suspicious of legit singing.

As well, many stage musicals these days are presented non-realistically; they can take place everywhere or nowhere, or both simultaneously. It was easy to film *Anything Goes* or *Oklahoma!*, but how does one make a movie of *The Fantasticks*, Harvey Schmidt and Tom Jones' endlessly long-running off-Broadway show of 1960? A piano and harp accompanied players on a bare stage (really a space at one end of the room where the audience sat) as they enacted an absurdly simple tale, almost a parable. It was something like How the Boy and Girl Learned the True Meaning of Life. And the explanation was: first it's too hard, then it's too easy, and at last it's just right.

A movie can't be that small. So the *Fantasticks* film (1995) re-invented the show's innocence using a magical carnival run by an equivalent of the show's compère, El Gallo (Jonathon Morris), who puts the two kids (Joe[y] McIntyre, Luisa Bellamy) through trials of purification. At times, the carnival is just a carnival; at other times, it's a sorcerer's playground. So when the Girl ventures into its little silent-film cinema, the carnival chief shifts shape from usher to projectionist to pianist. Then they all vanish and the keyboard goes on playing by itself.

Further, the chief is very open about his supernatural powers. When a motorcycle cop stops the little parade of carnival wagons as they ride into the movie's version of the show's wonderful nowhere—a green and pleasant land—the chief tells the cop to believe in the unbelievable:

CHIEF: When I'm in town, anything's possible.

Amusingly, the carnival crew takes in Teller, of the magician act of Penn and Teller, the one who never speaks. But *The Fantasticks* gives him lines. He and his comrade, Barnard Hughes, have fallen on hard times:

HUGHES: We take the odd jobs—abductions, medicine shows.... When things are really bad, a musical or two.

Unfortunately, the film was crudely cut back before release, and much of what I've described above is missing from what was shown in theatres. At that, the movie was not widely seen, as if, having bought the rights to the show and filmed it, the producer despaired of attracting customers. Some of the relatively short score is missing as well, including the opening, full-out statement of "Try To Remember," one of the most charmingly delicate pieces the New York musical has ever produced.

The difficulty in filming a show whose unique staging plan is built into its very composition dogs not only offbeat little bits like *The Fantasticks* but a smash of the Big Broadway sort, high-powered and imposing. Once, Big Broadway flourished a pile-on of marquee names, for instance Ethel Merman, Bert Lahr, and a Cole Porter score: *Du Barry Was a Lady*. Later, it could mean the follow-up to a huge hit, as when R & H brought forth *Carousel* after *Oklahoma!*.

Today, Big Broadway is likely to be *Jersey Boys* (2005), the bio of Frankie Valli (whom we last met authenticating era in the title song of *Grease*) and the other three of the Four Seasons, because the subject is bankable nostalgia. Further, the show's director, Des McAnuff, got a huge hit out of the slightly comparable *The Who's Tommy* (1993), a staging of one of the first of the two-disc rock song cycles. *Jersey Boys* enacted its chronicle-like story in the non-realistic, concept-show manner pioneered by Rodgers and Hammerstein's *Allegro* (1947), utilizing an almost breathless momentum broken only by the familiar Four Seasons hits, very stylishly set forth. There were no backdrops or side pieces on wagons. Instead, bits of furniture and the like would slide on when needed (very much as in *Allegro*, in fact) while the four singing leads took turns narrating.

There was no way the rather unexpected director, Clint Eastwood, could film (in 2014) so theatrical a presentation. So he naturalized it with real-life settings. Further, Marshall Brickman and Rick Elice's screenplay kept very, very close to their stage script—a procedure we really haven't seen much of, though it dates back to Warner Bros.' *Desert Song* in 1929. Eastwood even let the Four Seasons speak directly to us, though the practice has a different flavor on screen than on stage. Similarly different, and perhaps the one genuine touch of Hollywood in the entire film, is the use of Christopher Walken as a mobster, one Gyp DeCarlo. In the stage show, this character was just another member of the ensemble. But Walken's merrily baleful presence and eccentric line readings—he sounds like someone *imitating* Christopher Walken—enlivens the film considerably.

That all but verbatim use of the stage script tells us how much more faithfully Hollywood has lately been in its Broadway adaptations; think of all those ravaged Cole Porter scores, the cooling of *Pal Joey*'s sleazy heat, the literalizing of *A Chorus Line*, losing its parable-like air of pilgrims seeking sanctuary. *Jersey Boys* did make one odd change in the dialogue, when, originally, Frankie Valli says, "I'm going to be bigger than Sinatra." In the movie, he says he'll be "as big as Sinatra." Is Hollywood still so in awe of the notoriously touchy singer that it fears his anger from the beyond?

Stephen Sondheim's *Into the Woods* (2014) is also quite faithful, and this we find shocking, as Sondheim pioneered the most ambitious wing of the modern musical, often moving outside the comfort zone of many in even the first audience. Further, *Woods'* mash-up of fairy tales is replete with the authentic Grimm violence. We keep thinking these tales are about Cinderella and her glass slipper, but they'll more likely tell of limbs getting hacked off and monsters wondering what sauce you go with.

On the other hand, it's wonderful actually to *see* all the magic, as in the way the beanstalk cuts its way right through the earth to dare the heavens. Even the day-to-day of the action's various storylines is laid out for us as it could never be on stage, for instance when the principals of the plot-driven title song proceed through their fairy-tale village to enter the woods. A crane shot shows them separately following paths into this testing place of valor, eros, compassion, and adaptability—a wonderfully airy visual in a film that necessarily spends most of its time claustrophobically edging around in a forest.

The very engaging cast was largely drawn from relative newcomers, though Meryl Streep's Witch and Johnny Depp's cameo as the Wolf lent some movie-star prestige. Sondheim's scores maintain a high espressivo level, yet he writes for "Broadway" voices—men who carry a tune in the Robert Preston rather than Alfred Drake manner and women more like Angela Lansbury than Barbara Cook. Still, Streep is especially effective in "The Last Midnight," in a slow build of volume as the wind comes up and the camera circles fiercely around her. There was no dubbing in the movie; on the contrary, a few vocal passages were sung live during the shoot.

Jersey Boys retained the narrator function from stage to screen, but the original *Into the Woods* offered a weird take on the narrator function in that he starts as a genial television-quiz-show-host sort of fellow—obviously incongruous in the storybook setting—who is then dragged into the narrative himself. Director Rob Marshall decided to let the Baker (James Corden), the nearest thing to a protagonist in this ensemble of leads, narrate in voiceover, thus keeping the film's dramatis personae consistent. In the film, everyone we see is from the same time and place, with no intrusions from the modern world, in accordance with a newish rule in the filming of concept musicals: the meta-theatricality must be tamed. Or let's just say "naturalized." Marshall did allow a subtle in-joke at the first sight of the castle where the king is holding his festival: the soundtrack discreetly quotes a theme from Sondheim's *A Little Night Music*.

Here's a question, or, really, two: one, did any of our Broadway songwriters create a movie career as distinguished as their stage career? And has a Hollywood version of a stage show ever improved on the original? *Into the Woods* looks better in the cinema than in the playhouse, because its story is magic and so are movies. Theatre must style everything; film *shows* it to us. But how many other Hollywood adaptations outperform their source title? They do occasionally preserve historical portrayals—Yul Brynner's King of Siam, for instance. Or they give us competitive assumptions, as with Rosalind Russell's Madam Rose (even if some of it is Lisa Kirk's). Still, even the celebrated 1936 *Show Boat* is too short a boat, half the show, and the longer Broadway films, such as *Camelot* and *Hello, Dolly!*, have that sixties bloated quality.

As for the first question—how well did the Harms group colonize Hollywood to exploit the unique advantage of the camera?—the answer is: not well enough. But then, there was too much interference by jerks in power. As Lorenz Hart wrote, in *Pal Joey*, when Vera deplores Joey's lack of intelligence, "I know a movie executive who's twice as bright." These executives would tell experienced theatre craftsmen to keep their ideas to themselves. They went score-shopping for hit tunes, playing one team against another. They ripped songs out of shows that were famous *because* of those songs. They wanted to cut "Over the Rainbow" from *The Wizard of Oz*. They *did* cut it. And Arlen and Harburg had to fight to get it into the release print; they didn't have to fight to keep great songs in their Broadway shows.

In fact, not a single one of our Broadway songwriters conquered Hollywood in any real sense, because movies aren't a writer's medium the way theatre is. Few of the Hollywood honchos could bear to be around songwriters at all—and there was that third audience, haunting producers' philosophy of art, something that never concerned people on Broadway. The American musical—at least from something like 1925 on—was written for New York, with the strong possibility of a post-Broadway tour to first-and second-audience towns.

Let us make our farewell with three final titles that sum up the approaches common in Hollywood's Broadway today, to see how they compare with those in the past. For instance, the backstager. And that would be *Dick Tracy* (1990), though technically it's a police-detective thriller. It gives us Stephen Sondheim's only produced original Hollywood musical (others were initiated but not filmed), with five superb numbers that are, however, often so submerged in the action that most viewers probably don't consider *Dick Tracy* a musical at all.

Though commercially successful, the film is not highly rated (its Rotten Tomatoes score is 64%), but it is cleverly brought off and, interestingly, goes out of its way to honor the elements of Chester Gould's comic strip. This was founded on the notion of a square-jawed law-enforcement hunk in eternal war with bizarre foes named for their salient physical drawback— Pruneface, Flattop, Lips Manlis, even the uncommunicative Mumbles.

Warren Beatty directed and played Tracy himself, in the trademark dark suit and yellow overcoat with matching fedora (as in the strip), meanwhile filling the screen with Gould's villains. But the movie expands its real estate from Gould's simple comic-strip art to the more elaborate pictorial of the comic *book*, establishing locale with the "splash panel": a big view of things, in this case of an unnamed metropolis. We see a graveyard with the skyline behind it and a vast, shiny moon; or a waterfront scene boasting two ocean liners. The only major difference between Gould's world and that of the movie lies in Beatty's characterization of Tracy as ever-ready in physical confrontation but hesitant in battles of words. In the comic's very first episode, way back in 1931, it took Tracy only two strips to take his fiancée, Tess Trueheart, into his arms (while they're doing the dinner dishes) and propose. But Beatty's Tracy is forever tongue-tied.

His arch-foe, Big Boy Caprice, however, is never at a loss for words, whether quoting Nietzsche or Thomas Jefferson, coaching the chorus line at his Club Ritz, or even telling his hostage Tess (Glenne Headly) why he's barking orders at his henchmen:

BIG BOY: You gotta tell them everything. They crave leadership.

This is Al Pacino, thrillingly over the top as he creates a unique gangland style—when to wax sarcastic, when to throw a line away only to burst into a temper explosion on the next line, when to slam the piano keyboard cover down while the pianist is playing. And there's a homeless kid (little Charlie Korsmo) whom Tracy and Tess adopt, and the Club Ritz pianist (Mandy Patinkin), and the Club Ritz diva (Madonna), who tries to take Tracy away from Tess.

So there's plenty to sing about, because Sondheim can turn the floor numbers of a nightclub into character pieces. "Sooner or Later (I always get my man)" could be Madonna's performance spot or it could tell about her interest in Tracy or even, obliquely, about Tracy's victories in law enforcement. Or "More," another of Madonna's numbers on the nightclub floor, functions as an out-of-story character number for the Material Girl herself. Or "Live Alone and Like It," sung by Mel Tormé in voiceover, refers to the adult principals, all single yet all getting more and more involved with one another. "Don't ask me to like it," says Tess, when the song is over.

So *Dick Tracy* is a musical—except when it isn't. *The Broadway Melody*, with its Francis Zanfield revue, let its music be heard from first note to last. *The Fleet's In*, with Jimmy Dorsey's band, strongly featured its vocalists. *Dick Tracy*, unfortunately, keeps overpowering its Sondheim with distracting plot action, a Hollywood tradition, as we've seen. "Back in Business," a carol devoted to the joys of a crime wave while Tracy is sidelined in jail, scarcely bothers to establish itself as a nightclub number before the editing of plot vignettes takes over (though at least the vocal isn't drowned out by dialogue).

It seems that Beatty, who also produced the film, wanted Broadway's best songwriter for its vocal spots but was really interested in exploring how love and its baggage affect a man dedicated to his work. Songs just get in the way—even though Beatty was personally involved with Madonna and, to an extent, tilted the picture toward her singing. And she is much better here than in *Evita*, skating sardonically on the thin ice of how the role she plays in the movie resembles the role she plays in life:

BEATTY: Whose side are you on?
MADONNA: The side I'm always on. Mine.
BEATTY: No grief for [your murdered former gang master]?
MADONNA: I'm wearing black underwear.

She plays yet another role here, masquerading for much of the movie's second half as The Blank, a faceless villain all in black who intervenes to save Tracy's life yet also to frame him for murder. Whose side is she on, indeed?[4]

And whose side has Hollywood been on? Because it hasn't been that of Broadway's songwriters. This is especially blatant in Richard Condon's movie of *Dreamgirls* (2006). Surely all my readers know the most apparent points in the *Dreamgirls* saga—of its look at the rise and break-up of an extended family surrounding a Supremes-like singing trio in the 1960s and 1970s; of the show's stupendous 1981 Michael Bennett production using five very mobile lighting towers to frame the action on an open stage; of its tremendous impact as a musical at once dramatic and touching, almost a modern *Carousel*. Seldom does a show rip open its principals' vulnerabilities while concentrating on so many of them—the three girls, their

---

4. Like almost all the film's bad guys, The Blank comes directly from Chester Gould, much as Gould drew him. In the strip, however, The Blank's motivation is simpler than Madonna's: he's killing off the members of his old gang while wearing cheesecloth pasted over his features. Unmasked at last, he is no Madonna, so ghoulish-looking that Gould shows his face in only one panel. "My little show is over," he says, in the adventure's final speech balloon.

songwriter, their manager, and their high-strung fellow performer with the beautifully judged name of James "Thunder" Early, a billing that could have come right off an Apollo Theatre marquee.

Dreamgirls eschewed the traditional First Couple-Second Couple structure and had no certain protagonist. Is it Effie, the troubled lead singer moved, to her fury, to backup? Is it Deena, cuter and suaver, who takes over the lead spot—the Diana Ross figure, more or less? Is it their manager, Curtis Taylor Jr. (as he proudly, insistently, calls himself), who loves first Effie and then Deena as he juggles the twin choices of black music—crazy-rave soul on one hand and "passing for white" smooth on the other, Bessie Smith or Nat King Cole? Curtis wants his art glamorous and nationally influential, but isn't he the villain of the piece for telling artists what their art should be? He would say it has nothing to do with race, that it's about success—and, as I noted at the start of this book, to share in political and social power in America, a minority group must first assert a presence in the popular arts. So Curtis is right, but only in a sense. A Curtis sense. And by the story's conclusion, his family of talent has devolved into a group of regretful survivors—except for Jimmy Early, who rebels and is punished, destroyed. In the stage show, Jimmy simply disappeared; in the movie, Curtis' rejection kills him.

Who owns the art? If it's Hollywood, Richard Rodgers would answer, "The producers, and they can keep it." True, *someone* enabled the making of *Love Me Tonight*. Yet "Who owns the art?" is the question that dogged Broadway songwriters throughout their decades in the movies, and *Dreamgirls*, too, asks the question. It's so packed with memes that it's virtually an epic disguised as a backstager. But then, so is *Show Boat*.

Dreamgirls' high-powered look at show business meant it had to be filmed, but it took so long to reach the screen that Tom Eyen, who wrote the book and lyrics, had died, leaving his composer, Henry Krieger, to create the new numbers with other wordsmiths. Nor could the first stage cast, so excellent in suggesting how much lay behind the characters' protean relationships, preserve their portrayals, twenty-five years after the New York opening. There was some movie-star casting, especially in the use of Eddie Murphy as Jimmy, though he gave a superb performance and, like everyone else, did his own singing. And we should note the ceremonial use of one of the original Broadway dreamgirls, Loretta Devine, in a new-for-the-movie role as a club singer memorializing the departed Early in "I Miss You, Old Friend," by Krieger and Willie Reale.

Scenarist and director Richard Condon clearly wanted his *Dreamgirls* on the dark side, interpolating scenes running the high temperature of sixties America that Bennett hadn't presented. Condon's main concern, however, lay in finding a cinematic transformation of Bennett's unique staging, in camera work as creative as Bennett's dancing towers and ever-changing playing areas had been.

Condon succeeded, partly through the rat-a-tat editing that jumps frantically from shot to shot, emphasizing the quicksilver nature of the story's character interactions, from Effie's feuds with everyone to Jimmy's lord-of-misrule challenges to Curtis' authority. Krieger and Eyen seem to tell us that black music is autonomous by nature, unwilling to be stabilized by masters white *or* black, and Condon's camera races through the set-ups as if looking for a protagonist—one character to center the action, inform us who owns the music.

But Condon knows when to soar, too, as in the early scene in which the three Dreamettes (as they are first called, later to be billed as the Dreams) learn Jimmy's "Fake Your Way To the Top" to go on at the last minute as his backup. During the music, we move from this backstage coaching to the number as it appears on stage, accomplished on Broadway through a short blackout, the movement of the towers, and an announcer and brass musicians entering the playing area.

So Condon goes utterly *camera* here, in the film's first money shot: Jimmy at the keyboard and the three girls picking up their music. The pro pianist taking over. The drummer cutting in, the playing heating up. And as we're swept into the rightness of this act of destiny, the screen revolves around Jimmy to "materialize" the auditorium, the excited audience, the performance itself. And the orchestration is as visual as the shot, genuine music theatre by other means, ripping open the very physics of the narration.

Wonderful. But Condon destroyed *Dreamgirls*' identifying innovation: its many sung dialogues. Much of *Dreamgirls*' score is performance numbers, but much else is conversations—very striking ones—in music. Let's be blunt: this is the rhythm-and-blues opera. Condon included the most famous of the musical dialogues, the sextet just before Effie's mad scene, "And I Am Telling You I'm Not Going," as she discovers that she has been fired from the act and confronts her now-rejecting "family" with her typical cocktail of injury and belligerence. *Dreamgirls* buffs regard this scene as the very heart of the show, a driving quarrel fired by Eyen's uncanny ability to keep every principal's lyrics in character—Deena's calling Effie "Miss Blame It On the World"; Effie's helplessly pointless rejoinders; newcomer Michelle's beat-down of Effie as "a second-rate diva who can't sustain." It's startlingly well-phrased characterizing from Eyen, who till *Dreamgirls* had been nothing more than New York's enfant terrible of downtown camp.

These sung dialogues bunch up especially in the action's second half, but Condon replaced them with spoken lines, even the moving scene in which

Ellie and her estranged songwriter brother finally make up. Those attend-
ing *Dreamgirls* on Broadway, particularly when the vibrant first cast was
still playing, recall a public constantly cheering—for the over-the-top designs in the fashion-show sequence, for certain special effects...but above
all for the bold black opera of it all in the sung dialogues.

Thus, even today, nearly a century after *The Love Parade* and *Love Me
Tonight* guiltlessly *sang* their stories at us, Hollywood continues to nourish
its approach-avoidance complex over the notion of mixing music and "real
life." It might well be the defining characteristic of the movie musical, more
even than its use of the magician-camera. It is certainly its greatest point
of contention with the Broadway form. But note that we are not uncover-
ing a difference between Broadway's songwriters and Hollywood's songwriters. The difference is between Broadway's songwriters and Hollywood's
producers and directors. In New York, the writers most often define the
art. In California, the writers are employees; the business defines the art.

If *Dick Tracy* is a backstager folded into a policier and *Dreamgirls* is a
backstager built around the world of Motown, *Chicago* (2002) is a crime
drama and not a backstager. Yet all of its numbers are performance pieces,
because the stage *Chicago* (1975), billed as "a musical vaudeville," was con-
ceiver-director-choreographer Bob Fosse's "presentational" musical. It
had a story, drawn from Maurine Watkins' 1926 comedy on the show biz
of murder, but the songs stood more or less outside the action to recall the
days of Marilyn Miller, Eddie Cantor, Ted Lewis, Helen Morgan. Thus,
when the prison matron entered for her establishing number—heralded
by an announcer, as if in a variety show—she was not in the gray linen of
her day job but all dolled up, as if headlining at the Palace. And the number,
"When You're Good To Mama," recalled Sophie Tucker's specialties, such
as "You've Got To See [your] Mama Every Night" and "Papa, Better Watch
Your Step." Similarly, when the chief murderess' dreary husband got his
solo spot, "Mr. Cellophane," it echoed Bert Williams' theme song, "Nobody,"
and he wore clownish attire with an oversize white collar, as a tramp.
A nobody.

Chicago had to be filmed. With its superb Kander and Ebb score, its per-
tinent satire on how crime pays, and its flashy Fosse staging, it suggested a
sexy package ripe for exploitation at a time when Hollywood had lost its
touch in knowing what musical to film. So let's film *Chicago*—but no one
could figure out how to do it, because the songs acted as parergons to the
action rather than elements of it. That is, they seemed supplementary to
and separate from the story. What kind of musical is that?

Years passed, and nothing happened till the O. J. Simpson trial made
Chicago's aquittal of the guilty so au courant that a movie version became

irresistible. And Rob Marshall, as director and choreographer, figured out how to restyle the stage show's vaudeville acts for cinema, and it occurs within a single second of "All That Jazz," in the movie's first sequence.

As always in film, we start in "real life," as Velma Kelly (Catherine Zeta-Jones) arrives at a club to perform her sister act, unfortunately without her sister, whom she has just murdered. Velma's opposite in *Chicago*, Roxie Hart (Renée Zellweger) is also there, watching the number, entranced. This is what life is for: getting noticed by Doing a Number. It's *The Broadway Melody*, *Swing Time*, *A Star Is Born*, *Gypsy*, *Funny Lady*, *Dreamgirls*, *Jersey Boys*. It's show business, sometimes known as American Life. As Velma sings on a little stage amid writhing dancers, Roxie stares at this ... star:

> VELMA: (singing) And *all*
> (chord!)
> VELMA: *That*
> (chord!)

And now comes that single second, on *Jazz!*, for, suddenly, Roxie herself is leading the number on the little stage, in a shot that wrenches the showbiz away from Velma. Roxie will Do a Number—and Roxie, too, will kill this night.

From then on, every *Chicago* song is a kind of show-biz version of itself, announced by the "All That Jazz" pianist (Taye Diggs) and generally performed within a theatre setting. For "When You're Good To Mama," the matron (Queen Latifah) dons exotic finery and waves a feathery fan, her ample bosom addressing a stag crowd as eloquently as her song does. The "Cell Block Tango," for six murderesses, is an elaborate chain of pas de deux, one for each killer and the man she was involved with, the ultimate act styled with the appearance of a red bandana (except for the innocent Hungarian girl, whose bandana is white). Back in a theatre set, Roxie's drab husband (John C. Reilly) sings "Mr. Cellophane" on an undressed stage, and the auditorium he plays to is very nearly empty of spectators.

Thus Marshall translates the stage show's theme from metaphor to a visual reality: now we actually see the effect show biz has on society: it devours us till nothing counts unless it's a form of entertainment. News is entertainment, politics is entertainment, crime, science, education, sports: if it isn't entertainment, then it isn't *playing*.

And as long as it is entertainment, nothing else about it matters, as we learn when Roxie and Velma are exculpated. Velma suggests the two team up in vaudeville, and, in lines written for the movie by our *Dreamgirls* director, Richard Condon, Roxie sees a glitch in that proposition:

ROXIE: I hate you.

But Velma and American life have the cure ready:

VELMA: There's only one business in the world where that's no problem at all.

And onto the wicked stage they go, in Marshall's new choreography to Fosse's "Hot Honey Rag" combinations, the two women moving in synchronization in a brand-new sister act: as sisters-in-crime.

So perhaps Broadway has managed to influence Hollywood in one new way, leading film into the surreal theatricality of the concept musical's evaporation of the border between real life and illusion. Movies already are illusion as it is; a pile-on of illusions would be a sensory overload. Theatre can do it; movies couldn't. But now they can, in *Evita* and *Chicago*. It's a small victory for the Harms group in its eternal war with producers catering to the second and third audiences.

So it seems that Harvey Weinstein, of Miramax, the studio that filmed *Chicago*, wanted to dilute the Kander and Ebb score with a number for Anastacia, popular with the kids, major members of our new fourth audience. Weinstein applied also to Janet Jackson, and even tried to get Kander and Ebb to collaborate with her, though in the end another team wrote the Anastacia solo.

But Kander and Ebb were contractually empowered to keep interpolations out of the film. They themselves wrote a new number for the closing credits, "I Move On," for Zellweger and Zeta-Jones; and Weinstein had the right to include Anastacia's song on the soundtrack CD. But he needed Kander and Ebb to agree to let any interpolation by others into the film itself.

So Hollywood gave New York a call. This should be a cinch. I mean, Come on, guys, it's Anastacia. It's Janet Jackson. It's kids, it's rock stars, it's *now*.

Kander and Ebb didn't take the call, and Broadway wins at last.

BIBLIOGRAPHY

There are no books focusing on the Hollywood work of Broadway songwriters besides this one, though there are plenty of volumes on the movie musical itself. Having mastered the history of the form for *The Hollywood Musical* (St. Martin's, 1981), I had the chronology and its developments already in hand. Further, being well up on the achievements of the Harms group (and their colleague Irving Berlin), my preparation for the present book consisted of my personal observations of the films themselves, set within the context of each New York writer's movie career.

Nevertheless, the reader might want to do some exploring, and the starting point is the coming of sound. Harry M. Geduld's *The Birth of the Talkies: From Edison To Jolson* (Indiana, 1975) spends much time on the technological background. Alexander Walker's *The Shattered Silents: How the Talkies Came To Stay* (William Morrow, 1979) is far more interested in how Hollywood used the technology aesthetically; Walker's lively narration makes one feel like an avid moviegoer in a city filled with theatres wired for sound. We take in each new feature with its individual innovation—the first musico-dramatic use of the soundtrack in Walt Disney's *Steamboat Willie* cartoon (1928); Rouben Mamoulian's mixing of two separate sound feeds on a single track in *Applause* (1929). Walker also captures the paradox that the first talkies, now regarded as vital history, were at the time thought of as trash obliterating the holy beauty of rapturous silent film. Says Walker, "No wonder the intelligentsia felt resentful." Doesn't it always?

Scott Eyman's *The Speed of Sound: Hollywood and the Talkie Revolution, 1926–1930* (Simon & Shuster, 1997) bears on its cover a screen "grab" of an open-mouthed Al Jolson fomenting that revolution. It's an arresting shot and an arresting book, knowledgeable but also writerly, with a solid appreciation of the backstage of it all. Of the irruption of Marilyn Miller into Hollywood to film *Sally* for Warner Bros., Eyman tells us, "Miller was a prima donna, a drama queen, and spoiled rotten. She was Jack Warner's kind of woman, and they quickly began an affair." Weighing in on the mystery of when the studios adopted pre-recording as opposed to live singing on the set, Eyman suggests that not till *42nd Street* in 1933 did the industry as a whole finalize the switch to pre-recording—rather later than many writers have supposed.

Katherine Spring's *Saying It With Songs* (Oxford, 2013) looks at the same period through the use of theme songs and other vocals in, mostly, part-talkies and stopping short of a full-length look at the score of *The Broadway Melody*, when the movie musical's chronicle properly begins. The marriage of the piano and sheet-music interests around 1900, which created one of the nation's biggest industries, became by the late 1920s a yet more influential ménage à quatre among the recording, radio, and moviemaking interests. Noting how a huge seller like De Sylva, Brown, and Henderson's "Sonny Boy" publicized the Al Jolson vehicle *The Singing Fool*, Spring traces the movie men's eagerness to capitalize their output with more and more of these song hits. The tail wags the dog—and perhaps this was why, ever after, producers have sought to keep pointed plot and character numbers out and contentless ditties like "Sonny Boy" in—or, at least, to add a what-have-you by Anastacia to a pure story score like *Chicago*'s. The irony is that *Chicago*'s songs deliberately refer back to the days of the contentless ditty, though "When You're Good To Mama" collects the information of Sophie Tucker's feminist anthems, anti-authoritarian in an authoritarian age. This creates a very crowded text.

Two volumes itemize virtually every title in the first four years (1929—32) of the full-fledged musical, the period in which the flame of the form illuminated the land, sputtered out, and was re-ignited at last by *42nd Street*. Yet the two books complement rather than duplicate each other. Richard Barrios' *A Song in the Dark* (Oxford, 1995) and Edwin M. Bradley's *The First Hollywood Musicals* (McFarland, 1996) command a startlingly detailed knowledge of this in part elusive era, and the authors seem somehow to have seen every surviving title. I've attended private screenings of little-known films with buffs who call out the names and career data of very minor players as they appeared, but one has the uncanny feeling that Barrios and Bradley could tell you who was passing outside the theatre during the showings. They're lively writers, too, with different approaches. Bradley peppers his chronicle with quotations from personnel of the day, while Barrios waxes sarcastic about its excesses. Captioning a still of "Li-Po-Li," the atrocious Asian number in *The Show of Shows*, Barrios calls it "Chinese Junk."

Assisting these very personal reviews of the epoch is *The Movie Musical From Vitaphone to 42nd Street* (Dover, 1975), Miles Kreuger's collection of every article, advertisement, photo, review, and news flash from *Photoplay* magazine. It's a very useful resource, showing us how the first musicals were looked upon in their own day, and the brief reviews, each with a still and bare-bones credits, acquaints the browsing newcomer with the wit and wisdom of grouchy James Quirk. He certainly missed the boat with *The Jazz Singer*: "Al Jolson with Vitaphone noises.... Without his Broadway reputation, he wouldn't rate as a minor player."

Max Wilk's *They're Playing Our Song* (Moyer Bell, 1991) consists of interviews with a host of songwriters; for those who had died, such as Jerome Kern and Lorenz Hart, Wilk quotes the recollections of their associates. Much of the book treats working in Hollywood, as when Richard Rodgers recalls *Love Me Tonight*; *Hallelujah, I'm a Bum*; and *State Fair* as "the only three experiences I ever had with California that were enjoyable." (And *State Fair*, of course, was written in New York.) Jule Styne didn't care for movie work, either: "It was [an assembly-line] belt, it was a factory.... California didn't draw on your talents, because you were *told* what to do." Of his first show on Broadway, *High Button Shoes*, Styne told Wilk, "I *learned*—oh, did I learn what I didn't know!" Styne brings up a key issue here, because on *High Button Shoes* he was collaborating with (besides the lyricist, Sammy Cahn) George Abbott and Jerome Robbins. Styne mentions also the designers, Oliver Smith and Miles White—all artists from whom one got an education in the mating of narrative and music. In Hollywood, you were collaborating with those infernal producers.

A classic on a fixed point of the Hollywood musical map that deals with the contributions of New Yorkers is Arlene Croce's *The Fred Astaire and Ginger Rogers Book* (Dutton, 1972). RKO, where the two stars made all their pictures till the later reunion at MGM, was a New York-centric place, and, as I've emphasized, Pandro Berman was one producer who appreciated writers' contribution to moviemaking. Of the nine Astaire-Rogers RKOs, seven were assigned to Youmans, Kern, Berlin, and the Gershwins,

so, to whatever extent the movie musical should be considered with the American mu
sical generally, this RKO series is essential. A labor of love, Croce's book troubled to
find stills (or actual frames) to illustrate her observations, and she included little grabs
at the right and left that, when the book's pages are riffled, create a flip-book effect of
Astaire and Rogers dancing.

For some time, I would hear the buffs wish for a book on the roadshows of the
1960s, and Matthew Kennedy's *Roadshow!* (Oxford, 2014) was the answer to their
prayers. When I told critic Ken Mandelbaum about it, he replied, "I'm already reading
it, and I hope it never ends!" Full control of the topic, scholarly research, and a sense of
humor create a fascinating voyage through the ego collisions and artistic confusions
of a form that had grown too grandiose to control. And note that this is a distinctly
Broadwayized Hollywood, a time of Rodgers and Hammerstein, Lerner and Loewe, and
other subjects of the present book. *Camelot*: Richard Harris, peeved at lordly Jack
Warner, halts production till Warner humbles himself before Harris. *Hello, Dolly!*: Gene
Kelly tells screenwriter Ernest Lehman, "If you ever talk to another one of my actors
on the set I'll kick your fucking teeth in." Who's the most treacherous star? Rex
Harrison. Who's the most forgotten star? Gertrude Lawrence, with a bio so dire Fox
kept repackaging it and it still flopped three times.

Before the Internet Movie Database, the only information resource on the Hollywood
musical was Stanley Green's *Encyclopedia of the Musical Film* (Oxford, 1981), which
I have quoted several times herein. In the chronology of writers on the stage musical,
Green takes his place way at the beginning, after Cecil Smith and David Ewen and
before Gerald Bordman as a kind of old guard. Smith and Bordman were happy to share
their opinions, but Ewen and Green maintained a neutrality about everything. Green
in particular reads as almost stubbornly noncommittal, an odd attitude in a world
whose aficionados hold passionate views. But he makes few factual errors, a real
achievement in a field as full of minutiae as the musical, with all those songs, characters, players, writers, and revisions. The work under discussion is full of interesting
backstories on films and amusing recaps on how numbers were originally presented.
It's also a great place to dig for trivia. Who knows Lucille Ball's middle name? Hint: it
links her with a Sondheim character. An actress.

Now to the picture books. Thomas G. Aylesworth's *Broadway To Hollywood* (Gallery,
1985) is apropos, dealing with the film versions of stage shows. Unfortunately, the
author has little of interest to say and no command of the topic whatsoever. Some of
the illustrations are unusual, but he lacks familiarity with them. A rarely seen shot of
the 1936 *Show Boat*'s playing of *The Parson's Bride* is captioned to point out only Charles
Winninger and Allan Jones (whose name is misspelled). But principals Irene Dunne,
Sammy White, and Queenie Smith are in the still, too, prominently at that. Aylesworth
is most befuddled when discussing the music; he doesn't know one song from another.
Of *Kiss Me Again*, First National's movie of Victor Herbert's *Mlle. Modiste*, he says "new
songs were included," and names them—all from the show, one of them being "If I
Were on the Stage," the extended solo that contains "Kiss Me Again," one of Herbert's
most familiar titles. If you don't know the music, you don't know the musical.

Ken Bloom's *Hollywood Musicals: The 101 Greatest Song-and-Dance Movies of All Time*
(Black Dog & Leventhal, 2010) is a great way for the newcomer to acclimatize him or
herself with this vast world. Indeed, most of Bloom's choices deal with Broadway songwriters, from *Sunnyside Up* to *Chicago*. And there is a real sense of command here; the
very first movie still gives us an extensive view of *Hello, Dolly!*'s Fourteenth Street
parade, creating a visual teaching moment in how wastefully elaborate the sixties roadshow musical became. Each film selected benefits from a varied layout, with many

seldom if ever seen shots and actual frames as well. Again, they're well chosen, as in stills of the first two *State Fairs* side by side, showing the four Frakes in what appears to be the same moment in their respective films. As well, profiles of specific artists and a Behind the Screen feature supply fascinating supplementary information, and Bloom has his fun adding isolated quotations, such as Bob Fosse to *Cabaret*'s producer, Cy Feuer: "You never thought I could direct this movie, did you? You hired me only for the fucking choreography"; and *Seven Brides For Seven Brothers*' director, Stanley Donen, about *his* producer: "Jack Cummings' only contribution to the film was to make it more difficult."

It's Desiree, incidentally.

INDEX

General discussion of songwriters' contributions are indicated with **Bold** page numbers.